Copyright © Marsha Erb, 2002

All rights reserved. No part of this publication may be reproduced, stored in a retrieval system, or transmitted in any form by any process — electronic, mechanical, photocopying, recording, or otherwise — without the prior written permission of the copyright owners and ECW PRESS.

NATIONAL LIBRARY OF CANADA CATALOGUING IN PUBLICATION DATA

Erb, Marsha
Stu Hart: lord of the ring

ISBN 1-55022-508-1

1. Hart, Stu, 1915- 2. Hart family. 3. Wrestling — Alberta — Calgary. 4. Wrestling — Biography. 5. Wrestling promoters — Alberta — Calgary — Biography. 6. Wrestling coaches — Alberta — Calgary — Biography. I. Title.

GV1196.H376E73 2002   796.812'092   C2001-904082-2

Cover and text design by Tania Craan
Back cover photo of Stu and Bret Hart: by Jim Wells, courtesy *Calgary Sun*
Layout by Mary Bowness

Printed by AGMV MARQUIS

Distributed in Canada by
General Distribution Services,
325 Humber College Blvd.,
Toronto, ON M9W 7C3

Distributed in the United States by
Independent Publishers Group,
814 North Franklin St.,
Chicago, IL, USA 60610

Published by ECW PRESS
2120 Queen Street East, Suite 200
Toronto, ON M4E 1E2
ecwpress.com

This book is set in Bembo and Copperplate.

PRINTED AND BOUND IN CANADA

The publication of *Stu Hart* has been generously supported by the Canada Council, the Ontario Arts Council, and the Government of Canada through the Book Publishing Industry Development Program. Canadä

Lord of the Ring

An Inside Look at Wrestling's First Family

MARSHA ERB

ECW PRESS

This book is dedicated to the memory of
my father Cyril Coleman Erb 1924–1996
and Helen Louise Hart 1924–2001

*He's a walking contradiction,
partly truth and partly fiction . . .*
— Kris Kristopherson

Acknowledgements

I would like to thank the many individuals and organizations who contributed to the research, editing or production of this book. My sincere appreciation goes to my publisher Jack David and my very talented and patient editor, Michael Holmes, both of Toronto. Further thanks to my agent, Robert Mackwood of Vancouver, as well as Brian Scrivener of Bowen Island, B.C.; Dolores Vyzralek, chief librarian of the North Dakota State Archives; the helpful staff at the Calgary and Edmonton public libraries; the Edmonton Public School Archives; the Tofield Museum Society; the Calgary and Edmonton city archives; the Calgary Boxing and Wrestling Commission; the Glenbow Museum and Archives; the Court of Queen's Bench clerks in Edmonton and Calgary; Mary and Ron Taylor and Charlie Sears of Tofield; Phil Klein of Edmonton; former Calgary mayor, Rod Sykes; and Alderman (now MLA) Jon Lord of Calgary. As well as Susan Dumont and Nancy May of Calgary for their research assistance; Calgary lawyers, C.D. (Chris) Evans, Jim Butlin, Tom Walsh and Ed Pipella (for their recollections); Jane Rotnem of Calgary (for her comments on the early manuscript); journalists Allan Fotheringham (for his advice and encouragement) and Christine Mushka of *The Globe and Mail* (for her encouragement and reads of the early manuscript), Dave Stubbs of the Montreal *Gazette,* Ned Powers of the Saskatoon *StarPhoenix* and Dave White, formerly of the Edmonton *Journal* and Regina *Leader Post*; former NWA world champion, Dory Funk Jr., of Ocala, Florida, and Wladek (Killer) Kowalski of Boston; Jim Thomson of Calgary and the late Mr. Justice Michael O'Bryne of Calgary (who were with Stu in the Navy in both Alberta and Nova Scotia); Hart family friends, Eileen Simpkins O'Neil of Ottawa, and the late Ed Whalen of Calgary; and members of the Hart family: Bruce Hart, Ross Hart, Elizabeth Neidhart, Keith Hart, Smith Hart, Alison Hart, Georgia Annis, B.J. Annis, Ted Annis, Jock and Diana Osler, Davey Boy Smith, Natalie and Jennifer Neidhart. My thanks also to my sister Theresa Erb of Mons, Belgium, for her encouragement and support.

But, most of all, I would like to thank Stu Hart and the late Helen Hart for their trust, cooperation and belief in this book.

Foreword

This book is a tribute to one of Canada's most colourful characters. Stewart Edward Hart has led a life of contradiction. Today, he remains what he has always been: hard and soft, inflexible and agile, brutal and gentle. He is a man whose character was formed in the wake of the development of Western Canada — a place where all things can happen, and often do.

I first met Stu Hart in early 1999, after having spent the previous fall working on the civic election campaign of Craig Burrows. (Burrows lost, but three years later he was elected to represent Calgary's Ward 6 as a City Councillor.) Bruce, Ross, Georgia, Ellie and Diana Hart, as well as Davey Boy Smith, all either worked on the same campaign or made regular appearances in the campaign office, located on Bow Trail next to the Odyssey Restaurant, a family run Greek pizza house. We campaigners often crowded around a table there, or at the Toi Shan, another family run place across the street, to wind down and talk at the end of an evening. Sometimes the discussion touched on Stu and the rest of the family. At a post-election wrap-up party in November, Ross and I chatted extensively about Stu's history. The more he discussed his father, the more fascinated I became. I

remember saying that someone should record Stu's stories before they were lost. Ross nodded in agreement.

By January I had convinced myself that I had the time to take on a big project. I spoke briefly with Bruce, Ross and Ellie about whether their father would be receptive. They knew that I had worked as a journalist for several years before enrolling in law school. And I was still enough of a journalist to recognize a good story when I heard one. By the time I was introduced to Stu in mid-January, he was as ready to proceed as I was. In his own way Stu is a raconteur, but it took months to acquire the reams of material which would eventually become *Stu Hart: Lord of the Ring*.

Bruce and Ellie were there when I first sat with Stu at the dining room table. So were Susan Dumont and Kathy Anderson, two friends who were pushing me to take on the project.

When I suggested we arm wrestle, Stu smiled and then looked directly into Kathy's camera lens. Stu and I connected instantly, for reasons I have never quite been able to explain. In some ways he reminded me of my father, who died in 1996. He, too, was larger than life. A character: crusty on the outside, but a softie at heart.

The more time I spent with Stu, the more I realized he was one of kind — a man not likely to walk this way again.

Over time I started to feel amazingly close to Stu. I spent my Saturdays, and many evenings, month after month, accumulating hundreds of hours of interviews, tracing his ancestry through his own recollection and with the help of archival material. I tried to reconstruct his early years, from his birth in Saskatchewan in 1915 to his first athletic endeavours. Invaluable bits of detailed information came with my own independent research and helped fill in the story. So did Stu's wife Helen, his children, friends and the men he wrestled, employed and trained. The more I listened, the more I realized that what I had come to think of as "the project"

Lord of the Ring

could not be completed in the two years I had originally planned: Stu's life, and the Hart family history, was just too dense with fascinating events.

The story gradually wove itself together, despite the pressures of my "other" life — particularly in the book's final stages. Working full time as General Counsel for the Tsuu T'ina (Sarcee) First Nation was demanding, but Stu literally consumed all of my evenings and weekends.

And, with such a large, diverse and successful family, new material kept appearing as I worked — the tragic death of Owen, the subsequent lawsuit against the WWF and Vince McMahon, and the toll both took on the family, Stu's Order of Canada, the controversy created by Diana Hart's book, the loss of Helen in November 2001 and Ed Whalen a month, to the day, later. All of it became essential to the narrative.

Stu's declining hearing was an impediment throughout the process. His hearing aids had a habit of disappearing in places like the washing machine. But Bruce, Ross, Ellie and other family members were always there to help fill in the blanks.

I quickly learned that Stu likes to tell a story his own way — that is, he has a habit of leaving out some of those salient details that help flesh out events and put them in context. When Stu does not want to answer a question, because the answer is "No," he often says "Not necessarily." The interviewer is left to translate.

When I began researching Stu's early life, and the roots of the Hart and Stewart families, independent of his recollection or known family history, help came from unexpected places — the Court of Queen's Bench file from 1926, which detailed the land dispute that altered his family's fortunes miserably; archivists in North Dakota — where his maternal grandfather sat as a respected territorial legislator; the Tofield Museum near Edmonton, where

Stu's family eked out an existence for four years; the Calgary and Edmonton libraries, and New York newspapers which recorded Stu's pro-wrestling debut and development as professional wrestler; as well as files from local newspapers, the Edmonton Eskimos and the Boxing and Wrestling Commission in Calgary.

New material came from Stu himself from time to time. At a party in a log cabin on Park Hill in Calgary in December 2001, marking my appointment to the Alberta Bench, he regaled my niece, Angela Vogel of Saskatoon, with talk about wrestling and self-defence for women.

"Never try to dismantle a man with a kick in the groin," he cautioned. "You could miss and have yourself in worse trouble. You see these little bones on the front of your ankle?"

He tapped the spot on Angela's foot with his cane.

"Drive the heel of your shoe into that spot. He will be forced to fall forward. And when he does, just kick him in the face and get away as fast as you can."

Accuracy and detail have been a preoccupation throughout this project. And while nothing is ever perfect, I believe that *Stu Hart: Lord of the Ring* is an accurate chronicle of the life and times of an amazing Canadian. This is not a book about pro-wrestling *per se*, but it does include a great deal about the business as Stu's life work.

It is, however, a book about sacrifice, perseverance and achievement. All of which Stu Hart has experienced in great abundance, and for which he has been an inspiration to so many — both at home and around the world.

Prologue

May 31st, 1999. Stu Hart was in pain. His knees ached badly but he refused to use a cane — as if doing so would be to concede defeat in one of the toughest battles he had ever fought. A detached, surreal feeling produced by great devastation obviously had swept over him. It now served as a shield from the events of the past week.

No one would fault Stu Hart, at 84 years of age, for believing he would not have to bear the anguish of outliving another child. Losing Owen, the youngest of his brood of 12, in such a bizarre and senseless way, was unimaginable.

At the McInnis and Holloway chapel on Elbow Drive, mourners overflowed into the parking lot outside: a sound system carried parting tributes to fans who stood mesmerized. Visible signs of pain and respect mixed with the sound of the voices and music from within. The stillness of the morning was broken by a light spring rain.

Stu Hart had watched as his six remaining sons — Smith, Bruce, Keith, Wayne, Ross and Bret — served as pallbearers.

The funeral service had started at 11, and the most poignant moments included eulogies given by Owen's widow Martha, and by brothers Bret and Ross. Each spoke of the tenderness known

and shared with a husband and brother. Martha, between tears and warm, smiling reminiscence, shared the letters she'd exchanged with Owen while he was on the road. Everyone understood when she confessed: "I don't know how to let go of him." Owen and their children had been Martha's everything. There had never been another man in her life, not even a boyfriend, and it had been the same with him. First loves. By the time Owen's friend, country singer Colin Raye, strummed his guitar and sang "One Boy, One Girl," the couple's favourite song, no eyes were dry — not even among men considered the toughest in a tough-guy world, the wrestlers who were Owen's peers and colleagues. Bret had already expressed the family's pain and devastating loss in an eloquent column published in the *Calgary Sun*, and it had a similar effect on readers. The column was distributed widely on the Internet and read by thousands around the world.

Friends and family were gathered in small clusters around the Hart's yard once Owen's funeral was over. Stu hobbled to the chair his eldest daughter Ellie had put out for him.

He recognized many of the funeral guests immediately — Hulk Hogan, the Undertaker, the Rock, Pat Patterson, Owen's tag-team partner Jeff Jarrett, Mick "Mankind" Foley, Terry Funk and Dory Funk Jr., both National Wrestling Alliance World champions, Road Dogg Jesse James, Billy Gunn, Chris Jericho, Chris Benoit and dozens more from the industry circuit. Even Killer Kowalski had come up from Boston.

Stone Cold Steve Austin was noticeable in his absence. The WWF's biggest star had a complicated, awkward history with Owen Hart. Hart, by all accounts one of wrestling's best and safest workers, had somehow botched the execution of a piledriver during one of their matches — Stone Cold suffered serious,

Lord of the Ring

career-threatening head and neck injuries.

As the afternoon wore on, some of the wrestlers made their way down the steep steel steps to the basement bowels of the Hart mansion to the infamous pain centre known as the "Dungeon." For some like Chris Benoit, Chris Jericho and Terry and Dory Funk, it was a familiar place. The Funks had worked out there with Stu and the Hart boys on many occasions. Benoit and Jericho had learned some of their craft in the Dungeon, honing their skills under the tutelage of the old master himself and his talented sons. As the wrestlers gathered, Bruce Hart was left with the impression that they were on a kind of pilgrimage. Hulk Hogan, who was visiting for the first time, walked around the mat and slapped his big hands against the heavy, wood-panelled walls. For the Rock it was a different kind of nostalgic journey — his own father, wrestler Rocky Johnson, had spent time with Stu Hart on the mat in this very room. But for everyone, whether they had been trained there or not, the Dungeon was a sacred place, the stuff of legend.

Outside, Stu was never left alone for long. People pressed in around his chair, some had buried children of their own and sensed the depth of his loss.

He was as tired as he looked, but he had a job to do — allow all these people to say the words he already had heard hundreds of times: "I'm so sorry, so terribly sorry." The tragedy of his son's death had been covered widely by media around the world — not only because Owen was a World Wrestling Federation star, but also because of the bizarreness of the failed stunt which plunged him 78 feet to his death from the ceiling of the Kemper Arena in Kansas City.

Across the yard, Vince McMahon Jr., the man who controlled the WWF and, by contract, Owen Hart, stood with his wife Linda and several others between the house and the marquis intended as a shelter from the intermittent spring rain. He was not entirely listening to the conversation, distracted as he was by the movements of the man in the chair across the yard.

Vince and Linda McMahon had travelled with Stu in one of the 16 white limos which carried the huge Hart family home from Queen's Park Cemetery. The limos led a long meandering procession that included at least 100 private vehicles escorted by police on motorcycles. Along the way, motorists, blocked by police to make way for the mourners, had stepped out of their cars. Young and old alike took off their baseball caps or lowered their heads and stood silently, a gesture of respect for both Owen Hart and the family that would have to live without him.

Stu had made an effort to be kind and gracious to the McMahons in the most difficult of circumstances. They talked, but not about his son. It must have been puzzling for Vince. He was not aware that Stu made a practice of handling a difficult situation by stepping back, compartmentalizing, focussing on something — anything — else.

Standing there in the yard, Vince would still have had in his mind the unsettling exchange with Stu's superstar son, Bret "the Hitman" Hart. It had taken place just after the interment. They had stood together for a few minutes under the huge trees that provided a sad moment's respite from the fast-paced, hardball world that occupied most of their daily lives. Vince would later tell the media that he had been shocked by Bret's words.

He claimed Bret had accused him of destroying his career, his marriage, and his life. . . .

Lord of the Ring

Reminiscence led many of those gathered at Hart House back to an earlier era of pro-wrestling, when Stu himself was a young champion and the toast of Western Canada. Inevitably, thoughts turned to the intertwining of two family dynasties, the Harts and the McMahons. Because of the international scope and financial success of the WWF, Vince was certainly more powerful and better known. But among those who knew both men on a personal level, there was no comparison. Stu Hart was beloved, a character who had left his mark on countless others.

McMahon must have known that despite the graciousness of the Hart family — the unspoken decision to leave accusations and unanswered questions for another day — the horror of Kansas City was still on the murmuring lips of many of those assembled.

It must have weighed heavily.

McMahon had done what he could to make amends — flying in wrestlers and their families to attend the service, providing catering for the Harts. He would have been acutely aware that many blamed him for the tragedy which cost Owen his life. On this day, however, even the Hart family unity would be threatened by divided opinion.

As he was pondering these things, he noticed Bruce Hart, Stu's second oldest son standing nearby. Bruce and his brother Ross ran the Hart Brothers' wrestling camp in addition to working as local high school teachers. Bruce held a well-known disdain for McMahon, cultivated long before either Bret's messy departure from the WWF and subsequent signing with Ted Turner's WCW, or the tragic events of the previous week.

Vince had taken over Stu Hart's "Stampede Wrestling" in 1984. The promotion controlled a lucrative territory of more than two dozen venues in the Northwestern United States and Western

Canada, with Calgary as its nucleus. By either taking over or driving competitors out of business on both sides of the 49th parallel, Vince had what he needed to take the McMahon family promotion national. In doing so he changed pro-wrestling completely — the WWF as we know it was born.

A viable, profitable resurgence in Calgary would take an act of God.

McMahon had systematically dismantled the old territorial system of pro-wrestling — in which individual promoters each controlled large areas of North America, trading wrestlers back and forth and controlling the gates of matches in a dozen or more large centres at a time. In the old days, promoters met annually in places like Las Vegas, St. Louis, Chicago, Dallas, Tulsa, and Toronto, under the National Wrestling Alliance banner; there, they'd sometimes elect the new world's champion and engineer the match that would be the chosen wrestler's championship bout. The new champion would then make the rounds as a star attraction throughout all the territories, keeping gate receipts healthy for all of the participating promoters.

Vince had acquired Stampede Wrestling in a way that angered Bruce. On a handshake, he'd picked up the company's TV spots and all of its top talent — including Tom "the Dyna-mite Kid" Billington and Davey Boy Smith (Bruce had brought them both over from England and helped train them to become the charismatic stars known as the British Bull-dogs). Even Bret Hart, his brother-in-law, Jim "the Anvil" Neidhart and later Owen himself became part of the McMahon empire.

Eventually that sad spring afternoon, Vince McMahon approached Bruce Hart.

The 1980 Commonwealth Wrestling Champion recalls Vince's words clearly. With his chin thrust forward, McMahon said: "Well,

Lord of the Ring

go ahead give me the best you've got." It was the kind of baiting frustrated men sometimes do.

"This isn't the place," Hart said, understandably annoyed, but at the same time remarkably aware that Vince McMahon, too, was a man in pain — a man who had travelled all the way from his comfortable home in Connecticut to face the parents, siblings and friends of one of his best wrestlers after a flawed and senseless accident had taken him from them. Bruce respected Vince for facing the family, but was in no mood to deal with him — or the insensitivity of his actions immediately after Owen's death.

Vince, knowing full well the extent of the tragedy, and ostensibly directing the Kemper Arena Pay-Per-View, had ordered the show to continue.

Later that afternoon, one of the promoters from the old days took Vince by the arm and steered him toward Stu Hart's lawn chair. Linda McMahon, son Shane, daughter Stephanie and two bodyguards followed.

Stu saw him coming and with all the effort his knees — destroyed by a thousand squats a day over the course of years — could bear, rose and reached to shake hands, his arms opened to half embrace a man who had been like another son not so long ago.

The cordiality was vintage Hart, part of why he was revered by so many.

Stu Hart has always had an ability to weather any emotional storm, no matter how tumultuous. His children often refer to him as stoic. In his heart Stu knew there was no reason to go into battle with Vince McMahon.

Unless someone could bring Owen back, what was the point?

It must have been puzzling for Vince, the way Stu called over Dory Funk, Jr. to talk about alligator boots and old wrestlers. Vince

was left to smile and nod politely, not quite realizing that he was being spared, in a gentle and kind way, from difficult words.

Stu Hart, despite his unofficial position as the patriarch of pro-wrestling, respected around the world for his training techniques, has always had an unexpected tenderness. Even so, he knew how to inflict pain just as he knew how to endure it; it was something he may have been more skilled at than anyone else milling in the yard outside his home that day. Still, holding court from his chair, Stu presided over those gathered like a benevolent godfather. It was a stature he had earned over the course of 70 years. He had travelled a long distance from his humble, uncertain beginnings, desperate times for himself, his parents and sisters. They were years he often recalled with a shudder. A time of remarkable hardship, of struggling through prairie winters in an unheated 6-by-9-foot canvass tent dampened by melting snow and made leaky by sparks from an open fire.

Sometimes he could hardly believe those days were part of his life at all.

There had been so many achievements. Stu and his beloved Helen had shared so much — every kind of joy and pain. Now, there was a sense of foreboding. A new, unsettling chapter had begun. They braced themselves for what was yet to come.

Sunday, May 23, 1999. Another warm, spring day in Kansas City, Missouri. Owen Hart stepped off his flight from Calgary, sports bag slung over his shoulder, and his long stride took him quickly out of the terminal and into the vehicle waiting for him. He had many friends all over the United States; one of them usually picked him up when he when he blew into town for a match with the World Wrestling Federation.

Owen headed over to the Kemper Arena, paying little attention to the floral splendour erupting everywhere. He was focussed on one thing: he wanted to check in before the WWF's Pay-Per-View later that evening. Specifically, he wanted to go over the circus-like entrance he was scheduled to make.

When approached by a script writer about pulling out his old Blue Blazer costume to spoof WCW's Sting, Owen had misgivings. In fact, he did his best to get out of the stunt — but to no avail. Eventually, he got the assurance he was seeking. Everything would be set up the right way, properly, professionally.

It wasn't the first time Owen had to glide into a ring. His brother-in-law and former tag-team partner Davey Boy Smith recalls Owen doing a similar bit in a match with Steve Blackman. That time it had gone off without a hitch. In Kansas City, however,

things were different. This time the descent was vertical and the set-up was new and unfamiliar.

Despite any second thoughts Owen might have had that day, he carried deep within him an ingrained fearlessness. It was something he shared with his 11 brothers and sisters, something instilled by their father. Stu's sons had honed their mat skills under the careful tutelage of a professional credited with training many of the pro-wrestling greats of more than four decades. His own sons had entered that pantheon.

Owen, blonde, blue-eyed and the youngest of Stu Hart's eight sons and four daughters, truly believed the informal family mantra: *If you live right and be strong, nothing can go wrong.* The Harts' sense of invincibility had been rocked, of course, with Dean's death in 1990 after a long battle with kidney disease; and they struggled again, when young Matthew Annis, 13-year-old son of Stu's daughter Georgia, died of flesh-eating disease in July 1997. Still, although badly shaken, the Hart credo was intact on that warm May afternoon.

A clean-living family man, Owen had grown up under the watchful eyes of many siblings. Even though he was a tough kid in his own right, who grew into a beefy, athletic man, he had all of those older brothers ready to spring to his defence whenever he needed help. He rarely did, but the comfort of having their backup gave him confidence in everything he did.

Owen was like his father in many ways. He had strong, handsome features, a high forehead and cheekbones. He was a superb wrestler, noted for an acrobatic style that was paired with a no-blink approach to a challenge. Few could flip off the ropes the way that he could, cleanly, expertly.

In many ways, he had wanted to live a quiet life: as a physical education teacher, out of the spotlight. But the substantial income he could so easily command from something that had

Lord of the Ring

been taken for granted by the Harts for so long was the catalyst that pulled him from the University of Calgary, where he had studied for three years on an amateur wrestling scholarship. By the late '90s it had become more and more difficult to simply wrestle a few bouts, collect his paycheque, and head home to Martha, their daughter, Athena, and son, Oje — whose name is a derivative of his father's first and second names, Owen James.

Owen actually left pro-wrestling for a time to travel the world with Martha. When they returned to Calgary and he tried to get into another line of work, the fire department — despite his athletic prowess — turned him down. He went back to the WWF — the money was just too good to ignore. In the spring of 1999, he had signed on for another five years, well-established internationally as a star.

Moral questions bombarded wrestlers like Owen Hart in the late '90s. Storylines became more and more outrageous each week. But Owen was not one to compromise his ethics. He and Martha agreed that no matter what he would not sell out his beliefs.

It just wasn't worth it.

As his brothers and sisters would recount many times, Owen could always be relied upon to do the right thing. He shared the old-fashioned family values of Stu Hart, and it would never have occurred to either of them to abandon them. Like his father, Owen married the first woman he fell in love with. Forty years apart, the romances were the stuff of poets, novelists, movie producers.

Sunday night at the Kemper Arena was to follow the tried and true pattern of all WWF Pay-Per-View events. Frenzied fans, a backdrop of flashing lights, pyrotechnics and mind-numbing, ear-piercing, hard rock music. There would be 20,000 in attendance, with millions more watching around the world — everyone waiting for the testosterone to kick in and make something happen.

It is often hard for wrestlers not to get caught up in the hype: egos are fuel-injected with each performance. Many have slipped into the shadows, some lured into dependency on painkillers, which mask real injuries, or lead them towards other kinds of drugs. The ring-rat groupies, druggies and hangers-on attend wrestlers like vultures. But Owen had no trouble avoiding it all. He had a clear sense of himself and what he wanted out of life. He didn't have the kind of ego that demanded constant public stroking.

For the better part of the decade the WWF had been caught up in a power struggle with its only North American rival, World Championship Wrestling. In 1985, media mogul Ted Turner had given McMahon the national air time he needed to position his WWF at the top, drive out the old alliances and turn the pro-wrestling game into the huge cash cow it became. It wasn't long, however, before a shrewd Turner, who realized wrestling always attracted viewers, decided he should have a bigger piece of the action. As well, fans of Turner's previous programming, Georgia Championship Wrestling, began to complain. The show returned. In 1989 be bought the sinking WCW from Jim Crockett and positioned the relatively cheap programming favourably on TBS. The new WCW became successful by upping the ante, acquiring many of McMahon's big stars, producing fast-paced, outrageous television, and pushing the envelope with radical storylines. At one point, for more than a year and a half, WCW's Monday night television ratings topped the WWF's numbers. In an unfamiliar position, as the number 2 game in town, the WWF had to stay on its toes.

The competition led McMahon to an "anything that sells goes" approach to what used to be simple theatre — big men acting out comic soap opera story lines embracing classic allegory — good triumphing over evil. Good guy ("babyfaces") versus bad guy ("heels" or "villains") was the standard fare for decades. McMahon and Turner took wrestling into uncharted terrain. These days televised pro-wrestling has less and less to do with displays of physical strength and controlled, scripted athletic skill than with hero worship, morally ambiguous characters and bizarre story lines which at times have focussed on the occult, the sinister and the sexual. Today's pro-wrestling is often wrapped in sleaziness. The fans, gradually desensitized by "shock television," have increasingly blurred the heel and babyface distinction.

The bad boy reigns supreme.

More and more frequently, McMahon has written himself, his wife and his adult children into scripts. It's as if his in-ring persona — the evil billionaire Mr. McMahon — is constructed to tell fans: "It's all okay because I'm doing it, too." Perhaps it is a way to legitimize the WWF's unstated philosophy: the only rule is that there are no rules.

For McMahon, the pressure is to make each event more of a spectacle than the last. In 1987, after Wrestlemania III at the Pontiac Silverdome, the Associated Press reported the reaction of a 17-year-old fan; it serves as an eerie foreshadowing of what would come 12 years later: "It can't get any better than this, they'll have to kill somebody."

By the '90s, McMahon stopped bothering to pretend that pro-wrestling was a serious, "fair," athletic enterprise. The term "sports entertainment" was born. But as the decade progressed, the emphasis seemed to have less and less to do with "sports."

Plots became more daring, the sexual antics more revealing, the vocabulary more foul. This appears to be incongruent with the fact that the largest sector of fans is clearly teenagers and prepubescent kids. Pro-wrestling's influence on impressionable youth is debated now in much the same way as it was in the 1950s, when Stu Hart was still building his territory. But in those earlier,

more innocent times, the public complained about swearing, spitting and the use of foreign objects. By 1999 it was unique if a wrestler *didn't* clobber an opponent with a metal chair or ring bell, or if a middle finger wasn't flashed at the referee and crowd.

Owen Hart had always been popular — because of his boyish good looks and charm. But that Sunday night in Kansas City, he was uneasy.

Hart didn't like heights, but told his wife Martha that the pressure coming from the WWF to spoof Sting's glide-from-the-sky routine was overwhelming. He felt he just couldn't keep saying no — he had morally rejected other outrageous storylines, involving lewd antics with ring temptress Debra — and expect to keep working. Owen knew that McMahon was capable of cutting him from the action, that his job would be snapped up by one of a hundred wannabes in a New York minute.

Other wrestlers knew it, too. Weeks after Owen's death, wrestling superstar Hollywood Hulk Hogan would describe what he thought of Vince McMahon on *Larry King Live:* "He buys the horse, he races the horse, then he eats the horse." Not even Owen's superstar brother Bret had total creative control, although for a while, Bret was in a far better position, as the company's top wrestler, to have his objections heard. Still, in the end, even Bret would succumb to McMahon's manipulation.

By the end of May, 1999, Owen Hart's values were clearly at odds with the WWF's product. He saw wrestling as his job. As soon as he finished his matches, he was on his way back home to Martha and the kids. On the road, he didn't check into luxury hotels or live it up the way some wrestlers do. He saved every cent — because the money meant that soon he would be able to quit wrestling and live a quiet life with his young family.

When Owen was born in 1965, Helen Hart was told that it was

Lord of the Ring

time for her to stop having children. She had delivered a dozen healthy babies in 17 years, and by this time Owen's older siblings were turning into young adults.

As the youngest, Owen had both his dad and older brothers at football games and amateur wrestling meets, at least some of the time. Stu had always longed for one of his sons to take up Olympic wrestling, and edged Owen towards that goal. Years earlier he had unsuccessfully attempted the same thing with Bret when he started showing interest in the family business. Stu himself had twice missed out on the Olympics, when both the 1940 and 1944 games were cancelled because of the War. His attempts to lure Owen away from the pro-wrestling circuit and into the legitimate amateur world failed. According to his brothers, Owen was not interested in that level of competition. He didn't like the idea of being an Olympic athlete and all it entailed. Either way, Owen had the skills to do whatever he pleased.

Growing up, the Hart kids adapted to the way their dad made a living. Stu often worked long hours just to keep the promotion going. Helen too, keeping the books and business in order. Together they juggled the challenging job of looking after their growing brood.

Still, it was clear to each Hart child that, despite the sometimes tough discipline they were subjected to, they were special to their parents — wanted and loved.

At times, the older children were like second parents to the younger ones. Bruce, the second-eldest son, had that kind of relationship with Owen. Bruce was 15 in 1965, and the warmth of their relationship would endure for Owen's entire life. During his teen years, Owen was often driven to wrestling by Bruce. The older Hart made time for his little brother, teaching him holds and helping him improve his technique. As a result, Owen was closer to Bruce than any of his other siblings. By the time Owen reached

the WWF, where his brother Bret reigned as superstar, a remarkable closeness developed between him and "the Hitman" as well.

Stu and Helen had more time to fuss over the youngest kids, but their time was still spread as widely as the cat and dog hair left behind the herd of family pets that raced through the house. For years they had struggled to raise children spaced as little as 12 or 18 months apart. Owen capitalized on being the last. By the time he arrived his parents had settled into a more relaxed approach to parenthood. As parents, nothing they faced was new.

Keith, the third Hart son, tells a story about Owen's rite of passage, when he finally moved out of the girls' room and in with the boys. From almost the moment Owen arrived, the girls treated him like a big doll. By the time he reached kindergarten, Owen's seven older brothers had written him off — it was just as bad as having another tattletale girl around. Then one day at dinner their mother announced that Owen would be moving into the boys' room. Little Owen glanced around the big table at the smirks on the faces of his seven older brothers. The knowing looks and nudges were not lost on him. Not long after the move, sister Ellie and brother Dean got into a tumble. Their dad, who had strict rules against the boys getting into physical combat with their sisters, demanded to know what was going on. Owen, sensing an opportunity to redeem himself in the eyes of his brothers, let three little words slip from his pre-school lips, which would change his stature among his brothers forever: "Ellie started it." The boys cheered, and the solidarity among them was permanently and irrevocably sealed.

Stu and Helen had planned to have a large family, and that was the reason behind the big house. But the turn-of-the century brick mansion earned its own fame because of the parade of wrestlers who had gained notoriety in Stu Hart's basement gym.

Lord of the Ring

Owen's dad was often perceived as a brute — a man many assumed was a mean s.o.b. The kids liked the myth, especially because they knew the truth.

In many ways Stu was just a big teddy bear — as long as you didn't do something stupid, like get him mad. Because when you did, there was hell to pay. It might entail being propped up on the mantle above one of the huge Hart House fireplaces while Stu pinned you there with a couple of fingers — demanding to know if you were going to behave, while you believed you were going to crash onto the hearth.

Generally, it was the kind of intimidation that was enough to keep the boys in line.

Stu Hart has always been a slow-to-anger kind of guy, intimidating but respected, and he, too, never shrank from a challenge. Like his brothers before him, Owen had watched his father invite tough-guy braggarts down to the Dungeon to teach them a little respect. In his 80s, Stu could still put 25-year-old wannabes in holds that brought the blood rushing to their faces and gave them red eyes for hours after their futile efforts to release themselves. When Stu finally let them go, they would peel themselves, exhausted, off the mat and look at Stu Hart differently. Even if unspoken, it was admiration they felt as they nursed their own injured pride: an old man had held them to the mat and they couldn't move a muscle.

Keith recalls being a teenager and going down to the Dungeon to practise with one of his buddies. He'd tell the friend: if my Dad hears and comes down, make sure you get off the mat right away. It never failed — ten minutes later, Stu would be asking Keith's buddy if he was learning some holds. Sooner or later he'd question, "Did he show you this one?" In a matter of seconds the kid would be in a hold, wishing for dear life he had listened to Keith and stepped off the mat right away.

Owen learned the ropes at an early age. It was inevitable; pro-wrestling was as ordinary to a Hart boy's daily life as comic books, cartoons, hockey and football were for other Canadian youngsters. But life at Hart House was far from ordinary. Keith says it was more like living in the middle of a circus. Colourful characters appeared and disappeared on a regular basis. Midgets would wander through the house, wild animals sat in cages on the porch, and athletes like Andre the Giant and Killer Kowalski played with the kids. As a small boy Owen was terrified of the man named "Killer." He was apt to run and hide the minute the big wrestling legend stepped onto the back porch. It took a while to convince the littlest Hart that Kowalski really hadn't killed anybody.

Some of the wrestlers would hang around the house for good stretches of time, and so would some of the animals. Once, a huge black bear was stuffed under the front porch for the winter, so it could hibernate in peace. The kids still remember the spectacle of the bear being pulled out in the spring and walked around on a chain until it had fully regained its senses.

During their high school and post-secondary years, the Hart boys were not allowed to work for their dad's Stampede Wrestling promotion unless they used the money to further their education. As youngsters, they would be handed a bundle of programs to sell around the box office and just outside the Victoria Pavilion or Stampede Corral. The kids were out there rain or shine, and there they remained until they had sold their quota. Only then would they be allowed to come inside and watch the matches. In the end, each of the Hart boys would end up on the payroll of Stampede Wrestling — in one way or another.

Stu and Helen wanted their children to graduate from university so that they could make informed decisions about their future. Stu appreciated how hard it had been for him to get an education when the odds were so against it, and Helen, academic-

Lord of the Ring

minded in her youth, had to give up school to help her family. Together they would attend parent-teacher meetings and Stu, like a giant in his son or daughter's seat at school, would flip through notebooks rifled from the desk and wonder just how much attention was being paid when the covers had so many hand-drawn cartoon characters and doodles.

The "university first" plan worked for the eldest children, who did go on to earn degrees and teaching credentials. Even so, every one of the boys, Smith, Bruce, Keith, Wayne, Dean, Bret, Ross and Owen, participated in wrestling, and each of the four daughters married men who had wrestled at some time or other or had made it their careers. Elizabeth (Ellie) married WWF wrestler Jim "the Anvil" Neidhart. Georgia married Bradley Joseph (B.J.) Annis, a marine engineer, body builder and gym owner who sometimes wrestled. Alison married wrestler Ben Bassarab. Diana married "the British Bulldog" Davey Boy Smith, a WWF and WCW star.

Despite the common perception, Keith insists that none of the boys were pushed into wrestling. But wrestling has a way of capturing a young boy's imagination, and Owen was no exception.

As a small boy, Owen invented wrestling storylines. His brother Keith, now a firefighter and occasional wrestler for Ross and Bruce's promotion, remembers Owen staging matches between Heathcliff, the cat, and a stuffed monkey. After a while, Owen simply had to bring out the monkey and the cat went after it with a vengeance, sending anyone nearby into hysterics.

When Owen arrived at Kemper Arena the rigging for his stunt was already set up and ready for a dry run. The repelling harness which connected him to the rigging line was, reportedly, a flimsy contraption with a few narrow straps, hook rings, ropes and

cables designed for sailboats — not for stunt like this. The harness was connected to the line with a quick-release snap. The apparatus was literally taped to Owen's body.

During the trial run everything went smoothly. But no one told Owen that the rigging was designed to hold 30, not 230 pounds. No one mentioned that it could take as little as 10 pounds of pressure on the quick release to send him into a free fall.

Number seven son, Ross, confirms that McMahon pressed Owen to bring back and revitalize the "Blue Blazer" mystery character, complete with chicken feathers and electric blue Spandex. Owen was reluctant, tired of the costume, the mask and the repetitive story lines. But in exchange for reviving the character and carrying out the stunt, Ross says Owen was to land the Intercontinental Belt — next to the World Championship, which Bret had dominated in recent years, the most important title the WWF had to offer.

Owen did all he could to dissuade Vince McMahon from going ahead with the entrance as scripted. During the weeks before the Pay-Per-View, the usual lead-up matches were scheduled in venues around the United States. After a match in California, Owen detoured from his usual route home to Calgary. He flew instead to Stanford, Connecticut, to talk to McMahon directly. His efforts to get McMahon to let him bow out of the stunt were met with stubborn refusal.

Owen's job that night in Kansas City was to glide smoothly from the rafters and into the ring like a comic book superhero, trounce "the Godfather" character, and capture the Intercontinental Belt. It was a stunt McMahon himself described as routine.

At the appointed hour, just after 7:30 p.m., Owen Hart, dressed in coveralls to hide the blue Spandex, climbed a wooden ladder and took his place on the catwalk scaffolding high above the packed arena as he had done in the test run just hours earlier.

Lord of the Ring

He took off the coveralls, put on the rest of his Blue Blazer costume and stepped into the harness attached to the rigging suspending him above the throng below. Rock music blared at a fever pitch. Owen, wanting to put the stunt behind him, moved to the outside of the scaffolding and stepped over a railing to position himself for the glide down. He would have been able to see that the fevered crowd was eagerly waiting for the match to begin. The din of music and voices must have seemed incredible from his bird's eye perch, some 78 feet above it all.

But as Owen's hands left their grip on the scaffold railing, the quick release on the rigging suddenly sprang open. The harness failed to hold. The Blue Blazer was hurled into a crashing free fall.

When the catch opened, Owen started screaming. He kept screaming as his body plunged. He struck a ring post, then slammed onto the mat. Owen's left arm was smashed, the principal artery to his heart had nearly been severed when he hit the ring post and his lungs filled with blood almost immediately.

Next, silence.

A stunned split-second of shocked disbelief engulfed the arena; then mass confusion set in as paramedics rushed to the fallen superstar.

Fans sat confused, many started to weep, not even sure that what they had witnessed was real. Others kept asking over and over whether this was part of the script, some sort of ingenious sleight of hand, or whether something had gone horribly wrong.

Why didn't Owen jump up and wave to the crowd and show everyone that he was really just fine, that it really was part of the storyline?

The horrible truth was becoming all too apparent.

The paramedics tried desperately to stabilize him, but to no avail. Announcer Jim Ross told viewers that something had gone very wrong, that Owen Hart was receiving an external heart

massage. Owen was carried out of the arena on a stretcher. He died in the ambulance en route to hospital, without even a familiar face nearby. No one from the WWF was in the ambulance with him, even though his condition was clearly critical.

Fortunately, the fall was not televised on the Pay-Per-View because a pre-recorded interview with Owen was being aired at the time. Owen was expected to hang in his harness for almost ten minutes before coming down the guide lines, leaving time for the interview to wrap up and have the cameras pick up the last few seconds of his ring entrance. No one expected him to come down so fast. Fifteen minutes after Owen was taken out of the ring on a stretcher, Vince McMahon ordered the show to continue, as if nothing had happened. The decision was considered callous and reprehensible by the Hart family.

Some of the wrestlers who performed later on the card wept openly, barely able to complete their moves; others were simply stunned and going through the motions. A shocked television audience heard the announcement an hour later: Owen Hart was dead at age 34. It was a freak accident that not even the most sadistic script writer could have penned.

In Calgary, Stu and Helen Hart were putting the finishing touches on the Sunday night dinner table. Their eldest son, Smith, and daughters Ellie and Alison had already gathered, along with Ellie's daughter Jenny. The rest of the family was expected as soon as the Pay-Per-View was over. The phone rang and Smith picked up the receiver. Spencer Tapley, the manager of the Westgate sports bar, nicknamed by Bruce Hart "Mark the Shark de Carlo," was on the other end. He had been watching the Pay-Per-View with Bruce. They wanted reassurance that the news about Owen having an accident and being taken out on a stretcher was a rib, part of the script.

Lord of the Ring

Smith turned to his mother and repeated what he was told. Helen looked back at her son, the colour gradually draining from her face. Ellie, the oldest Hart daughter, volunteered to run over to Diana and Davey Boy Smith's place where some of the Hart clan had gathered to watch Owen's match. An overwhelming dread began to take over as she drove the few blocks.

But the bitter reality hadn't reached Davey Boy's yet either. A stunned Jim Ross talked about the seriousness of the situation while Diana and Ellie debated fearfully. Could it really just be part of a sick, twisted script?

The way Jim Ross spoke, it sounded too real.

Mercifully, the television cameras panned the crowd while the paramedics worked on Owen. The family watching at Davey Boy and Diana's were spared what the fans at Kemper Arena were not.

The phone rang again at Hart House. It was Martha. She had received a call from Vince McMahon, telling her Owen had been had been seriously injured. McMahon was unsure of Owen's condition, and unable to give any further information. A little later Martha received another call, this time from the chief surgeon at the hospital in Kansas City.

He confirmed her worst fears.

She called Stu.

"This is the hardest thing I've ever had to tell you," she began, her voice breaking, overwhelmed with pain.

Ross had just walked into his dad's house when Martha phoned. He wasn't aware that Owen was wrestling that night, or that he was scripted to do a stunt. It fell upon him to phone his sister Diana. Diana burst into sobs of painful disbelief. She and Owen were the youngest, so close in age they'd grown up like twins.

Diana's husband Davey Boy Smith was having a beer with his former brother-in-law, Ben Bassarab. Earlier in the afternoon,

Stu Hart

Davey and Diana had taken Davey's Harley-Davidson for a spin out to Bragg Creek, a picturesque little hamlet nestled in the foothills of the Rocky Mountains, just south of Calgary. On the way back, they stopped at Elbow Springs and had a look at the house Owen and Martha had just finished building. The couple had planned to move in the following Wednesday.

Davey had dropped off Diana and watched a few minutes of the Pay-Per-View before heading out. About an hour later his cellphone rang. It was Diana, crying, "He's dead, he's dead." Davey couldn't get Diana to collect herself enough to say who she was talking about. Gripped with fear, he drove home as fast as the Harley would take him and was met by his 14-year-old son Harry. Harry told his dad that Owen had taken a fall in Kansas City during the Pay-Per-View and was dead.

"No way, he's not dead, it's just an angle, you'll see," Davey confidently brushed off his son's words. But when he got into the house, he quickly realized the accident was no angle. Shock continued to descend like a heavy black curtain.

Bruce Hart hurried home to pick up his wife, Andrea, and their kids, and went to his parent's place, too. Georgia and her husband, B.J., had just returned to Calgary from Saskatchewan, where they had collected daughter Angie from Notre Dame Collegiate at Wilcox. They heard from the family on B.J.'s cell that there had been an accident and were expecting an update as they headed up the hill to Hart House. On the way they saw sports reporter Tammy Christopher in her TV vehicle at the stop lights on Bow Trail. They rolled down the window and asked what she had heard. It was Tammy who confirmed the devastating news. Both vehicles headed up the hill.

The phone at Hart House kept ringing and ringing. It had to be an angle — it just couldn't be true. The easy banter that accompanies a dining room table that sits 25 disappeared. Food

Lord of the Ring

was left untouched. The brothers and sisters held each other close, trying, without much success, to comfort each other.

The extended Hart family clustered together, sharing what little they knew, surfing television stations, trying to find out more about what had happened or taking turns answering the telephone. Their movements were automatic, semi-conscious. How such a thing could happen was a question echoing in every Hart mind.

A few thousand miles away, Owen's older brother, wrestling superstar Bret Hart, was sitting on a commercial air flight to Los Angeles, on his way to an interview with Jay Leno for *The Tonight Show*. An airline steward approached him, explaining that there was an emergency call he needed to take. Numb, Bret walked off the plane in Los Angeles and was met by wcw's Eric Bischoff, who had already chartered a plane to take the Hitman home.

Keith Hart was at Calgary's Fire Station Number 4. An alarm came in and the crew was about to pull out to respond. Then, the shift captain pulled Keith off the rig and told him what had happened. Dazed, he too headed for the family home. His cell rang; it was local television personality and long-time Stampede Wrestling ring and tv announcer Ed Whalen, offering to help. Keith gratefully dispatched him to handle the press calls. A wrestling friend called, too, hoping that Keith would tell him the news rapidly circulating around the world about Owen's death just wasn't true.

Instead of heading straight to Hart House, Keith drove over to Owen and Martha's place on Sirocco Drive to check on Martha. He was relieved to see Martha's sister, as well as other members of her family. Martha was totally and completely devastated. She had just lost the love of her life, the father of her two young children.

The news ricocheted through the wrestling world. In the days that

Stu Hart

followed, Stu kept wondering, "What the hell was he doing up there in a harness? Why didn't he say no to Vince?"

More calls came in from all over the globe, most not believing what they had seen and heard. There were so many the family had to set up an answering service just to have a little peace.

By Monday evening, an angry and broken Hart family listened to the tributes pour in. Nearly 24 hours had passed since the tragedy that had claimed Owen. Stu stared at the television screen, barely moving, locking his feelings deep inside, the pain on his face evident. But he did not fall apart, his stoicism deeply imbedded in his personality. McMahon's decision to continue the program disgusted most of the wrestling fraternity. Worse, McMahon allowed the show to continue as if nothing had happened, including going ahead with a storyline in which McMahon himself was beaten up by "Stone Cold" Steve Austin, carried out on a stretcher and transported to hospital. Not one member of the family could understand the WWF's insensitivity.

When friends arrived, Stu rose silently and mechanically and embraced the first person in the door. The depth of the loss was as plain as it was piercing.

Helen, arms folded across her chest, rocked quietly on the edge of her chair, her thoughts clearly anywhere but in the kitchen. Perhaps she was thinking about the last time she and Stu had seen Owen.

It was just days before his birthday, on May 7, and he had stopped in to drop off a box of Greek sausages he had brought home from a trip to Eastern Canada. He sat and talked to his parents for a while, but didn't stay long because he had promised Martha he would be home by 4. Hugging his parents, Owen told them he was going to have dinner with his sister Alison on his birthday. As his parents stood together on the front veranda, Owen ran to his car and waved goodbye. "Owen was always running,"

Lord of the Ring

Helen recalled with sadness.

Owen's sisters Georgia and Ellie and his nieces Natalie and Jenny huddled together in the kitchen with Smith. Their safe, insular world had changed overnight. The Hart mantra — *If you live right and be strong, nothing can go wrong* — had died in the Kemper Arena.

Martha and Bret prepared to travel to Kansas City to make arrangements to bring a beloved husband and brother home. They would find Owen's body wrapped in layers of plastic and a huge Canadian flag.

Two

Stu Hart was sitting quietly in an oversized, worn leather chair in his living room reading the Sunday edition of the *Calgary Sun*. He still hadn't had a chance to scan Bret's celebrity column in the sports section. Weekends were always fast-paced around the Hart home, especially during the summer months. Ross and Bruce ran the "Hart Brothers Wrestling Camp," affectionately known as the "School of Hart Knocks," and young wrestlers-in-training kept a steady pace running up and down stairs to and from the basement Dungeon, or were scattered around the yard watching the action in a wrestling ring set up on the side lawn.

Whenever a novice like Adrian Gilmore (who wrestled under the name "Crazy Horse Eddie Mustang") or Carl Leduc, son of one of the Leduc wrestling brothers of the 1960s, caught sight of Stu shuffling through the house, they would raise a question about a wrestling hold or some legendary figure from the past and Stu would end up telling stories drawn from his own days as both as a wrestler and a promoter.

Stu loved the banter, and would reminisce freely about the early days of Stampede Wrestling and its predecessors. And his sons and daughters were always glad when their father had a fresh ear to hear his many anecdotes. Every Hart sibling had heard them all — many times.

Stu's Saturday afternoons were absorbed with the ritual of stocking up on groceries at the nearby Westbrook Safeway store for the Sunday night dinner his family shared around the huge dining room table, its burgundy tablecloth reaching to the floor, the antique sideboard and cabinet gasping under the weight of enough china and glassware to feed dozens. Stu and his second oldest daughter, Georgia, prepared the big meal while Helen organized the table and made sure her favourite sprigs of parsley were evident.

It took a lot of work to turn out a meal for as many as 25, the family, wrestlers, friends and anyone else who happened to be around. Sometimes the Sunday night ritual even included canvassers who were passing out tracts for a religious sect, if they happened to arrive at supper time. Helen would invite them in — they balanced out the group of athletes around the table.

In the good years, roasts and steak prevailed, but in leaner times the meal was more likely to be a huge mound of spaghetti and meatballs. The financial situation of the Hart family jumped around like a free-range chicken, but they always believed that, sooner or later, good times, economically, were never far away. Helen, who enjoyed a good turn of phrase and irreverence, called the house "Hart Acres" because of it.

The Sunday night dinner remained a ritual even after the kids had all grown up and moved out on their own. They liked to bring their own families and hang around the house talking to their parents and to each other. The house was as inviting as it was comfortable. No one worried about doffing shoes at the door to spare the huge Persian carpet in the living room or the hardwood floors bordering it.

Children had long run the floors at high speed, in a circle that

Lord of the Ring

included the kitchen, with its swinging saloon-style door, the dining room, and into the living room, past the old leather furniture and massive coffee tables that had all seen better days, and on into the library with its Scottish antique furnishings and fireplace mantel, lined with congratulatory messages for Stu and Helen since their 50th wedding anniversary in 1997. A bronze bust of Stu's head kept the focus on the man who had brought it all together.

But by July 1999, there was a tenseness around the dining room table. Battle lines had been drawn between Bret — who was supported by Keith — and Ellie, Bruce and Diana. The factions were becoming openly hostile. Bret strenuously disapproved of Diana and Ellie's husbands' continued affiliation with the WWF after Owen's tragic death. His sisters thought of themselves as realists. Where were wrestlers supposed to work if not for the WWF or WCW? They had families to feed. They didn't have huge nest eggs like Bret — substantial savings built over many years with the same WWF he now loathed. Bret's stellar career continued into his mid-40s, and did not let up until a concussion took him out of the action in 2000.

Stu thumbed through the sports pages that July afternoon until he found Bret's column. He had heard his daughters discussing his son's comments about Davey Boy Smith's plan to return to wrestling after a long recovery from a serious spinal staph infection. Davey's condition was still fragile, but he was getting stronger every day. In his July 10 piece Bret wrote: "Saw a strange sight yesterday. Dogs rolling in manure and loving every minute of it. For some reason it made me think how the British Bulldog will do anything to work for the WWF." Bret was implying that Davey was grovelling his way back.

Davey disputes this with indignation.

Bret continued to blame Vince McMahon personally for Owen's death. His own controversial history with the McMahon-owned WWF could only fuel a dark, cynical attitude toward anything connected with his old boss. While Bret had good reasons to resent Vince McMahon and his company, anger may have made him myopic to differing points of view.

Davey had made a statement to the media shortly after Owen's death, asserting that Vince McMahon had been a kind of father figure to Owen, and it did not sit well with the Hitman. Bret went to Davey's house, sought out his sister Diana and told her what he thought about Davey's comments. He didn't get the sympathetic response he had expected.

The incident thinned out the Sunday dinner ranks. If Bret showed up, Ellie and Diana made a B-line for the door. Both sisters knew why Bret was angry and they made an effort to give him a wide berth. But even some other members of the family would note that their brother might have been ignoring some of the facts.

Davey recalls quitting the WWF in 1997 as a gesture of loyalty to Bret, after Vince McMahon had publicly betrayed the Hitman during that year's infamous Survivor Series, humiliating him in front of Canadian fans in Montreal, when the World Championship belt was snatched from him and delivered to Shawn Michaels. Before the Pay-Per-View event, Bret had made it very clear that he did not want to give up his championship belt in Canada, and invoked his contractual right to veto any script that called for it. Montreal would see his last big match before he moved to WCW — a move Bret lamented but accepted essentially to accommodate McMahon himself. McMahon verbally bowed to Bret's demands, then changed the script without the Hitman's knowledge.

Davey jumped ship after Montreal. His show of loyalty came with a heavy financial burden for a man supporting a family. He confirms that it cost him $100,000 to buy out his contract so he

Lord of the Ring

could join WCW.

Davey and Bret had shared a lot of history, wrestling in North America, Europe and Japan with both Stampede Wrestling and the WWF, and Davey believed he owed his career to Bret's brother Bruce and his father, Stu.

But less than 18 months into his new contract with WCW, Davey was checked into the hospital with a spinal staph infection that nearly destroyed his career. While still recovering at Calgary's Rockyview Hospital in the spring of 1999, WCW's Eric Bischoff's terse note arrived. He had been dropped from WCW's roster. Davey believes that Bret failed to go to bat for him. "Bret's in it for Bret," he says bitterly. Three years later Davey's wife Diana would put a different spin on the situation. She believes that Davey was not in a position to wrestle anyway, given his injury-related addiction to both under- and over-the-counter pain killers.

At the time, however, Davey got a lift from another member of the Hart clan. When Owen arrived at the Rockyview to visit his brother-in-law they worked out a plan to get the recovering wrestler back into the WWF. Owen convinced Vince McMahon that they would make a lively team. Davey was re-signed to tag with Owen just a few days before the Kemper Arena tragedy. The announcement that Davey was returning to WWF was held back for several weeks out of respect for Owen and his grieving family.

To Davey then, Bret's comments about his return to the WWF were just plain unfair. As Bruce points out, when script writer Vince Russo moved from the WWF to WCW after Owen's death, Bret did not object to working with one of the men who had been involved in the script Owen was to carry out in Kansas City.

Stu was becoming increasingly worried about the way the children were treating each other since Owen's death and the announcement of the multi-million-dollar lawsuit against Vince McMahon, the WWF and Titan Sports, McMahon's company.

He understood how important it was for Owen's widow to protect the future interests of her children by filing a wrongful death and negligence lawsuit, and he and Helen had agreed to support Martha in the battle by becoming plaintiffs in the action. Ordinarily such lawsuits can take years to resolve. But a judge in Jackson County, Missouri, set an early trial date, taking into account Stu Hart's advanced age. Legal wrangling over witnesses resulted in loss of that date, but also forced the parties to seriously consider the possibility of settlement.

Despite the litigation, Stu was filled with a need to be conciliatory. Not a man to hold a grudge, at least not for long, sooner or later he would let controversy drop in an attempt to maintain civility. Stu and Vince McMahon, Jr. shared a lot of history — even if it was not always pleasant. Vince did not do business like his father, Vince Sr., or his grandfather, Jesse McMahon, before him. Jesse and Vince Sr. had always co-operated with other wrestling promoters, and Stu had known them both well. But Vince Jr. had essentially dismantled the NWA when he took the WWF national. For many, the modernizing was an inevitability, something that needed to happen in a world where satellite communications brought so much to the living rooms of the continent. To others, it was an act of callous greed. But national television made the competition too fierce for most of the independents.

Vince Jr.'s awareness of what the medium of television could do for wrestling revolutionized the business. He was shrewd, cunning and ruthless. But Vince also made stars out of many wrestlers, including Bret and Owen, and they enjoyed the financial benefits that went with stardom. Vince Jr. promoted his wrestlers like rock stars — and *with* rock stars, like Cindy Lauper — and his original approach made them incredibly marketable.

When Hulk Hogan left the fold, after giving damaging courtroom evidence about the use of steroids in the WWF and implicating McMahon, Bret was in the right place at the right time. Hogan's testimony battered the WWF's reputation as well as McMahon's own ability to operate as freely as he once had. It also shattered the increasingly fragile relationship between Hogan and McMahon. Suddenly, Vince was without a top star. One had to be invented, quickly. He needed someone with excellent wrestling skills, someone clean and not on steroids. He needed someone who was charismatic, with commanding, articulate microphone skills, and hungry for success on a major scale.

There in his own talent stable was Stu Hart's big, good-looking, well-trained, articulate, clean and very suitable son. Bret, a consummate self-promoter, used the opportunity wisely.

On that July day in 1999, as Stu placed Bret's newspaper column on the coffee table, Lana Keela, his late son Dean's old pit bull, slept at his feet. She was as grey and stiff in the legs as he was. Stu gave her a gentle pat on the head. The house was quiet — a rare state. He sat back in his chair. Helen was upstairs absorbed in one of her books and the only other adult around was his son Smith, who was occupying himself under one of the old Cadillacs in the driveway as his five-year-old son Matthew played with the other resident dogs nearby.

The house is full of Stu's favourite things — the leather furniture, the collection of antiques, the Chippendale and Queen Anne chairs, and the six huge chandeliers prominently positioned throughout. Every drawer in every desk and cabinet is crammed with memorabilia and photographs, old wrestling programs and personality profiles of wrestlers who had worked for Stampede Wrestling. The walls in the dining room are filled with family portraits and pictures of memorable moments. Three walls in the living room are lined with black-and-white studio photographs of

Stu Hart

the children, all taken when each was about six, and arranged eldest to youngest. It's an impressive legacy.

It's almost amazing that Stu had been able to accomplish anything, given the abject poverty of his early days. This house represented how far he had travelled, from the boy who had literally nothing except the inadequate clothes on his back and a home-made slingshot, to the man with the golden touch. No one else could really understand the extent to which he had struggled, especially during those years living out of doors on the open, windy Alberta prairie, experiencing every kind of weather in a land which offers such a wide range of extremes.

In many ways, the house is Stu. But just a year earlier, he and the children had been embroiled in an intense battle to keep the old mansion from developers who fought to turn it into a clubhouse for a seniors' complex which would surround it. They had intended initially to tear it down, but the historical society would never have permitted it. The development plans were quickly altered to accommodate this reality. Stu had never really wanted to sell but was prone to being manipulated until he acquiesced. Things changed before the city was asked to approve the plan, and the developer, despite pushing the envelope as far as possible, finally gave up fighting with all "those" Harts.

Now, Stu Hart glanced up at the 12 framed photographs of his children. There was Dean, his feisty number five son who had lived such a tragic, short life. Dean, who had so much to offer, spent most of his adulthood battling Bright's Disease caused by a combination of accidents, fights and substance abuse. He succumbed to its effects at the age of 36, in November 1990, while awaiting a kidney transplant. Each year in November, members of the family gather in the dining room and light a candle in remembrance of Dean and pray together.

Continuing around the room, over the faces of all those boys

Lord of the Ring

and girls whose innocent smiles at age six were so without a trace of guile, Stu's eyes rested on the last framed photograph. A blonde, blue-eyed youngster's slight smile, frozen in time. His eighth son and youngest child, Owen. Gone now, senselessly. The pain of that loss was clearly visible in Stu's face, in eyes as blue as those of the boy upon whom his gaze was fixed.

"He was so full of humour and life. Sometimes it's hard to believe he is really gone," he said, glancing towards the door, half expecting it to swing open and the one so missed by so many to run into the room. "There wasn't a soul on earth who didn't like him. He didn't drink, he didn't smoke, he didn't do drugs. He married his high school sweetheart and they were so happy together with their little ones. He was such a good boy. I miss his laughter. We all do."

Stu leaned back in his big chair and rested his feet on the massive wood-and-glass coffee table. The silence was suddenly broken by the crack of the screen door. There was a child's footsteps, running, bare feet slapping the hardwood floors until the Persian carpets muffled the sound as the small boy entered the living room. Behind little Matthew Hart trailed the rest of the family canines, large and small, all barking and wagging their tails. The dogs ran over to lick Stu's hands. But Matthew did not immediately notice his grandfather's bulky form. He was focussed on a burgundy leather sofa, and he quickly, expertly climbed up on its arm, carefully positioning himself to take a flying leap onto the middle cushion. It was clearly something he had done many many times. As he prepared to leap, he hesitated. His grandfather's forbidding presence had come within his peripheral vision. He could feel the disapproving gaze.

The small boy and the old man eyed each other. Matthew's huge brown eyes and round chubby cheeks were framed by tousled dark brown hair. Stu broke the silence with a calm but steady direction, repeating a sentence he had obviously used on many such occasions: "Young man, I strongly suggest that you move on." Without a word, Matthew climbed down from his perch and ran off towards the stairs to the second floor, the little entourage of dogs behind him.

Lana Keela was too old and tired to join them.

Stu's thoughts wandered back to earlier that morning, when he had watched Bruce and Ross guide young wrestlers through a series of moves. He enjoyed following their progress. After doing back flips off the top rope, they would steal a glance at Stu, seated in his usual ringside lawn chair, hoping he was watching. Stu would nod his approval, which was really all they wanted.

The young athletes, many of them hockey and football players, reminded Stu a lot of himself when, at just 14, he got his chance to hone his skills on the mats at the old Edmonton YMCA.

Stu could see himself 70 years earlier, a sturdy farm boy hanging around the wrestling room at the Y. The amateur wrestlers were working out. He could almost trace the features of faces purple from exertion, bodies that gleamed with sweat and pain as they mauled each other. Young Stu soaked up every move.

Stu smiled, remembering his condition as he dragged himself off the mat after that first day. His body had been tied into so many knots he could barely walk. He didn't know it at the time but the aches and the pains would become a permanent fixture, something he would live with for the rest of his days.

Edmonton was great. Everyone was sports crazy, which was understandable since there wasn't all that much else going on. When he first arrived in what was then just a big prairie town, there were only a few buildings more than a storey or two high. The stately Canadian Pacific-owned Hotel Macdonald, the domed provincial legislative buildings and, sprawling south of the North Saskatchewan River, the University of Alberta

Lord of the Ring

anchored the city on the escarpment. Edmonton presides over the most beautiful river escarpment in Western Canada. And to balance it all, there was that big, endless blue-grey prairie sky, so often streaked with rose, purple, orange and amber, the atmospheric influence of the cold, crisp Canadian north.

Stu was overwhelmed in Edmonton. Scared, in fact, but deep down he knew that his father finally losing the farm in Tofield, after putting himself and his family through four years of misery and deprivation, was a blessing in disguise. Whenever those years come up in conversation, Stu still visibly recoils, as if the constant chills and cold had returned to his old bones.

In a flood of memories he is once again on a rumbling old train with his mother and older sisters, Sylvester and Edrie. On the way to the intimidating city from little Tofield, 50 miles east. The fence posts were topped by two inches of snow that January day in 1929. Stu was four months shy of his 14th birthday, both thrilled and terrified of the great unknown ahead. He was worried, too, about his father, who had been thrown in jail on trespassing and vagrancy charges for camping on the road allowance outside the property he had lost 10 months before for unpaid taxes.

The Royal Canadian Mounted Police had arrived at Ketchamoot School in the Tofield district to pick up Stu and his sisters. An officer told the teacher the Hart kids would not return because their dad was in jail. It was against the law to live on a municipal road allowance. The extent of the humiliation the three Hart students endured that day as they filed, heads down, out of the school and climbed into the waiting patrol car would be remembered by each of them for years to come. Despite what the RCMP said, Stu knew that it was just one more episode in his father's long battle to hang onto land that altered circumstances had taken from him.

That train trip reminds him of his mother. His sisters with their clear young complexions and light brown hair, huddled

Stu Hart

close to her. Edrie's looks were so similar to Stu's, with her prominent cheekbones, angular face and large blue eyes; her long light brown hair was pulled back and usually tied at the nape of her neck. She was the smallest of the Hart children at 5'3". Sylvester was three inches taller, with a small oval face and hair also tied neatly in a long plait at the back of her neck. In an old school picture from 1926, both girls wore the loose cotton dresses of the day; Stu wore a white shirt and a pair of overalls he recalls digging out of a rejected clothes box at the back of the schoolroom, outgrown by an older child.

His mother, Elizabeth Hart, had a slight five-foot-five-inch frame, her honey brown hair was streaked with grey and swept back in a bun that a few bobby pins could not quite successfully hold in place. Her thin face was wind-burned and lined with the strain of the past five of her 53 years, living on the open prairie, cooking over a campfire, trying to sleep in a flimsy canvas tent in the dead of winter. On the way to Edmonton, Stu believed his mother was as worried as he and his sisters were about what was about to happen to them. Years later he would understand just how hard that time had been for her.

In 1929, Mrs. Hart was clearly anxious about her husband and the hopeless situation his stubbornness and insistence on prairie justice had forced upon them. But she was not one to complain. Elizabeth had been raised in the pioneering tradition — to endure and to survive. She did both in her own quiet, unquestioning way.

The Hart family had eked out an existence in two threadbare canvas tents, fighting the sweltering heat and blackflies of prairie summers and the sub-zero temperatures of winter. Despite years of sacrifice their land was lost. The cattle and horses were gone, too — sold to pay real estate fees on land that another man now owned. At 14, Stu couldn't understand how that could be right. How could his father, a hardworking, devout Baptist who recited chapter, verse

Lord of the Ring

and line from the Bible, be treated this way? How could he be thrown into jail like a common criminal when all he had tried to do was buy land, cultivate it and raise a family like everybody else? Why had fate robbed him of his dreams and dignity?

For Stu, there were no answers. He could only wait and see what would happen next.

Edward Ernest Hart had taken a half-section of land near the small farming town of Tofield in 1924, nine years after the birth of his only son, Stewart Edward Hart on May 3, 1915. It was a dream come true for Edward that December day — he had signed on for a crop share that would in time pay for his own property. He had always wanted good, productive land to farm and build a future for his family. He did not want to work the chalky, alkaline or clay-hardened earth that made his early attempts at homesteading and crop sharing a resounding failure. He'd learned the importance of quality land the hard way.

Edward had come upon the half-section during the fall harvest, when he'd joined a crew of rag-tag farmers like himself who couldn't quite make a living on their own homesteads. He'd hired himself out and made enough to keep the family afloat in Forgan in western Saskatchewan; he'd moved the family there five years earlier from a farm on the outskirts of Saskatoon.

Sometimes guilty about dragging his wife and children through such a rough life, he was grateful that Elizabeth never complained. Elizabeth was highly educated for the times and had taught school for several years before she met Edward. She had been raised in relative comfort in the Devil's Lake area near Bismarck, in the old Dakota Territory (now North Dakota) where she had earned her teaching certificate. Her father, Donald Stewart, had served as a twice-elected territorial legislator after he'd emigrated from Scotland with his English wife, Elizabeth

Curtis. The Stewarts had initially settled in Ontario before moving on to the Dakota Territory.

Donald Stewart had strong features, dark brooding eyes, a neatly trimmed beard and a stubbornness that was easy to detect. Bismarck newspapers in the mid-1880s painted him as a highly principled and respected man who would verbally assault anyone who even hinted at accepting personal benefit from public office. But after serving four years, he found himself weary of petty local political disputes, and he packed up family and trudged north to the small farming centre of Saskatoon, which would later become an important city in the new province of Saskatchewan.

Elizabeth Stewart was born in 1878. After teaching school for several years and helping out on the homestead in Saskatchewan, she decided that she wanted a family of her own. At the age of 29 she threw in her lot with a handsome, blond migrant farm worker with cobalt blue eyes, strong, angular features and, like her father, a self-righteous, stubborn nature. At 26, Edward Hart was full of optimism. He had lived through enough hardship and disappointment since his birth in 1881 in Bruce County, Ontario, to last a lifetime. He believed he was due a break. When he found the half section in the Tofield district, he was sure the beautiful land was his ticket to prosperity. By this time he had three children, two daughters and a son who had been named Stewart in the family tradition, after his mother's maiden name.

The property was treed and gently rolling, with a natural slough that attracted swarms of migratory birds. It was four miles from a school and seven miles from the town of Tofield, which offered the basic amenities and had a grain elevator. Edward could easily picture a sturdy farmhouse and barn, outbuildings and fences enclosing his herd of cattle and horses. He was sure Elizabeth and their children would settle in well, and certain the farm would be productive.

Lord of the Ring

Edward's family had migrated west from Bruce County, near present-day Peterborough, to Brandon, Manitoba, when he was still a boy. His father, John, had been a skilled carpenter and his mother, Fannie Sargent, was happy to move west since she had family already settled there. They had seven sons and one little girl, Emily. John and Fannie wanted to settle in a place that offered real opportunity for their offspring, and they had been impressed with the advertisements posted in the Bruce County dry goods stores — glowing reports about vast tracts of land for settlement and towns that were springing up overnight. There was bound to be lots of work for an enterprising carpenter.

But while the children were still small, John was caught in a blinding prairie blizzard as he trudged on foot to his in-laws' farm 20 miles away. He moved along fence lines and managed to find his way in white-out conditions, but was stricken with pneumonia. A few weeks later he died, leaving Fannie to raise eight children on her own.

The boys dropped out of school as soon as they had mastered the fundamentals to earn what they could to supplement their mother's meagre income. None complained. They were firmly entrenched in the spirit of the day. Parents provided life and love, and the children, each in their turn, went out into the world to make their way as best they could.

When Edward's time came, he found work on neighbouring farms and later learned the butcher's trade. He wandered from threshing crew to threshing crew, back and forth across the prairies, and when the field work dried up he joined logging crews in the British Columbia interior or operated a river boat. By the time he met Elizabeth, back in Saskatchewan, he had decided to settle down and work towards what he really wanted — a farm of his own. They married and their three children were born over the next eight years. But crop sharing, working as a butcher and living with his father-in-law on the outskirts of Saskatoon wasn't what he had in mind. For a time he toiled away on a crop share near Bulcher, Saskatchewan, a town that would all but blow away with the dust and the tumbleweed. A few years later he found what he thought was a better crop share at Forgan, another wisp of a town near the Alberta border. The land there was a disappointment, too, and he and Elizabeth struggled over the next five years to keep their children and livestock fed.

Young Stu learned to ride a horse, milk and feed the cattle and tend to the endless chores a farm demands.

In 1924, at 43, Edward thought everything he had worked for was finally coming together. The half section next to the Tofield Coal Company would change everything. All he had to do was seal the deal with the owners, a consortium of American land speculators.

It was good land, near a prosperous town. Tofield has always been a quiet, affluent farming centre, nestled among rolling hills and farmland which by the 1890s had been settled by farmers from Eastern Europe, Scandinavia and the northern territories of the present-day United States, where open land was becoming harder to find.

The friendliness of the early settlers stood in sharp contrast to the district's history as a battleground of the powerful Cree and Blackfoot Nations, whose war cries pierced the otherwise late summer winds across the serene prairie grasslands and injected an energy and excitement now reduced to folklore.

Nearby Beaverhill Lake was a magnet for migrating game birds, and the fresh water swelled with jackfish. Wild meat was plentiful and berries grew in abundance. It all sounded like a little paradise; but in winter Tofield was, and continues to be, as cold and desolate a place as can be found anywhere. Temperatures can fall as brutally low as -40 degrees Fahrenheit and stay there for weeks at a time.

Lord of the Ring

Edward wanted to build a cabin and break ground. It was important to get his first crop in the following spring and meet his share payment. Stu was old enough now to help out. He was big for his age, strong and sturdy, and by spring he would be 10. Already competent on a horse, he could work with little supervision.

On December 11, 1924, Edward travelled by train to Tofield to sign an agreement for sale and a chattel mortgage to secure payment for realtor's fees which the vendors had refused to pay. Edward put up his cattle and horses as security — something he would later regret.

When he got back to Forgan, however, he became ill. Soon the rest of his family and most of his neighbours were quarantined with whooping cough and scarlet fever. To make matters worse, 16 head of cattle had wandered off in a snowstorm. No one was well enough to round them up. It took the family months to get back on its feet.

By the time Edward arrived back in Tofield, with his family, goods and livestock, it was already July 1, 1925 — two months behind schedule. He hadn't even finished moving his livestock off the train when a stranger told him his half section had been resold to the owner of the dry goods store, James Jobb. It seemed someone thought Hart had abandoned the sale when he hadn't shown up in May as expected.

To get to Tofield, Edward and his family had walked their cattle and horses 50 miles to the Rosetown, Saskatchewan, train station, camping in the ditches along the way. They then rode in a boxcar with the livestock into Alberta. As uncomfortable as it was, Stu thought it was a grand adventure. It was the first time he had been on a train since the family had arrived in Forgan five years earlier. He had no clear recollection of that trip, and seeing new places and people was more exciting than anything he had experienced in his young life.

37

Stu Hart

As young Stu gazed around the dry goods store, Edward argued with Jobb and tried to pay the storekeeper for the clearing work his hired man had already completed. But Jobb refused to step back from the sale, even though he told Edward that he wouldn't have touched it had he not been assured that Edward's purchase was abandoned. Edward refused to concede defeat. He bought two small canvas tents, walked his family and livestock out to the half section and set up camp in a sheltered spot close to the dirt road. In his pocket was the signed contract of sale for the land, and he was determined to carry on. He would hold off on building a cabin, however, until things got sorted out.

Camping in the summer was one thing. But as the days grew shorter and the Canada geese aimed their V formations due south, the family hoped something would break. It didn't. Jobb had dug in his heels too. He sued Edward and applied to the court to have him evicted from the land. When the first heavy snows came and the temperatures dropped, the case was still not resolved. Even then, Edward would not be moved. Sub-zero temperatures set in and life took a steep downward plunge for the Hart family. Jobb was confident that the harsh winds and frigid temperatures would rid him of his "squatters."

He was mistaken.

Edward barricaded and insulated the tents with evergreen boughs and anything else he could get his hands on. But living in a pup tent in sub-zero weather without a stove was no picnic for Elizabeth, Stu and his sisters. The winter months dragged on and it was so cold at times that even the air itself seemed frozen. The magical effect of hoar frost on the trees and bushes, like the magnificent flashes of colour streaking the sky from the northern lights, was all but lost on the Harts as they battled to keep from freezing. Stu and his sisters helped their father milk 18 or 20 head of cattle a day in every kind of weather. Sale of the milk and

Lord of the Ring

cream sustained the family and fed the livestock, but little more. Stu recalls how cold his hands would get in the open wind while milking the cows, and his practice of sinking his hands into the soft flesh of the cows udder to warm them enough to keep on with the tedious task.

Stu and his sisters walked four miles to school. The warmth of the little stove there was a welcome luxury. It was a kind of oasis from a cold, harsh life that had become all too familiar. The walk home, over frozen, snow-covered fields was all the more miserable because they were usually hungry. Sometimes they had lunch to take, but not often. Charlie Sears, who still lives in Tofield, remembers Stu and his sisters from the Ketchamoot School. The other pupils, he recalls, often shared sandwiches of thick homemade bread with the Harts, but the kids endured a fair amount of taunting about the way they lived.

At that time in western Canada, serious poverty was viewed as a condition directly related to some character flaw, not as a result of circumstance or lack of opportunity. The poor were treated accordingly. The Harts were clearly the poorest family in the district, without even a proper roof over their heads.

Stu describes the Tofield years as the worst imaginable, but they may well have given him insight into the hard times people sometimes face when circumstances are out of their control. He would later lend a helping hand, time and time again, to those less fortunate. Civic workers recall seeing Stu Hart leave Calgary's City Hall in the 1970s and '80s, after having paid his Monday morning wrestling match fines to the Boxing and Wrestling Commission. These fines were levied for wrestlers' improper conduct, offences like swearing or spitting. Then, on the way to his car, he'd help street people from the back alley into his Cadillac. He drove them to a nearby shelter. Stu would never turn down a request from a church or charity to help the less fortunate, and he would come to support fund-raising efforts for at least 35 different charities, clubs, churches and causes during the decades of his association with pro-wrestling.

At night, the Hart's little tents were as dank and cold as any Calgary alley. Stu slept on a rough frame cot, his mattress made of pine bows stuffed in a gunny sack. The tents had no heat at all and the wind whistled around them, attacking any loose bit of canvas, relentlessly giving the occupants the uncomfortable sense that the whole apparatus, their only shield from the full force of a prairie winter, might blow away at any moment. Stu struggled to keep warm under his pile of flannel blankets and tanned cow hides. It was hard to get comfortable and the only other relief came from the flat rocks his mother heated in an open campfire and wrapped in a feedbag, or from the warm-blooded body of his dog. He was glad for the warmth of his pet; possibly, it kept him from freezing. His parents huddled together, his sisters huddled together, but for Stu there was the dog. For the rest of his life, Stu would value his animal friends and treat them with great kindness.

The roof of the tents were covered with pinhole burns from sparks from the campfire, and on wet days they leaked. When it snowed heavily, Stu had to slide what accumulated off with his hands before the weight caused the tent to collapse.

In the mornings, he woke up bleary-eyed, body aching from the contortions of trying to keep warm, only to be greeted by frozen boots or moccasins. Most of the time he would sleep in his clothes because it was too cold to take them off. Stu would rub his face and hands with snow to clean up. He only felt warm sitting close to the campfire, or when he stood between the cattle, their bodies steaming in the harsh climate.

Stu remembers being sent out on a horse at 12 or 13 years of age to search the flat prairie landscape for missing livestock, usually horses that had wandered off. Sometimes, as his horse

Lord of the Ring

meandered along under a clear, starry sky, his ears got so cold he was sure they were frozen under his flimsy cap. Often at nightfall he would be stranded out on the prairie, too far to get back to his parents' camp. When he finally got off his horse in a farmer's yard, his thighs would be numb from the cold, making it a chore to even dismount. Sometimes he would be as much as 15 or 20 miles from home. If he was lucky, a farmer would take him in, feed him and give him a place to sleep. The next day he would continue his search and eventually wind his way back to the camp, usually with the missing livestock.

Sometimes, on warmer evenings, the family gathered around the open fire after eating whatever Elizabeth had prepared in the black cast iron pot suspended above the fire. Often it was stew made from a rabbit Stu had snared, or a partridge brought down by his slingshot or some beef left over from a butchered animal. The family would listen to Edward play "Red River Valley" or "Golden Slippers" on his harmonica. Occasionally Edward read from the Bible by the light from the campfire. Later on, Stu acquired a 50-cent Marine Band mouth organ and learned to play, too. That was the sum total of their entertainment: no radio, no newspapers, magazines or books. They were as isolated as they could be, left to whatever small amusements they could conjure. There were no arguments among Stu and his sisters, no fighting or bickering. In such close quarters they were forced to be tolerant of each other on every level, and to be patient. These traits would be useful for Stu in later life, but they would also foster his tendency to suppress his feelings.

Those years were so hard it would be a long time before Stu would be able to draw meaning from them. Without realizing it, he was learning lessons about life: about how harsh it can be even to those who work hard to succeed. As a young boy, he could do nothing but watch as his hard-working, decent parents sank

41

deeper and deeper into abject poverty. Yet he never once heard his mother complain or his father speak about life with bitterness, or in words that so much as hinted at defeat. In his later years, Stu would hear his own children describe their grandfather as "pink" with kindness and courtesy. Stu was learning how to survive and to take adversity in his stride, acquiring a self-sufficiency that would serve him well later on.

In late 1926, two years after the Hart family arrived in the Tofield district, the Alberta Supreme Court finally decided the case between Jobb and Hart — in Edward's favour. It was a bittersweet victory for Edward because by this time he had all but depleted his resources in the legal battle and was living hand to mouth. The legal system had worked for him, but not nearly quickly enough. Still, Edward built a nine-foot square cabin and started clearing land as fast as he could. Things were looking up, but almost at the very moment they did, another enemy closed in — the tax man.

Barely holding the land a year, Edward suddenly faced three years of outstanding taxes, which included the years the land was tied up in court.

He didn't have the money. And the tax man is never patient.

Jobb jumped at the chance to pick up the land in the judicial sale and the realtor pulled out the chattel mortgage Edward had signed. He seized Edward's livestock, selling everything to pay the outstanding realtor fees — even though the land now belonged to another farmer.

Edward hired Joseph Clarke as his lawyer. Clarke had served on Edmonton's city council for several terms and later became mayor. "Fighting" Joe Clarke, as he was known locally, had long been the champion of the underdog. And he was no stranger to colourful legal battles, many of them on his own behalf. He once had to fend off an assault charge in Whitehorse after a boisterous

Lord of the Ring

encounter with a Yukoner, and he had sued a church minister in Edmonton for slander. But his most distinguishing battle, well-recalled by many decades later, was the fist fight he had with the Mayor of Edmonton while he was a councillor. They shocked their more subdued colleagues by whipping off their jackets and jabbing at each other in the council chambers during a debate that had escalated rapidly. Clarke's name is still prominent around Edmonton because Clarke Stadium was named in his honour. Stu Hart would later play professional football there for the Edmonton Eskimos.

For some inexplicable reason, Clarke advised Edward Hart to pitch his tents on the road allowance adjacent to the property and take up residence there to protest what had happened to him. Clarke's advice was intended to embarrass Edward's adversaries, but it is far from clear what could come of such a plan since the land had already passed to Jobb in the judicial sale and it was the dead of winter. But Edward took Clarke's advice and stubbornly moved his camp to the grid road allowance close to the property line in January 1928. He again barricaded the tents with whatever he could to help break the wind. The little hovel had every appearance of a pile of rubble. It later shocked some of the other local farmers to discover after the fact that a family had lived there. Edward refused to concede that he had lost, and he was determined to stay on, even if only on the road allowance.

Finally, after 10 months, Jobb called in the RCMP. Edward was arrested and hauled off to jail in Edmonton. He was sentenced to serve six months, but Clarke immediately appealed and arranged a surety for Edward's release, putting up his law office furniture to help secure it.

After picking up the children from Ketchamoot School, the RCMP put them and their mother on the train to Edmonton, where they became wards of the province. The Salvation Army,

43

which at that time dispensed social welfare programs, housed them in the modest, two-storey Raymond Hotel. It would be the first time in years any of them had slept in a real bed, in a room which was warm and inviting despite its shabbiness. To Elizabeth and the Hart children it felt like heaven. Stu and his sisters, unfamiliar with the "luxuries" of hotel living, promptly caused the bathtub to overflow. Water leaked into the lobby below. Stu laughs with slight embarrassment at the recollection of the hotel desk clerk stomping up the stairs and lecturing the Hart children on the use of bathroom amenities.

Clarke found Edward a job skidding in a logging camp. A few weeks later, he was able to get his family together and rent a small shack in Edmonton's Bonnie Doone district. It had to be scrubbed from ceiling to floorboards because it had housed dogs for six months before the Harts moved in. Modest as it was, it was again an improvement over the tents.

Edward went back to Tofield to check on their possessions and found that the tents were gone and the cabin burned down. All the family keepsakes were lost; the only thing of value left was a milk separator and a little saddle horse named Myrtle that had been overlooked in the seizure and sale. He took Myrtle to Edmonton along with the separator.

Later on, Edward scraped together enough money for a small three-room house on 83rd Avenue with a barn and four acres of land where he tethered a cow and raised chickens. He acquired a workhorse and wagon and did landscaping around Edmonton. It wouldn't be long before Edward would do a short stint in jail for fighting with a man who had unfairly chiselled him out of a labouring job — work was scarce enough as the Great Depression set in.

Stu and his sisters were packed off to school. Stu went to Rutherford, while the girls were old enough to attend Strathcona

Lord of the Ring

High School. Stu discovered right away that his education had suffered in Tofield, despite his attendance at Ketchamoot. He worked hard to catch up, and with the help of his mother graduated from Strathcona High School and took two years of business courses at Strathcona Commercial. He completed his formal education in 1935. His sisters learned secretarial and office skills at Strathcona Commercial as well, and later on Sylvester moved to Vancouver to work as a secretary. Edrie stayed in Edmonton and worked at a dance studio for a time and in various offices.

The family's move to Edmonton was, for Stu, the best thing that had happened in his short life. Not long after he started school, he discovered athletics. He excelled in any sport he took up, and soon he became intrigued with amateur wrestling. Unknown to him at the time, it would set the course for the next 70 years of his life. Wrestling would become the instrument Stu Hart would use to avenge, without bitterness, his early family struggles.

Three

At the Edmonton YMCA in the fall of 1929, a husky 14-year-old farm boy was struggling to maintain his crouched position and to keep the kid sitting on him from turning him over. It was a battle of sheer will. The farm boy was clearly getting the worst of it — the tell-tale canvas burns on his forehead, elbows and knees, and the strain of exertion on his young face said it all. During this match, the other kid had shoved his head between his knees, pushed his elbows together behind his head and grape-vined his legs. His head had been pushed down his chest to his belly button. Even before the exercise was over, the farm boy's neck was starting to feel like it had grown several inches.

When the pain from the "stretching" was just short of the most Stu Hart could possibly bear, the kid on top of him suddenly broke his hold on a signal from the coach. Young Stu rolled over on his back, his eyes bloodshot, head dizzy and neck throbbing.

It was Stu's first taste of wrestling, and even though his body had been twisted into several unnatural positions, he knew from that moment the sport was for him. Stu had been hanging around the wrestling room for weeks after his swimming lessons, watching the young amateurs maul each other. Finally, the coach invited him to join the other boys on the mat, since his young athletes always needed a fresh body to practise on. Stu, still wearing his trunks from swimming class, eagerly accepted.

On the way home, his body aching, Stu made the decision to work out every chance he got until he had mastered, in a scientific way, every move he had been put through that day. He developed a plan to focus on building up his body so that he could be stronger and tougher than the other boys. He would learn to understand how the human body worked and exactly what its absolute limitations were. It would be a good two years before Stu would be able to hold his own — most of the time he was on his back or his face.

From the first time he attended the YMCA swimming classes offered free through his school, Stu vowed to save up enough money to pay for a full membership at the Y. It cost $5, but would be his passport to hanging out there. It took him months of odd jobs, but he scraped together what at first seemed like an impossible amount of money, especially to a 14 year old. His life was going to change.

Returning home to Bonnie Doone after his first wrestling experience, Stu also decided to keep his plan to himself. His parents understood football and baseball, but wrestling was an unknown entity. His father, much to his surprise, had actually encouraged him to take up sports when the family moved to Edmonton. Edward had missed out on school activities, devoting all of his time to basic survival. When neither of Stu's parents questioned the canvas burns, the neophyte grappler said nothing.

Stu loved everything about wrestling, but it wasn't long before football and baseball occupied a lot of his time, seasonally, too. His nearly perfectly proportioned physique was well suited to every sport he took up. The side of the old barn behind the house in Bonnie Doone served as a backboard for Stu's rubber ball, which he threw over and over and over again. The thud of it hitting the

Lord of the Ring

weathered barn boards became a familiar sound in the neighbourhood. Stu was building a strong baseball and football arm, and he had set up a practice gym in the hayloft.

Needing to earn money, he scoured the neighbourhood for anything a 14-year-old could do to earn a few dimes. The Great Depression meant little to Stu. Of course, he had to hustle for part-time jobs, but the reduced standard of living which most Albertans suffered in those years really didn't affect the Hart household. They had endured their own personal depression, in many ways one far more devastating. What they might have to endure in Bonnie Doone was nothing compared to what they had already stared down. Stu laughs when he recalls it: "We had already been depressed beyond imagination. Anything we experienced in Edmonton was a pretty noticeable improvement."

Since he never knew when one job would begin and another end, Stu jumped at any and every opportunity to pick up part-time work. Asking his parents for money to join the YMCA or to buy sports equipment or even sneakers was completely out of the question. It would never have occurred to him. Instead, he knocked on the doors of neighbours, mowed lawns with a push mower, weeded gardens, hauled, lugged and fetched whenever he could. Fortunately, wrestling did not require a lot of expensive equipment, just trunks and sneakers.

Juggling school, athletics and a series of part-time jobs that first winter in Edmonton, Stu picked up a pair of ice skates at the Salvation Army thrift store for a few cents and taught himself to skate largely by watching other boys. Hockey was added to the list of sports he played with enthusiasm.

Stu's finances improved during the early '30s when he picked up a job delivering the *Edmonton Advertiser* door to door and hawking it on the streets of downtown Edmonton. He had to fight for a good spot on Jasper Avenue, and often when he found one, older boys would chase him away. But after he started gaining confidence on the wrestling mat, it was harder for anyone to dislodge him. Stu sold the *Advertiser* and *Edmonton Journal* wherever he could. As soon as the school bell rang at lunchtime, he raced over to the nearby Strathcona Hotel or to the train station. He'd unload as many papers as he could to visitors and train passengers and then race back to classes. But the hottest seller of all was the weekly *Edmonton Liberator*.

The paper was owned by the reputed head of the local chapter of the Ku Klux Klan and came out every Saturday. It sold as soon as it hit the streets because its publisher, J.J. Maloney, made a point of slurring anyone who crossed his path, especially Catholics. He milked the local Catholic-Protestant rivalry to the hilt, and he wasn't all that careful about his facts. A slander suit would eventually shut him down for good.

For several years, however, he kept the churches and community in turmoil. His public persona and appearances helped his newspaper's circulation. Stu remembers seeing him arrive at a gathering outside a local hall in a shiny black Cadillac, complete with a driver and a bodyguard. People lined the streets and pressed in around him like an early superstar, and they filled the hall just to hear him echo whatever he had already railed about in that week's *Liberator*. The sight of that Cadillac would stick in Stu's mind for many years as a symbol of prosperity.

Readers lapped up the outrageous copy that spilled out of the *Liberator*, and they spent the following week gossiping and speculating about it seated at lunch counters and coffee shops along Jasper Avenue. And Stu was there for the killing. He'd pick up 500 copies on a pledge to pay seven cents apiece for them, then he'd sell them for a dime. Fifteen dollars at that time was a lot of money, and by the time Stu was in his late teens, he was earning more than his father was hauling loam with a team of horses and

Lord of the Ring

doing odd jobs around Edmonton.

The change in seasons was not lost on the enterprising Stu Hart either. A few weeks before Christmas each year, Stu and his father would go down to Whitemud Creek and cut Christmas trees to sell in downtown Edmonton.

Stu paid for his sneakers and second-hand school clothes, and what was left over allowed him to help out at home. He was also becoming a voracious eater, wanting to bulk up for football and wrestling. His mother kept a big vegetable garden and spent the fall months putting up preserves and jams. The family still had a cow and chickens, and Stu started to focus on what would make him grow bigger and stronger. He was building up a fine physique through eating carefully, staying away from alcohol and cigarettes — neither of which he has ever been able to see any benefit in — and experimenting with healthy choices to build up his body. Years on a high protein, vegetable and dairy diet made its contribution, too. Stu Hart was never to have so much as a cavity throughout his life.

Working, playing sports and attending school took up every square inch of Stu's time. He stopped taking all that much notice of what the rest of the family was doing, but he was still a contributing member of the household. The family moved to a larger house in Bonnie Doone when Stu was 19. It was Stu who purchased the house with a $200 down payment, and it was Stu who met the mortgage payments on the $750 home. Later on, when he joined the armed forces, Stu would sign the house over to his father in case something happened. After the war, Stu found, to his dismay, that his father had signed the house over to Edrie without so much as a word. Edward's explanation was far from satisfactory. "It was all I had to leave to her." But Edward would outlive both his daughters and his wife by many years.

While he kept up with football and baseball, Stu never forgot wrestling. By the time he reached his late teens, he had developed into a well-trained amateur, and gradually formed a plan to qualify for Canada's Olympic wrestling team. Putting on weight and working out religiously, one day he saw a notice in the *Edmonton Journal* that piqued his interest. The Edmonton Athletic Club was calling in young athletes to try out for its junior football team. Every teenage boy in Edmonton who could play the game wanted to make the squad. Stu remembers going down to the football field for the tryouts and finding at least 500 other teenagers gathered for the same reason. He thought his chances slim because of the numbers alone, but he stuck with it.

After each practice boys would be cut; the names of those invited back would then be posted. Stu found his name day after day. The elimination process eventually wound its course and Stu Hart became a fully fledged member of the EAC. The EAC sponsored baseball, too, and Stu played both sports equally well. The club was a breeding ground for exceptional young athletes. Bob and Bill Karse played for the EACs at that time and would later find themselves in the NHL playing for the Chicago Black Hawks. Mac and Neil Colville were another strong brother team and they would eventually skate for the New York Rangers. Stu sometimes caught their games at Madison Square Gardens during his own years in New York City. Stu dreamed of making it in both football and wrestling, and thoughts of playing in the NFL lingered for years. Coach Bob Fritz made him believe he had the ability and said, when Stu was ready, he would find a place for him across the border. "If the war hadn't happened, I would likely have gone on to play college ball in the States," Stu recalls, noting that Fritz had talked to him several times about looking for a football scholarship for him either at Notre Dame or the University of Wisconsin, where the coach had ties. He would have taken a degree in Phys. Ed. or teaching and followed football as far as he could, hopefully

Lord of the Ring

to the NFL. To Stu the differences between Canadian and American football were subtle and the transition would have been a simple matter. Wrestling and playing football dovetailed nicely for Stu Hart. The skills were different but being a rough, tough wrestler never hurt him on the gridiron. Occasionally he would use wrestling moves to block an opposing player — he was a tough customer either forum.

Stu started to make a name for himself, not only with the EACs but as an amateur wrestler. Before his 15th year was out, he won his first serious competition — the Edmonton City Championships — in the middleweight class. He followed this by winning the Northern Alberta Championship, ousting two highly regarded young wrestlers from Athabasca. He quickly moved up the ranks to the Alberta provincials in Calgary and walked away with that title as well. By 1937 he would be the Dominion welterweight champion. He remained undefeated until he outgrew his weight class.

It wasn't long before Stu was invited to train with the pro-wrestlers, and he started hanging around at the ring doing go-for jobs. The work didn't pay much, but it meant he could sit through the pro-wrestling matches without having to pay for a ticket.

In 1938 Stu moved closer to his Olympic dream by qualifying for the British Empire Games in Melbourne, Australia. The city of Edmonton didn't have the money, however, to send Stu, or the featherweight champion, also from Edmonton, to the games that year. And there wasn't enough advance notice for Stu to even think about trying to raise or save the money to send himself to the other side of the world.

He shrugged off his disappointment and continued with his work around the pro-wrestlers. Soon he was setting up the bleachers, checking the ring and watching the doors. It kept Stu at the matches on weekend evenings and even sometimes during the week.

Stu Hart

His love affair with pro-wrestling reached a high point when, still in his teens, he witnessed a match between Jack Taylor, the legendary British Empire champion, and Tiger Duhlea, "the Hindu champ," from India.

Born in Regina, Taylor was ranked as one of the best wrestlers of his day, and was later acknowledged as one of the greatest of the era. He had been wrestling since 1903 and came from a family of athletic over-achievers. He was promoted through a New York wrestling office and had taken under his wing a young protégé who would later become known as "Mr. Wrestler." That young man's name was Joseph "Toots" Mondt.

Stu would meet Mondt in later years under quite different circumstances.

Taylor was Stu's pro-wrestling hero. He had read about him in sports magazines and newspapers and lapped up every word with admiration. He dreamed of someday shaking Taylor's hand. When he saw Taylor's name on the card one Friday afternoon in 1932, nothing could keep him from the match. Stu has never forgotten the excitement and euphoria he felt when he headed down from Bonnie Doone. He stood in awe as Taylor engaged in pre-match banter with the other wrestlers on the card, and he hung on his every word. From a prime seat in the bleachers, Stu watched spellbound. It was a 30-minute bout between Taylor and Tiger, and they engaged in take-downs, escapes, flying mares and drop kicks. Seeing all this performed by someone with real credentials was a defining moment. Finally, Taylor hit his opponent with a body slam, got him in a hold he could not get out of and forced him to submit.

Those were the best days of the pro sport for Stu. He loved submission wrestling, with its mental and physical skill and precision. The displays of strength also attracted him, and he was proud of his own rapidly developing body. He was smitten: notwith-

Lord of the Ring

standing his perpetually stiff neck or the seemingly permanent aches and pains in every joint and disk. He spent as much time as he could working out and developed a ritual of doing one thousand squats nearly every day. It wasn't long before his legs and thighs were bulging from the heavy workouts. Stu built up an amazing lower body; his back and shoulders were also huge. The effect was impressive on his already naturally sturdy frame.

When his son eventually told him about his plans to wrestle or play pro-football for a living, Edward was far from encouraging. If Stu did not plan to go into farming, his father simply wasn't interested in hearing about it. To Edward, farming was all there was, and he couldn't understand his son's lack of enthusiasm. For Stu it was simple enough. Farming with his father had been nothing but a nightmare, and he had no intention of ever putting himself in that position again. Stu associated farming with a life of drudgery and mind-numbing poverty.

In the late '50s, Stu would help his aging father acquire a small chicken farm in British Columbia in an attempt to appease the man's yearnings for farm life. But nothing short of a cattle and horse operation really interested Edward, and it wasn't long before he lost interest in raising chickens. For Stu, his father's failure at farming had become a blessing in disguise. Sports and a decent education would have eluded him had the farm experiment been even remotely successful.

Establishing himself in football in those sports hungry times, Stu continued to play for the EACs during the two years he spent at Strathcona Commercial, a technical school in Edmonton. It wasn't long before the Canadian Football League's Edmonton Eskimos took an interest in the rugged but skilled farm boy.

With the Eskimos Stu met a string of players who would figure in his life for years to come — Ted Heath, Neil and Mac Caldwell, the Karse brothers, Ernie Stephenson, Hal Sutton and

Tommy Hays were all contemporaries. Tommy's brother Harry would later become Mayor of Calgary and have a distinguished career as a Liberal cabinet minister and Senator. Harry's son Dan would follow in his political footsteps and eventually became Speaker of the Senate. Stu was with the team from the 1937 season until the last pre-War game played in 1939. He played many positions, but most often centre, and he had a real knack for snapping the ball. He could kick a ball farther than most and enjoyed being a strong, punishing blocker. Stu remembers making his share of field goals and having a certain celebrity by being on the team.

But standing in the newly built football stadium for his first practice with the Eskimos, Stu could not help but remember his Tofield years and Clarke Stadium's namesake, "fighting" Joe Clarke, who had represented his father after his arrest. It was hard for Stu's mind not to wander back to what his life was like then and how very much things had changed.

An article in the *Calgary Herald* recorded Stu's football accomplishments years later: "[Stu] joined the Edmonton Eskimos, then coached by Bob Fritz, and performed for them for two years mostly at centre but tackle and guard too. The Esks' major accomplishment during the 1939 season was that they were the only team that beat the Grey Cup-winning Winnipeg Blue Bombers, coming from behind 11–0 at half time to register a 31–11 upset victory. That was also the season that Stu received his most serious injury — a broken nose. It was the only broken bone he suffered during his entire wrestling and football career. 'I came around a lineman fast and bang — Paul Rowe hit me, breaking my nose.'"

By the late 1930s, Stu had developed into a handsome young man. It was hard for his chiselled features, the cobalt blue eyes he'd inherited from his father, or his gentle, soft-spoken manner and nearly perfectly proportioned build not to attract attention. But

Lord of the Ring

Stu was still not taking a serious interest in romance. He was flattered by the giddiness of the young women around him and their attention to his athletic accomplishments, but he restricted his exchanges with the opposite sex to the occasional chat over a milkshake. He was busy developing his body into a temple of pain, wrestling every chance he got and playing pro football. He believed that getting too involved with a woman would derail his plans. He had watched many of his buddies end up married with small children and working on an assembly line. He would start a family when the time was right; in the interim he was determined to stay the course.

Those days he hung out with Harry and Tommy Hays. He went down to Calgary with them several times and they frequented a tavern in the Palliser Hotel, which dominated 9th Avenue and most of Calgary's downtown. Despite not being much of a drinker, Stu enjoyed the camaraderie and bonding rituals practised at such watering holes. He loved to listen to the stories the Hays boys spun about the cattle business and admired the prosperous Hays ranch in the rolling hills around Millarville, south of Calgary. The Hays brothers exported more cattle to South America than anyone else around as far as he knew. Both brothers were talented livestock auctioneers, and Stu got a kick out of listening to their rhythmic chant at the auction pens.

He also picked up another job — as a bouncer at the Palace Garden Dance Hall. In late 1939 and the early '40s the place was always packed with young servicemen and women, whiling away their evenings as they waited to be sent overseas. Stu got to know many of the "cute little Wrens," but he continued to avoid any real involvement. Because of his size, Stu caught little grief from the patrons. Occasionally he ejected someone from the premises who had had too much to drink, and a few quick moves were usually more than enough to subdue anyone who thought they could take him on. His favourite ejection move involved grabbing the troublemaker's arms and pulling their hands between their legs while standing behind them and marching them to the door. There was never much resistance.

As the Depression ended, work became easier to find. Stu's sports connections, however, were still invaluable, always keeping him employed. He was invited to coach wrestling for the University of Alberta when Coach Emile Van Velzen decided he'd had enough. The job earned Stu a modest $75 a year. This, like the other income he'd earn through EAC contacts, was enough to keep him on his wrestling training program.

5'10½" tall and 191 pounds, he had been training hard and power eating. Vitamin E and wheat germ factored largely in his diet. Wheat germ oil was popular for energy, and drinking cod liver oil, eating raw eggs and meat were the rage among young athletes of the time. Stu filled up on peanut butter and milkshakes, and he got a juicing machine — the first of many he would use regularly for the rest of his life.

When the War began and organized sports activities were shelved, Stu looked around for what he should be doing next. He didn't want to enlist, at least not right away, not until he competed in the 1940 Olympics, scheduled to be held in Helsinki, Finland.

Instead, Stu toiled at Edmonton Pane and Glass Ltd. — another job landed through sports contacts — until Coach Van Velzen approached him once again. This time he persuaded Stu to go with him to Yellowknife in the North West Territories, where they would get into "some of the heavy sugar" to be made up in the mines.

Stu jumped at the chance to leave Edmonton for a while. His mother spent a significant part of 1939 in the hospital, having been diagnosed with diabetes. She had suffered in silence for a long time. Because going to a doctor cost money in those pre-

Lord of the Ring

universal medicare days, she kept her illness to herself. Elizabeth was stoic, not one to call in a doctor unless circumstances were dire. Unfortunately, by the time she did get medical attention, it was too late. She died that year. Stu's anger with her attempt to conceal her illness represented one of the saddest points in his young life. He could easily have provided money to pay for her care if he had only known. Day after day, he sat with his mother in the hospital, holding her hand, in much the same way he would 60 years later when his wife would also succumb to the effects of diabetes. Over the course of his life his thoughts would return to what could have been prevented back in 1939. The whole experience was so painful that even decades later he could barely speak of it. He's packaged that time, mentally labelled it and tucked it away, sharing the memory with precious few.

Stu arrived in Yellowknife just before Christmas 1939 and started cutting cordwood for Ptarmigan Mines. The money was not as good as he expected, but he was stuck there until the following spring. He found himself once more living in a canvas tent in sub-zero temperatures, but at least this time he had an eiderdown sleeping bag and a stove — far better equipped than his family had been just 10 years earlier.

Stu built up strength and endurance working the blade saw but as spring approached, he knew he wanted to get out before the black flies appeared. When the work started to slow down as breakup neared, Stu passed his time wrestling in the soft spring snow with whomever would take him on. He also kept an eye peeled for other opportunities to keep in shape. One day, while walking past a local tavern, he saw some local men struggling with a weight-lifting contraption someone had rigged. It was an axle of about four inches in diameter, with wheels from a mine cart attached to each end. The whole thing weighed about 150 pounds. The men were trying to lift it, military style, up to their chests, then jerk it over their heads. But they didn't know enough to bend their knees for leverage. Stu picked it up with one hand and jerked his arm straight up over his head 10 times, impressing everyone with his strength. Like Emile Van Velzen, Stu had acquired a reputation as being a strong, tough man. Still, he was a bit of a mystery around Yellowknife because he did not jump at opportunities to fight in the taverns the way many of the men, bored with life around the mining camps, did. Stu recalls being lured into a few barroom brawls, but most of the time he kept to himself.

Yellowknife was a small town, with a population of only a few thousand. Stu liked to watch the Northern Cree Indians ice fishing on Great Slave Lake. Their methods were unique — they would cut two holes in the ice, feed a fishing net into one hole and anchor it with a stick. When the net was sucked under water, the Indians would fish it out the other hole dragging up 40 or 50 big lake trout with it.

Competitive wrestling remained at the forefront of Stu's mind. He started to worry about how he was going to get to Vancouver for the Canadian Amateur Wrestling Championships. He had managed the trip to Montreal the year before, where he had placed second. It was a good showing for a first-timer, but not good enough for Stu. He needed to win the 1940 championship in order to qualify for the Olympic team. But there he was, stuck in Yellowknife, which to him seemed as far away from Vancouver as Helsinki.

As luck would have it, a sports contact came in handy yet again. Back when he worked out at the Edmonton YMCA, Stu had met Leigh Brintnell, 20 years his senior, who had achieved aviation fame by being the first pilot to circle Great Bear Lake, as well as being the first to fly the mountainous route from Aklavik, NWT, to Dawson City in the Yukon. Brintnell had contracts sufficient to keep his aircraft repair company busy repairing and maintaining military aircraft.

Lord of the Ring

One afternoon, as he wandered down a street in Yellowknife, wondering how to get out of his predicament, Stu came upon Brintnell, who was also operating McKenzie Air Services. The company flew in supplies and mail regularly and made a round trip back to Edmonton.

After hearing about Stu's predicament, the older man offered to take the amateur wrestler back to Edmonton on his next flight out. From there Stu took the train to the coast for the championships. He had not been engaging in his normal training and he was naturally apprehensive about the competition he would face. Another second place finish would not satisfy him. The months cutting cordwood had added to his strength and endurance but made him more sinewy, threatening to make him too light for his ideal weight class. His training had been limited to his work on the blade saw, doing push-ups and squats, and wrestling in the snow. But his drive to make the Olympics was overwhelming. He was counting on joining the national team for a number of reasons — he wanted credibility and personal satisfaction. Even his father, who thought adult sporting activities were a waste of time, would have to be impressed.

Edward, living with Stu's sister, Edrie, in the house Stu had bought, was still eking out a living. Sylvester had moved on to the west coast, leaving her hard Alberta life behind. Neither sister would ever have a family of her own. The model provided by their mother and father was no incentive for them to take on marriage or children. For both girls, married life and motherhood no doubt represented little more than drudgery and abject poverty.

Having been runner-up in 1939, Stu was not overly confident when he arrived in Vancouver for the nationals. But he did prevail. He would later recall very little about the championship match, except that he was pitted against Ted "Lefty" Gardiner. Stu managed to pin Lefty five minutes before time was to be called.

A Vancouver newspaper reported the win under a heavy-type, two-column sports page headline:

Light-Heavyweight Crown Adorns Head of Stu Hart Decisions Maurie Batkin and Flattens "Lefty" Gardiner in Dominion Meet

> VANCOUVER, May 24 [1940]
> Stu Hart of Edmonton, runner-up in Montreal last year, dropped W. "Lefty" Gardiner five minutes from time in their 191-pound light-heavyweight bout, to top the national crown. The Edmonton boy earlier decisioned Maurie Batkin of Vancouver. He beat Ted Gardiner with a crotch hold and roll at 14:55 to win the crown.

With his victory, Stu became the Canadian Amateur Wrestling Champion in the light-heavyweight class, a title he held until he became a pro in 1946. He was now Canada's hope for a gold medal in wrestling at Helsinki. Stu's dream suddenly had every appearance of real possibility. He was poised for the Olympics, imagining every moment leading up to the final match, and he continued to gear his workout routines to the end.

But almost as soon as he got back, the radio and newspapers began reporting the dismal news — the Olympic organizing committee was considering cancelling the games because of the War. Waiting for their decision was agony. Everything that he had worked toward for the past several years was tied up in his Olympic dream. It had never occurred to him that something could cost him chance, other than the appearance of a better ath-

Lord of the Ring

lete in Vancouver. Since that hadn't happened, Stu believed things were unfolding as they should. But when the games were finally cancelled, Stu's hopes for Olympic gold were dashed. His disappointment was profound.

Back in Edmonton, at the age of 24, Stu's father was still pressuring him to go into farming. But despite his disappointment, he still wanted to see where athletics could take him. And, although he had buddies enlisting in the armed forces and heading overseas, Stu still wasn't ready for military service. He firmly believed the war would end quickly even as he was disconcerted to hear about the young men he had attended high school with. Arthur Figg, who he knew from the EACs, hadn't come home. Harold Sutton, who had played football with Stu with the Esks, became a decorated hero but went down with his plane.

On the flight from Yellowknife to Edmonton, Stu had sat in the cockpit with Leigh Brintnell. The two talked about old times around the YMCA, and about Stu's plans. Brintnell told Stu about his war contracts, for aircraft repair, with Northwest Industries, a company he was running out of a hangar on 101st Street in Edmonton. He had 17 employees working sheet metal jobs, and he could use another man for what was now classified by the government as "essential services" work. Doing something to help the war effort appealed to Stu, so he took Brintnell up on the offer and spent the next two years in the shop, qualifying as a journeyman sheet metal worker. Brintnell would add hundreds more to his payroll, in both Edmonton and Winnipeg. Like the others, Stu travelled across the West on work projects but never ventured further East than Winnipeg. Years later the Hart children would find the old aircraft repair tool kit their father had used during the War.

Stu's initials were still visible.

63

Four

As 1941 entered its final weeks, Stu Hart's faith in his Olympic dream was beginning to show signs of wear. After Pearl Harbor it looked like a prolonged war was taking hold. He was still doing essential service war work for Brintnell and by that time the cancelled 1940 Olympic games had been forgotten. In the spring and summer of '41 he put his baseball team, Hart's All-Stars, through its paces, but Stu wanted a lot more.

At 26, he was once again questioning where he was headed. If the Olympics went ahead in '44, he would be close to 30, and competing against much younger athletes. But the War was a harbinger of realities Stu did not want to face. By the time opportunities appeared, he might be too old, or out of the loop.

Other questions kept coming to him as he cut sheets of Durrell aluminum and fitted new skins on airplanes the Canadian and American air forces sent in for repair. Was he repeating history? Was he replaying his father's foolhardiness, hanging onto a dream long after it ceased to make sense? Stu was starting to wonder whether his aspirations were unrealistic, too.

On December 24, 1941, Stu wrapped up his day shift at Northwest Industries around 4:30 p.m. Like his co-workers, he was looking forward to getting home reasonably early to spend a quiet Christmas Eve with his family. But before Stu left the hangar, he joined in a few minutes of revelry with the rest of the men and women on his shift. Thirty-five hundred people were on the payroll at the time, working around the clock to help keep Allied planes in the air. Stu enjoyed the merry-making, especially since he had missed out on all the fuss over Christmas as a child. There had been attempts at cheer in the damp cold of the little Tofield tents. He and his sisters decorated a spruce sapling with bits of paper from the packages that bulk tea came in, and his father read the Christmas story from the Bible by the smoky light of a kerosene lamp. But the desperateness of the family's situation only reinforced young Stu's belief that his prayers for a better life were not being heard. It also caused him to conclude that money, indeed, made the world go around, and that he would have to take some steps of his own to pursue the almighty dollar. He had been forced to examine the mystery, tragedy and passion of life at a young age, and the way he added it all up would impact on him as a person for the long term. But that evening at Northwest Industries, he raised a glass and wished his friends a happy Christmas.

A few minutes later Stu put away his tool box, slipped out of the hangar, and wheeled his racing bike out into the cold late afternoon. He kept his bike inside the hangar to keep the tires from freezing during his shift. Once outside, he noticed the brittle crispness of the air and pulled his knit cap down over his ears, zipped his parka up snug to his chin and wrapped his scarf tighter around his neck. Hoar frost had settled on the trees. Heavier snows were due to fall, and that would bank in the streets until spring. During the winter, Stu's bike travels might be interrupted briefly, but the snow removal operation quickly cleared the main arteries of the city and he basically cycled all year round. Travelling by bike

Lord of the Ring

helped keep him in shape, but on really miserable days he drove his 1939 "Super Deluxe" Buick. He had bought it from an older man who had fallen sick and wanted to unload it. Not everyone during the war could come up with $250, but Stu knew a good opportunity when he saw one. The Buick had chrome wheel wells and had come in handy when he was driving around his girls' ball team. It replaced an old Dodge he'd bought for $25.

Once the temperatures dropped to -40, the wind chill made travel by bike unbearable. But it took a lot to get Stu Hart into his car. Tofield had conditioned him to handle winter weather with relative ease.

As he made his way down Portage Avenue from Northwest Industries to downtown Edmonton, Stu could see streaks of white, rose and purple of the aurora borealis rolling across the sky. He knew that in a couple of hours the northern lights would be clearly visible, etching a moving rainbow in the starry frozen heavens. Stu's mind turned to his family at home now in the little house in Bonnie Doone.

Despite his many disappointments, he was grateful that the family had a warm, snug place to live. The house had just two bedrooms, a tiny living room, kitchen and pantry, and a small barn and outhouse out back. Stu slept on a couch in the living room. But considering the family's history, such a house was a luxury, and they were all content. Stu missed his mother, and during the holidays her unexpected death was most keenly felt. Sylvester had gone off to Vancouver to work in an office a few years earlier and she was still there, hundreds of miles west, where the weather was far less harsh.

Edward Hart had acquired a reputation as an eccentric, and for having a rather short fuse. He moved from job to job, because sooner or later his temper got the best of him. But Stu was comforted knowing that his father and Edrie would be able to manage

Stu Hart

well enough on their own, now that the house was paid for and their combined earnings covered their day-to-day needs.

Even so, Edrie fretted that the old hardships of Tofield could return. Despite the fact that the family had lived in Edmonton for more than a decade her worries were hard to put to rest. Edward, constantly harping about getting back into farming, only added to her anxiety. It was something that Stu chose to ignore; he wished Edrie would learn to do the same.

Stu sped down to First Street and on to Jasper Avenue. He covered the distance rapidly and pulled his bike up in front of the Hudson's Bay Company store. He could see people admiring the big display windows, bright with festive decorations. Because of its size and prestigious stone facade and historic crest, The Bay dominated the street. Stu hurried in to finish the last of his own shopping. Cars were parked along the streets and people were running in and out of the shops and restaurants, waving to each other before heading off in different directions.

A few minutes later, Stu was pulling back on to Jasper. He planned to head on over to McDougall Hill, continue down to the Low Level Bridge across the frozen North Saskatchewan River, and then up to 99th and on to Bonnie Doone. As he biked along Jasper, near Mike's Newsstand, he could hear a rising clatter — sirens and the screaming of brakes behind him. Immediately recognizing the sound of a fire truck, he moved his bike as close to the curb as it would go, positioning himself to allow the vehicle to pass. The fire engine was roaring down Jasper at top speed, having left the station by the Presbyterian Church just a few minutes earlier. It crossed the First Avenue intersection and, before Stu understood fully what was happening, a small car darted out in front of the big rig, cutting it off. To avoid certain collision, the truck yawed precariously, veered wide, and slid wildly into the curb where Stu Hart was sitting on his bicycle.

Lord of the Ring

The truck's right front fender hit Stu as it skidded out of control.

Stu rolled with his bicycle, end over end. The car, which the truck had managed to miss, careened into a half dozen vehicles parked along the street. Miraculously, it missed the many pedestrians.

The impact threw Stu and his bike 30 feet. People rushed to him from every direction. Stunned, Stu looked up and saw a police officer kneeling beside him. He blinked and recognized Jim Malcahey, who had been at Strathcona High School with him. Before the officer could utter a word, a woman's face appeared, someone Stu didn't recognize. She peered into his face as he was lying there on the pavement, bleeding and in shock. She crooned sympathetically: "So young to die." Suddenly her body went limp and she slumped over an alarmed and bewildered Stu Hart. The woman had fainted on top of him.

Malcahey pulled the woman off, got Stu into his police car and raced him over to the Royal Alexandra Hospital. He had broken elbows and thumbs, and a serious injury to his spine. His thighs were skinned raw and he had numerous cuts, bruises and abrasions, all of which kept him laid up for weeks. Had he not been in peak physical shape, the impact might have permanently crippled him. As it was, the injuries kept Stu in hospital until spring.

Stu's Bonnie Doone neighbour, Al Oeming, his co-workers, family and sports buddies were all a part of the steady stream of visitors he would have throughout the winter. One day, as Stu lay back on the narrow hospital bed, his upper body propped up on pillows, Al stopped in for his regular visit with a more sombre and worried expression than Stu had seen from him all winter. By this time Al was a student in zoology at the University of Alberta, a man usually quite laid back in his general approach to life. He had worked out with Stu when they were teenagers and the younger Al looked up to Hart as if he were an older brother. Al followed the sports regimen Stu had set for him, and it wasn't long before skinny, lanky Al Oeming started looking like an athlete, too.

Stu was puzzled by Al's demeanor and quickly extracted the reasons behind the furrowed brow and pensive expression. "He told me he had been called up for duty in the armed forces and he wanted me to help him decide which branch of the services he should join," Stu recalls.

"We talked it over and I told Al he should consider the Navy because I knew the sports officer, who was also the medical doctor down at the Nonsuch, the Navy base in Edmonton. Dr. Koby McCallum was a pretty good guy, so we decided to go down to see him, as soon as I was released from the Royal Alex."

The more Stu and Al talked it through, the more they agreed that the Navy would be the most interesting branch of the services, given the fact there wasn't an ocean to be found within hundreds of miles of Edmonton. A few days later, Stu had his release from the hospital and he and Al headed down to the Nonsuch.

When the two walked into the Navy recruiting office, Stu heard the clear and unmistakable voice of Dr. McCallum: "Stu Hart, you're just the man I want to see."

Before he knew it, Stu Hart had enlisted as well.

McCallum wanted Stu, but he also wanted the baseball team that Stu had been working with — all currently employed in aircraft repair at Northwest Industries. Stu promised to have a talk with them. McCallum signed up Stu's entire team of 20 aircraft service repair men and put them on divisional (reserve) strength. Most were family men, and the designation meant they were shielded from being conscripted away from their wives and children. They continued to work in aircraft repair, but they all ended

Lord of the Ring

up playing on the Navy baseball team. Stu enlisted for regular service but was put on divisional strength until he fully recuperated from his injuries.

Stu was promptly appointed athletic director of the Navy's Edmonton operations and put in charge of the baseball team he had brought in with him. His orders were to train the team until it could "beat everything in sight." Stu took his orders seriously, and even though he couldn't play for months himself, he worked the team hard. Soon they were ready for the "All-Service" competition. The Americans, of course, were the team to beat. Ballplayers were brought in the by the United States Navy and Air Force from all over North America to ensure victories and boost the morale of the 60,000 American personnel in the Edmonton area working on the construction of the Alaska Highway and at various military positions in the North.

Stu was thrilled to get back to sports and he missed no opportunity to train the team to a top-notch level. There were Navy, Air Force, Army, even some civilian teams playing during the summer of 1942. The Americans won every regular season contest, beating all the other teams in the All-Service League. The crowds at Kingsway Ball Park were 5,000 strong for each game and heavily stacked with Americans.

By the fall, as teams prepared for the league championship, Stu had recovered enough to play first base. He had a local man, Allan Young, pitching, and Ken McCauley served as what Stu called his "shrewd and wily" catcher. Stu's team made it to a sudden-death final against the U.S. team. The Americans were a select, handpicked group; some were former pro ballplayers. Mike Milner, their renowned star pitcher, threw major-league heat that was nearly impossible to hit. But the game was tied going into the last inning. At bat, Ken McCauley bunted and managed to get to first base. With his next offering, Milner overthrew and Ken darted to second. Another batter hit a long drive which bounced off the fence. The Americans tried to cut off McCauley but again overthrew: McCauley headed for home amidst a blur of screaming fans. The rag-tag bunch from north of the border had won. The Americans were shocked.

The Canadians went wild with excitement and the team earned a whole new level of respect. Stu recalls with pride that the *Edmonton Bulletin* reported that Hart's team had "accomplished the impossible."

"Milner's team were supposed to kick the hell out of us," he says.

In early 1943, Stu put in for a transfer from the Nonsuch in Edmonton to regular service in Cornwallis, Nova Scotia. Physically, he had fully recovered, and he hoped to see some real sea duty. But the Navy seemed less interested in him as a seaman than as an athletic director. By this time the Navy had him wrestling to amuse the troops. He appeared regularly, before thousands of enlisted men in drill halls. Some of the seamen and soldiers he wrestled would resurface, years later, on wrestling cards in Stu's own promotion.

Stu loved to grapple in front of the frenzied audiences, men who appreciated physical combat as much as he did. For Hart, submission wrestling, the pure unadulterated exercise of inflicting pain to overcome another man, was a thrill he could never really explain. He had a knack for knowing just how far a body could be safely pushed, and he often took things to the very limit, especially when his opponents were much larger. Stu garnered a reputation as a sports star and the troops were quick to lavish praise on him. There were always men eager to take him on, and Stu had lots of time to work out. His early fears, that the armed forces would prevent him from spending time wrestling, couldn't have been more unfounded. Still, it wasn't long before it became

Lord of the Ring

clear that the 1944 Olympics would also be cancelled. Stu's Olympic dream died a second-death.

The late Michael O'Byrne, a justice in Calgary, was with Stu during his Navy years. "They had him wrestling in both Edmonton and later at Cornwallis," he said. "Everyone liked Stu, he was so pleasant and agreeable, and the Navy had him entertaining the troops as a wrestler. He wrestled with Sandor Kovacs and Al Korman, who would both later become stars in Stu's Stampede Wrestling. But he wasn't just appreciated by the troops. The Wrens would show up in big numbers just to get a look at Stu. He was a very good looking young man."

When O'Byrne pulled Shore Patrol, which involved checking the dance halls for remiss soldiers, he always made sure he was teamed up with Stu Hart. "We'd arrive at some dance hall, find the wayward sailors, and if they gave me any trouble, I'd just point to Stu and say, 'Would you rather deal with him?' They never did; they always went quietly. Stu was a pretty big fellow then, and there wasn't a sailor around who wanted to mess with him." O'Byrne was no slouch either, and held his own in the boxing ring during his military service.

Jim Thomson, now a Calgary-based race horse trainer, remembers Stu during the Cornwallis years too. There were a lot of Prairie boys down there as seamen, he says. "We all had to do work around the base and we'd pull jobs nobody liked to do like picking up refuse, vacuuming some officer's house, carrying stuff around. Everyone, that is, except guys like Stu Hart and Gay Stewart (later a Toronto Maple Leafs and Chicago Black Hawks right winger), who were recognized as athletes. They would get what the rest of us thought were pretty cushy jobs. Stu was usually assigned jobs like rolling the tennis court. He'd put on a real show, as if it was really tough work, but everyone knew it wasn't." Thomson notes that all the athletes got similar treatment.

Stu Hart

While stationed at CFB Cornwallis, near Digby, Nova Scotia, Stu and another seaman, Mac Sommersgill, also from Edmonton, decided to hitchhike down the New England coast to Washington, D.C., where Mac's sister worked as a secretary in the Pentagon. They took the ferry service on the Princess of Acadia to Saint John, and then hitched down the New Brunswick coastline to Maine and, finally, Washington. It was the first time Stu had crossed the border into the United States, and he was curious. Servicemen in uniform clustered together along the streets and in the coffee shops and movie houses, smoking cigarettes and cigars, talking, laughing and flirting with the women who passed by, just like they did in Halifax. The two Canadian sailors felt right at home in their Navy uniforms.

As they wandered down a street looking for a place to have some lunch, they came upon a small, well-lit restaurant called Joe Turner's Kitmarr, not far from Pennsylvania Avenue. Stu peered inside the big front window lined with dusty pink geraniums and could see a long row of bar stools at a polished wooden counter, and a line of booths along one wall. But as he stepped back from the window, his glance fell on something else.

A poster advertised an upcoming pro-wrestling card in bold type. That was it. Stu slapped Mac on the shoulder and Mac followed Stu inside. The place was doing a brisk business, with waitresses hauling trays of food and dirty dishes in and out of the kitchen, and their customers eating and drinking coffee and talking among themselves. Someone was pumping dimes into the juke box, and tunes like Woody Guthrie's "Sally Don't Grieve for Me" rose above the din of voices. Hardly anyone noticed the Canadian sailors who were making their way towards an empty table in the back.

As they walked past one of the last booths, a middle-aged man who seemed somewhat familiar to Stu, looked up and said,

Lord of the Ring

"You've got a big neck, kid. Have you ever thought of wrestling?" Stu knew, from the telltale cauliflower ears, caused by years of pounding, pulling and mauling, that this man was a wrestler himself. Before he could say a word, Mac piped in: "Hey, you're talking to the Canadian Amateur Wrestling Champion."

The man in the booth introduced himself as a promoter, Joseph "Toots" Mondt. Stu immediately recognized the name from magazines and newspaper sports pages. Toots replied, "I could tell you wrestled because of the size of your neck. Where are you from?" When he said Edmonton, Canada, Toots wanted to know if he'd ever heard of another Canadian wrestler he knew, the fabled Jack Taylor. Stu told him he'd seen Taylor wrestle Tiger Duhlea in Edmonton in 1932. Toots smiled, nodded his head in approval, and said, "Young man, if you know Jack Taylor, you're a friend of mine."

Taylor had given Toots his first wrestling opportunity in 1916, in Greeley, Colorado. Taylor himself had been promoted by the infamous Farmer Burns, recognized as the inventor of pro-wrestling, along with Burns's other major star, the legendary Frank Gotch. The two had barnstormed all over the United States and Canada, and were considered to be among the first serious pro-wrestlers. Their stardom during that era exceeded that of some of the most noted boxers and baseball players, and their smiling photographs were frequently on the cover of *Physical Culture Magazine*, one of the most popular sports publications of the era.

By the time Toots and Stu Hart met, Toots had already been in the business for 30 years, had wrestled in most of the arenas in the States and had even made the rounds with the Ringling Brothers Circus as a strong man. He talked like a man who knew everything there was to know about pro-wrestling, and Stu hung on his every word. Stu's focus on amateur wrestling was about to change.

Toots sized up Stu quickly, taking in his broad shoulders and well-developed and obviously trained limbs. Stu weighed-in at just under 200 pounds. He had wavy brown hair, his father's cobalt blue eyes and his mother's dimples. A perfect "good guy" wrestler, or what the business would call a "clever, clean and classy babyface."

Toots wanted Stu to stay in Washington for the week, so he could add his name to the following Thursday's card. He saw an advantage in having a new babyface in the mix, especially one who was the Canadian champion. Toots assured Stu that the money was good, and that it would get even better once his name became familiar. He made a convincing case, and Stu wished he could jump at this chance to actually do something with all his years of vigorous training.

Stu and Mac, though, were duty-bound, and had to get back to the base in Nova Scotia. Toots made sure Stu took his business card, assuring him that when he got out of the service he could come down to his New York booking office, where there would be lots of work for him. A few days after Stu got back to Nova Scotia, he found a letter in his mailbox from Toots reminding the younger wrestler that his talents could be put to good use on his wrestling cards and that the work paid well. That letter is still among Stu's collection of papers, more than 50 years later.

Toots Mondt commanded the largest of the 26 pro-wrestling promotions in the United States and Canada which operated under the National Wrestling Association banner (the organization changed its name to the National Wrestling Alliance in 1948). He held matches throughout the major cities on the Eastern Seaboard, and his territory included New York, Washington, Boston and Philadelphia. Because of his mentor, the Regina-born Taylor, Toots had a soft spot for Canadians. He also had a reputation for being tough, even among the tough. Mondt could handle the wrestlers physically, and he ran his promotion with ease. No one

Lord of the Ring

talked back to Toots. Stu seems to have admired this approach, and emulated it himself in later years.

When the War finally ended, Stu was already 30. He'd experienced great changes in three decades. At least 20 buddies from Edmonton were killed during the war. He'd missed the Olympics Games twice, as well as the British Empire Games. Just as he had feared, amateur wrestling honours had eluded him. It was time to concentrate on earning a living. He decided to get out of the Navy as soon as possible and join Toots Mondt in New York.

Stu applied for immediate release from duty, but heard every possible argument about why he should stay. The Navy brass wanted to hang on to its valuable athletic director — they loved the work he was doing.

Getting closer to Edmonton for a while appealed to Stu. He secured a transfer to Esquimalt on Vancouver Island, which was the closest available naval posting. Within weeks of his arrival in Esquimalt, he appeared on a wrestling card to help raise money for local hospitals. One Navy-sponsored boxing and wrestling match paired him, as the Canadian Amateur Wrestling Champion and the main wrestling attraction, with the great Joe Louis, the boxing draw. Louis, who had served in the American Army, had been crowned the World's Heavyweight champ in 1937 and had, just before the war, obliterated boxer Max Schmelling, who had been incorrectly perceived as a Nazi. History records that the Schmelling and Louis match lasted only 124 seconds. It is often described as the pinnacle of Louis' career.

Stu remembers sharing a Victoria dressing room with Louis. A humble, pleasant man, Louis was extremely popular at the time. And although he was not a prolific talker, he questioned Stu about the differences between boxing and wrestling.

Boxers, says Stu, always had a competitive interest in wrestlers. They wanted to know why it was that wrestlers looked like they were pounding each other into oblivion, but afterwards left the ring with nothing more than a few bruises. Stu grinned at Louis as he told him as little as possible about what really went on in the "squared" circle. Years later Louis would do some celebrity refereeing for Stu. Despite the racial turbulence of the '60s, Stu never considered racial differences in or out of the ring. The question was simple: was the guy any good as an athlete? Nothing else was of any consequence.

Stu continued to seek his release and finally, after five months in British Columbia, May 1, 1946, he received an honourable discharge. His plan was to visit his family in Edmonton, then make his way to New York to see what pro-wrestling could do for him. But it took three months for Toots Mondt to organize the paperwork and get Stu a work visa before he was really on his way.

The wait caused some anxiety, but when the documents finally came through, Stu got on the train for Toronto, picked up his immigration papers and boarded the bus to New York. It was an adventure that rivalled only his first train ride from Tofield to Edmonton. The significance was similar: both trips changed his life — for the better.

The farm boy from Tofield was completely awestruck and more than a little intimidated by New York City. In 1946 the Big Apple was bustling and crowded, teeming with excitement. A rapidly growing metropolis, the largest in North America, its famous landmarks and architecture and imposing public buildings confirmed its reputation as the financial and trade centre of the continent. With the help of numerous New Yorkers, Stu managed to find his way on the subway system to 42nd Street and Broadway, where the New York booking office Toots Mondt shared with Mike Jacobs was located, on the 2nd floor of the Times Square Building.

Toots wasted no time in working out Stu's schedule, adding

Lord of the Ring

his name to the week's card, directing him to a cheap but clean local hotel where he could stay temporarily, and telling him how to find an apartment. The booking office was a rough-hewn sort of place. Dozens of framed portraits and posters of wrestling and boxing greats almost completely wallpapered the place. Many of the posters were yellowed and dog-eared from age. The room was cheaply furnished, decorated with a couple of broken-down couches and a few chairs. A rickety old desk loaded with papers, flyers covered with cigar ashes, dirty coffee cups and more posters dominated one corner of the dusty, cluttered room. The telephone rang incessantly and wrestlers came and went, picking up their schedules, none staying too long. It wasn't inviting, certainly not the kind of place one hung around in. It smelled like a mixture of decay, cigar smoke and sweat. The coffee pot was almost always empty and when it wasn't, the coffee was not worth rounding up a clean cup for anyway.

St. Nick's on 58th Street was one of New York's most well-known arenas. By 1946 it had already witnessed many boxing and wrestling matches in its long, infamous history. It seated 2,500 and was a smoky, seedy place when Stu Hart walked in for his first pro-wrestling match. He was scheduled to face Chick Garibaldi, one of the half dozen or so wrestling Garibaldi brothers.

Stu remembers that night in a kind of haze, with the din of the fans and the noise of the place almost thunderous in the echo-prone old arena. The wrestlers' dressing rooms were on opposite sides of the ring in those days. Maintaining the illusion of opposition and competitiveness between the heels and babyface contenders was still paramount.

The promoters took the wrestlers, threw them into a ring and expected them to launch into hand-to-hand combat in a convincing way. The object was not simply to pin the opponent to the mat, but to get the crowd worked up and taking sides as quickly as possible. If a wrestler didn't win at least a respectable amount of the time, he wouldn't get a chance to recover; he'd be lucky to get bus fare back home.

The crowd at St. Nick's that night was as loud and aggressive as any could be. Stu was introduced as a Canadian champion, which brought a round of screams, especially from the women. His handsome, chiselled features and near perfect proportions went over big. It wouldn't be long before squealing and adoring females would rush Stu as he walked from the dressing room to the ring. Faced with the task of keeping them off Stu, the ushers weren't always successful. By the time he stepped between the ropes, Stu's arms and shoulders would often be covered with lipstick.

The noise, bright lights and barrage of cigarette packages, balled-up programs and candy bar wrappings flying from the stands were a little distracting until his debut match started. As soon as it did, Stu's concentration shifted completely to the task at hand. He wanted to do well the first time out, and he knew his career to some extent depended on it. Toots still hadn't seen him wrestle, and he was there, chewing on a big cigar, ready to assess his new babyface.

Stu was pitted against a tough opponent. Chick and his brothers dominated New York wrestling. There were so many of them, all good-looking Italian-Americans who had made their reputations as villains the crowd loved to bait. Stu was confident about his skills and wasn't about to let Garibaldi rattle him, even if he was a seasoned pro. When the bell rang to start the 20-minute match, Stu and Chick quickly assessed each other, grabbed hold and lunged into the task of taking each other out. Stu used his arsenal of head locks, body slams, straddles and flying mares and took a fair amount of abuse himself. He liked to grab an opponent by the head, use an arm drag, then drop to his

Lord of the Ring

knees and force the other man down. On the mat he'd grab his opponent's knees and try to pin him.

"If you got him on his back, you could get him into a submission hold," Stu explains. "Back then, wrestlers just did their thing. It was not necessarily an issue as to who might win or who might lose. But if you lost too often, they'd send you home. That pressure was always there." Stu now acknowledges that some of the time, to make the action more exciting for the crowd, there was a plan as to how the match would progress. This was always a carefully guarded secret. It was important in the industry to keep the myth of antagonism alive to add to the excitement in the ring.

Chick did not plan to hand anything over to the Canadian without a tough fight. Stu looked every inch the babyface, though, with his curling hair, blue eyes and dimples. His taller, dark-haired opponent could dance a mean tune around the ring, and he used the usual battery of illegal tactics — hair pulling and eye gouging, especially — to get the fans screaming. Soon the crowd was won over by the newcomer and began chanting "Stu-Stu-Stu" like a ritual drum beat. Chick was adept at drawing heat, so Stu, the new kid on the New York mat, stuck to his trusted submission holds and managed to get the heel into one he could not release himself from. Twenty minutes after the match began, the referee was holding Stu Hart's arm up above his head: the new babyface had won.

Stu laughs when he recalls his early matches.

"In those days, pro-wrestling was pretty hard core scientific skill, with a little guerrilla theatre ladled on. I was doing pretty believable work." He adds, though, that it took a while to learn how to get a rapport going with the fans. Still, in those days, "If you didn't have the skills, you couldn't cover that up with any amount of pizzazz." Stu firmly believes that a wrestler has to prove himself in the ring — no amount of prancing around or screaming into a microphone can compensate for a lack of skills.

Stu Hart

Although Stu had been training for a long time, at 31 he still insisted on modelling himself after the great pros, like Jack Taylor, he had seen and admired as a boy, as well as the ones, like Frank Gotch, he'd only read about.

"The classy Canadian," as he was often described by New York sports writers, hopped the trains and buses around the pro-wrestling circuit, performing in venues as far from New York as Boston, Philadelphia, Toronto, Montreal, Houston, Dallas and Tulsa.

On May 28, 1946, a New York newspaper extolled Stu's virtues:

Hart Triumphs in Tournament Armoury Bouts
Canadian Pounds Four Opponents for the Count in Wrestling Show

> Stu Hart, the young Canadian strong man and escape artist, pounded four opponents to the mat for the count as he won a one-night elimination wrestling tournament before a half-filled but hilarious house at the Armoury last night.
>
> Cool, clever and clean grappling Stu disposed of Pat Welch of Atlantic City as the latter's airplane spin backfired on him and saw the agile Hart come out on top with a body crush in 12:39. His next opponent was George Macricostas, the game Greek, and here Stu met some real wrestling that was almost on a par with his but not quite, and he took the 20-minute decision.

Lord of the Ring

Next to fall before Hart's power crushes and hard-driving slams was Texas Babe Sharkey, ex-claimant to the world's grappling title. Overcoming the weight handicap of his hulking opponent, Stu tore into him with his characteristic well-planned attack and won a unanimous decision over the 20-minute route.

With but a few minutes rest, he took on Chick Garibaldi, who had pinned Bill Middelkauf of Miami and Don Blackman, the Black Panther, to enter the final bout. The go lasted 20 seconds as Garibaldi opened with a series of headlock slams which saw Hart follow up with the same manoeuver as he slammed Garibaldi for the count in short order with the crowd screaming in wild frenzy. He used a reverse body drop to do the trick...

Stu's media presence wasn't restricted to wrestling, as a newspaper in St. Paul, Minnesota, reported:

Stu Hart Gets Gals in a Fluster

Stu Hart's ears should be pink. A woman writer had this to say about the Edmonton, Canada wrestler the other day:

"In my opinion, Stu Hart is not only a fine athlete with speed, youth and ability to

Stu Hart

his credit but a friendly, charming personality as well. He possesses a boyish charm that will set the feminine hearts a-flutter. And I know the girls will just love his slow-dimpled smile."

Hmmm!

Well, Hart may be all of those things, but he's also a rugged 232-pounder who got his start as a baseball and football player in Alberta. He was still undefeated as an amateur wrestler when he turned pro in 1946. A veteran of four years in the Canadian navy, Stu has made rapid progress since the war in the pro-wrestling game. Television has been especially kind to Hart, establishing him as something of a national favourite. His favourite hold is the flying cross.

In peak physical condition, Stu cut a handsome figure and had, to the Americans, a charming "English-sounding" accent. He thrived in New York, and was consistently among the top draws, appearing on the new medium of television twice a week. Broadcasts emanated from St. Nick's Arena on Tuesdays and from Madison Square Garden on Thursdays. He was becoming a presence, meeting people, going to parties and dances, and concentrating on developing a name and reputation as a strong, serious Canadian wrestler. And he was earning money — $90 a week for wrestling every night. It wasn't a bad income, given that he rented a studio apartment for $12 a month, and that you could buy a new Chevrolet for about $800 dollars.

Stu lived at 137 Amsterdam Avenue, not far from the booking

Lord of the Ring

office. He picked up some odds and ends, an old couch, a bed and a table and chairs. Sometimes he let other wrestlers move in with him, because it was a rambling, roomy place. Sandor Kovacs and Jan Blears both bunked at Amsterdam Avenue for a while, but reconsidered when a large rat moved in too. The rat came up out of the toilet and usually hung out by the trash. Hearing it rustle near the garbage bag was too much for the two wrestlers, but they wouldn't do anything about the new tenant. Finally Stu took matters into his own hands. He swatted the bag and startled the rat. When it rushed out, he literally jumped on it with both feet. The rat's flattened carcass was thrown out the window.

Stu's early matches with the Garibaldi brothers pale, in his estimation, with the high-octane wars he had with Abe Stein, a brutal, scientific wrestler who enjoyed every moment of his villainy. He could work up a crowd faster than anyone Stu had ever seen. He loved to play on the anti-Semitic barbs he would bait out of the fans, and he'd throw back any insulting remark that entered his head.

Stu loved wrestling Abe because it was always such a wild time. The two had a good routine going and established such intensity they sometimes drew the fans out of their seats and brought the police running down the aisles to put a stop to the crush of bodies moving towards the ring and threatening to riot. A New York newspaper clipping found among Stu's memorabilia captures the spirit of one of their combat sessions; it's accompanied by a photograph showing police attempting to keep fans off the wrestlers:

Mat Show Riot Averted

> A two-minute extra-curricular scuffle between Abe Stein, target of anti-Semitic

barbs at the Forum wrestling show last week, and Stu Hart at the conclusion of their 30-minute preliminary mat match almost precipitated a riot at the Bronx Winter Garden last night.

For a while tempers flared and feelings ran amuck as referee Al Reich, officials and minions of law and order battled to separate the exhibitionists.

The ring was completely surrounded by an enraged crowd, including minors, who pushed, shoved and shouted. Several climbed into the ring with malice aforethought.

It all started when Stein of Hollywood, California, went after Hart of Canada as his foe was awarded the decision.

Soon Stu was hanging out at Dempsey's Bar and Grill. Owned by boxing legend Jack Dempsey, it was the "in" place to be, especially for athletes. Everyone wanted to stop by and chat with the ex-champ and eat the best corned beef sandwiches in town.

Dempsey's was outfitted with the usual counter and scattered tables and a few booths. The cook occupied a prominent position behind the counter and tended the spit, which kept the beef turning and cooking slowly. He'd whip up sandwiches on a butcher's block table, slicing the meat expertly with an imposing, razor-sharp knife. Stu quickly got hooked on corned beef, which he'd slather with hot mustard. Dempsey would saunter in and keep the place buzzing with anecdotes and excitement. His job was to shmooze and dispense unsolicited athletic advice. The possibility that the champ sign autographs and banter with the customers

Lord of the Ring

kept the place full all day long. He would tell patrons that he made a lot more money at his restaurant, and for refereeing both boxing and wrestling, than he ever had in the ring itself.

A photo of Stu shadow boxing with Dempsey soon went up on the restaurant wall. It was fun to watch how Dempsey handled himself, and Stu picked up some pointers. Sometimes an obnoxious customer would try to bait Dempsey into a fight. But the ex-champ was not easy to intimidate, and invariably the aggression of the customer soon disappeared.

One day, Joe Louis walked in; Stu immediately invited him to his table. They updated each other on their lives because they'd bonded while sharing the boxing-wrestling card in Victoria. Stu Hart would invite both Dempsey and Louis out to the Calgary Stampede as celebrity referees in the 1950s. Louis would actually wrestle for a while, in an attempt to earn enough to cover a huge IRS debt. But he didn't fare well — fans just couldn't accept the classy boxer rolling around in a wrestling ring. Refereeing proved a better fit.

Stu branched out to frequent the eateries off Broadway, but usually stayed within a stone's throw of the wrestling office. Eventually he walked into a deli next to Gaylord's Dancing Academy, planning to pick up some beef, rye bread and pats of butter, which were all still under ration. Other athletes had the same idea. As he stood before the ubiquitous rotating meat spit and huge bottles of pickled eggs, someone behind the counter recognized either his face or accent. Stu recognized the man, too. He had been the catcher for the U.S. team that had played in the All-Service League in Edmonton during the War.

"You look familiar," the catcher said, although 50 years later the man's name is lost to Stu. He wondered: "Have you ever been up around Edmonton, Canada?"

It wasn't long before the two were reliving that sudden-death

Stu Hart

All-Service League final. The catcher introduced Stu to some of the ballplayers who came in for their cuts as well: Babe Ruth, Joe DiMaggio and a collection of other Yankees. As Stu waited for the big circular saw to slice off his half-pound, he soaked up the banter.

Stu was introduced as a hot young Canadian ball player who was now on TV, wrestling. Because of the way the deli manager spoke of Stu's abilities on the ball field, and because he was a celebrity back in Canada, he was welcomed into the deli sports-culture.

Babe Ruth, who by 1946 was in the last years of his life, always greeted Stu with a "Hi, Kid" and a slap on the shoulder. It was something he did with just about everyone, making it unnecessary to keep track of names. Stu would remind Ruth about touring in Edmonton and Western Canada, but their talk was always interrupted by someone trying to pull Babe aside to get an autograph or to ask him something about his career. DiMaggio, too, was always being jostled; people pressed towards him, wanting to be close to the great man and talk about the 56-game hitting streak he established in the early summer of 1941.

Periodically the wrestlers did their pre-match workouts at Madison Square Garden Stadium, which at the time was the third Garden to occupy the imaginations of New York sports fans. Sometimes, however, the wrestlers worked out at Yankee Stadium, where the ring was set up over the catcher's box. Stu enjoyed getting to know the ball players, sharing their locker rooms. Even after he left the city, when visiting New York he made a point of catching a Yankees game or wandering over to the locker rooms at the Garden or Yankee Stadium, just to see who was around.

One day at a practice session at the Stadium, he met a young ball player who was quickly becoming an important contributor to the team. Stu was impressed by the skill he saw in the man, little

Lord of the Ring

knowing that in a very short period of time Mickey Mantle would become a household name.

When he first walked into the wrestling office on 42nd Street, Stu was told that the best place to work out, however, was George Bothner's gym. It was famous because every New York athlete of note since the late 1800s had trained or worked out there at some point. Just five blocks from Madison Square Garden and a block and a half from the booking office, it was typical of gyms of its day with a main room where equipment, mats, free weights and wrestling/boxing ring were set up. A few beat-up card tables, scattered along the room's sides, were occupied by old athletes and rounders who played cards and chewed on the stogies they weren't allowed to light. Pictures of wrestling and boxing champions like Dempsey, Strangler Lewis, Bothner himself (who was the middleweight boxing champ in the late 1890s), Toots Mondt and others hung on the walls. Stu visited often.

He also occasionally wandered into Stillman's Gym, where most of the boxers trained, but he preferred Bothner's — partly because of the constant parade of characters, athletes and musicians who provided endless entertainment with their mere presence. Athletes like Mantle, DiMaggio, Ruth and Ray Steel, and even singers like Al Martino, Mario Lanza and Frank Sinatra wandered through periodically. Sinatra, then a skinny, popular young star, capable of sending his female fans into a swoon by just walking down the street, would come in accompanying Martino or Lanza. They did some light fitness training and all but ignored the athletes who made the place the serious workout venue that had attracted the crooners to begin with.

Working out at Bothner's was never dull. Stu collected autographs from Sinatra, Martino and Lanza and remembers telling Sinatra how much he liked his work. Sinatra was not foreign to the pro-wrestling set. Stu recalls that Joe Scarpello introduced him to Sinatra. Scarpello had grown up with Frank — he could hold his own in the ring, and there was generally a lot of Italian support for him during his matches. Sinatra occasionally came to watch. Stu also remembers the rumours: people said Scarpello knew a man named Johnny Michaels, who was Al Capone's driver. . . . But no one knew if it was true or just bluster. Whatever, it added to the excitement.

In time, Toots brought in another promoter he'd worked with occasionally. Jesse McMahon operated his own promotion and he and Toots got on relatively well. Stu describes Jesse McMahon as a reasonable person to deal with — a very capable businessman McMahon and Mondt combined their efforts in the late '40s, and it made Jesse Mondt's heir apparent. "In mischief together," was how Stu would later describe the relationship, noting that they promoted both boxing and pro-wrestling.

But Jesse, too, was getting on in years, and in 1952 he turned his interest over to his son, Vince McMahon, Sr. This promotion would operate under the name Capitol Wrestling Federation until the late 1970s, when it was re-invented under the banner World Wide Wrestling Federation (WWWF). By that time McMahon's son, Vince Jr., was working at his side.

When Stu met Jesse McMahon in the '40s, Jesse stood about 6 feet tall, weighed 220 pounds, and had thick, medium brown hair. His looks would be passed on in substantial measure to his son. Vince Sr., like his father before him, passed on his interest upon retirement, selling it to Vince Jr. in 1982.

Vincent K. McMahon Jr. would re-invent the promotion yet again, and change wrestling forever.

Vince Jr. was born in 1945 but, depending on the history you chose to believe, did not come to know his father until he was about 12 years old. When Stu first met the youngest McMahon he

Lord of the Ring

was a skinny teenager: "A nice quiet kid," in Stu's estimation, who was busy lapping up everything going on around him and resisting pressure from his father to focus on becoming a lawyer or accountant and have a different sort of life.

In the summer, Stu's body-beautiful regime kept him on the beaches of Coney Island. But after he met fellow wrestler Paul Boesch, all of that changed. Paul worked part-time lifeguarding at Long Beach — an idyllic 10-mile strip of sun and sand on Long Island.

After hearing Boesch talk about the interesting people he'd met, Stu decided to relocate his tanning efforts. Stu, Sandor Kovacs and Jan Blears all went together. Boesch promised to introduce them to retired Olympic track star Harry J. Smith, who lived there year round. If they were lucky, he said, they would meet Harry's five beautiful daughters.

Harry set records as a sprinter and was a national title-holder. As a result he was something of a local celebrity. He wrote a sports column for the *New York Tribune*, so his profile was maintained long after he hung up his track shoes. Harry had also run the Boston Marathon, for 10 years straight, was King of Mardi Gras in 1909, and a serious contender in the 1912 Olympics. Unfortunately, he sprained an ankle before he could compete. His Olympic roommate was the fabled Jim Thorpe, the Native American who went on to win the decathlon and pentathlon at those Olympic Games. Stu met Thorpe on the wrestling circuit years after the gold medalist's athletic heyday. At that time he was promoting a young Native American wrestler, and Stu was left with the impression that Thorpe was very knowledgeable about pro-wrestling even though it had not been his sport.

True to his promise, on one Long Beach outing Boesch introduced Stu and Jan to the five Smith sisters, who were all sitting on a blanket, sunning themselves. They chatted with the good-looking trio of athletes. All the Smith sisters had big smiles and were both witty and smart. Most of the women Stu had met were Wrens or wrestling groupies. These young Long Island women were very different.

The Smith house was a short walk from where they spoke; a two-storey white clapboard building, it was set back from the street by about 20 feet. And when the Smith girls were ready to leave for home, Stu and Boesch and Blears walked with them, carrying their blanket, hanging on their every word. No one was as taken as Stu.

He remembers them all as pretty girls, who had competed in beauty pageants and been crowned Miss Something-or-other by the time they were in their mid-teens. To Stu, they were unique and intriguing, smart, energetic individuals who had a famous athletic father. But Stu took an immediate interest in Helen, the eldest.

Helen dazzled Stu. "She had big brown eyes that danced and a lovely warm smile," he says, recalling that first meeting. "It took me a year and a half to trap her, but it was the best move that I ever made."

The first things Helen noticed about Stu were his unbelievable blue eyes, his gentlemanly manner and cute Canadian accent, which she thought sounded a little British. A serious-minded young woman with an academic bent, Helen had graduated from Long Beach High School as valedictorian and had won the English medal. But her aspirations of going to university and becoming an English teacher were dashed when her father was permanently injured in a hit-and-run accident. He had been out walking at the time, and suffered such damage to his leg that he would never walk again without a pronounced limp. It was a long, slow recovery. The family's comfortable lifestyle had

Lord of the Ring

already suffered a major setback with the stock market crash of 1929, when Helen was still a child. After her father's accident the Smith household desperately needed another income, so Helen went to work for the Long Beach School Board as a secretary. The Smith's had owned two houses side by side, one to live in and one to rent out. The rented house was promptly sold to help meet expenses.

On the walk towards the Smith residence that day in 1946, the little troupe met Harry on his way home, leaning heavily on his cane and taking his walk slowly. Helen loved to recount Stu and Harry's first meeting.

"They took to each other right away — it was like love at first sight, immediate, unconditional, permanent."

Stu would quickly become the son Harry never had. The men shared a common interest in sports, and they would sit and talk for hours. Sometimes, even in winter, Stu and Harry would get up from a chat and go out for a walk, not pausing from their conversation long enough to put on a coat. They would walk and talk, oblivious to the world around them.

Helen's mother, Ellie, was less impressed. She didn't like wrestling — it was low brow, certainly not something an acquaintance of her daughter ought to be doing for a living. She was more approving of the nearby West Point and King's Point cadets.

Elizabeth (Ellie) Poulis Smith was the daughter of Greek immigrants who had made their way from Agrinion. She was actually born on Ellis Island, while her parents, along with other immigrants, sat in quarantine waiting to be granted entry into the United States. A talented artist and dancer in her younger years, Ellie raised all daughters to be conscious of their social standing. It was so well drilled into little Helen that when she was asked, in first grade, what she wanted to be when she grew up, her response was "princess." Helen, two months premature, weighed a mere three pounds when she was born on February 16, 1924. In the 1920s there was not much hope for her survival. She was placed in a shoebox, with a hot water bottle on either side. A nurse kept burning the end of her toe with a wooden match to keep her awake — fearing that if she fell asleep she would never reawaken. The burn marks were visible throughout Helen's life.

At 22 Helen was stunningly beautiful. Her long, dark, curling hair framed Rita Hayworth good looks. She was petite, and barely stood 5'2". Helen would retain this beauty throughout each decade. Her upbringing had been softened by attentive parents, a celebrity father and a household that, before 1929, did not want for anything. Her background was a neat opposite to Stu's early years of struggle and deprivation. She was as smooth around the edges as he was rough and tumble. But because of his early experiences, he would bring to their marriage a self-sufficiency that would never cease to amaze her.

Despite his humble beginnings, Stu Hart had an almost incongruent kindness about him, given the way he had chosen to earn his living. Wrestling has always pushed the limits, especially when submission wrestling still meant a test of strength and iron will — of violence without anger. Then, as now, pro-wrestlers protected each other from injury and worked together as a team. Being the first thing a wrestler learns and hones, this kind of practised gentleness became just as much a part of Stu Hart as his ability to inflict pain. But there's no questioning his enjoyment of physical battle — he would have thrived in the days of the Roman gladiator, upon contests of physical and mental will.

Helen's first date with the Canadian was like no other she had experienced. He took her to a wrestling match. She had agreed to go out with Stu partly as an excuse to wear a pretty new green-and-white dress which she and her sisters were to take turns wearing. New dresses always rotated among the sisters. It was

Lord of the Ring

Helen's turn and she was determined to go somewhere, anywhere, in order to wear it.

But the wrestling match upset her.

Stu was grappling with Sammy Fitzpatrick Cohen, and when he lost, Helen rushed out of the open-air arena and headed home. Seeing Stu slammed on the mat, stomped on and punched was too much. Stu managed to catch up to her and finally talked her into going for ice cream. They had a long conversation, during which Stu extracted information about Helen, who later recalled feeling a little like a puppy having its pedigree examined.

She started to see Stu regularly after their talk, because he was nice and polite. But she had no real intention of allowing the relationship to develop further — their interests were very different.

Helen liked the theatre, but Stu took her to the circus.

As divergent as their interests were, Helen conceded, it was never dull. The circus especially appealed to Stu, likely because of early deprivation, a life completely devoid of magic. There was no Santa Claus, tooth fairy or Easter bunny in his childhood.

Once, while Helen and Stu walked along the beach, she stepped on some tar that had accumulated, from the ships anchored further out. Stu knelt down and scraped the tar from her sandal with a popsicle stick in such a sweet and gentle way that Helen realized he really cared about her.

"I said to myself, don't take this man lightly."

Their first year of courting had to accommodate Stu's circuit travels, but whenever he got back to New York, which by then was home, Stu immediately got in touch with Helen.

Ellie Smith finally decided that her daughter was seeing far too much of the big Canadian, and she resolved to put a stop to their relationship. She sat Helen down for a long talk, detailing all of the reasons why she should end the friendship. Find a doctor, a lawyer, even a football hero — anyone but a wrestler — Ellie

Stu Hart

begged. The truth of the matter, though, was that no one was going to be good enough for her first born.

Dutiful Helen considered her mother's advice carefully and decided to stop seeing Stu. She rationalized that while he was kind and wonderful and had those bluer than blue eyes, there just wasn't enough in common for the two of them to continue.

"I remember we had been walking," Helen would say. "It was raining softly, and as we walked I told him we had to stop seeing each other because we didn't have enough in common and my mother did not approve. Before I could say anything else, he stopped me and said he didn't agree at all. He was not going to give up on this. He told me: 'I'm going to marry you,' and he handed me this bunch of wilted flowers from some wrestler's mother's garden. Then I looked into those blue, blue eyes and that did it again."

The young couple soon set a date: they would be married on New Year's Eve, 1947. Stu was booked to appear in Great Falls, Montana, in early January 1948, and Helen would be joining him as his wife.

Ellie was appalled. The thought of her daughter marrying a wrestler, no matter how good looking he was, or how impeccable his Canadian manners may have been, or how hard he worked, was abhorrent. In her opinion, no mere wrestler was fit to take her precious first born away to some Godforsaken place called Montana. Or worse, to Canada.

Helen's mother knew next to nothing about Canada. Like most New Yorkers, she could come to terms with Montreal and Toronto, but not some prairie town several days drive to the west. Stu's stories, about Edmonton or the Calgary Stampede, did not impress her at all. And in truth, Ellie never forgave Stu for turning her daughter's head and taking her 3,000 miles away. Stu was permanently out of her favour. Years later, when she visited the

Lord of the Ring

family in Calgary, he would become so nervous that whenever he drove his mother-in-law somewhere, he would invariably take the wrong route and have to listen to a barrage of complaints from the back seat.

Helen would patiently ask, "Stu, why are we going this way?"

Harry J. Smith, however, was ecstatic about having Stewart Edward Hart as a son-in-law. The two would maintain a close relationship, one built on mutual respect, for the rest of Harry's life. In contrast to Ellie, Harry liked the feel of Calgary, the western edge to it. He saw it as a town with a future.

Helen and Stu were married at Long Beach Catholic Church by Father Gallagher in the middle of a blizzard on December 31, 1947. Stu was 32, Helen was 23.

Right away they were on the road, driving Stu's midnight blue Dodge to far-off Montana in the dead of winter to meet Stu's January 5th booking date.

Helen loved to say: "We were married in a blizzard and I've been snowed in ever since."

Life in Great Falls, Montana, living in a small trailer, was dull for Helen. The town had limited amenities, a tiny library, no theatre to speak of, and after New York, seemed mind-numbingly boring. When Stu returned from wrestling he would step into the trailer and ask her what would always seem a nonsensical, rhetorical question: "So what have you got for me?"

She never knew what to say until she finally had this response: "Well, in November, I'll have something for you."

That "something" would be the first of their many children.

Smith Stewart Hart was born in November 1948. Helen went back to New York to recover with her parents and sisters.

Stu established and maintained a warm relationship with the other Smith girls. He paid extra attention to the youngest, Diana.

Stu Hart

She was in her early teens when Stu met Helen. Diana likes to recount how nice it was to have a "big brother" around, and Stu made sure she wasn't left behind — often slipping her money for hot dogs and ice cream. Even after Stu and Helen moved to Montana, Stu never forgot about his new "little sister." When Helen was ready to pass her dresses along to Diana, Stu would pack them up for her and send them off. When Diana opened the box and took out the neatly folded garments she would find a silver dollar taped to each bodice.

"It was such a treat back then: a dollar was a lot of money. I think I still have some of them, even now. He was always so good to me, in that quiet way." Later on Diana would meet her husband, Canadian journalist Jock Osler, on a visit to Stu and Helen's home. Jock was then a reporter for the *Calgary Herald*. He got to know Stu from the newsroom: Stu would often come through with a wrestler he was promoting in tow.

Soon Stu was helping with the bookings around Great Falls as well as wrestling himself. It took the pressure off promoters Jerry Meeker and Larry Tillman, who concentrated on the far flung corners of a promotion that covered several states and parts of Western Canada. Stu was beginning to realize that the serious money in pro-wrestling lay in promoting. The territory ran through the Pacific Northwest of the United States, as far east as Montana, and included western Canada from the Pacific Ocean to the Manitoba border. There were also venues in Alaska, the Yukon and the Northwest Territories. Occasionally, Helen travelled with Stu if the match was of particular interest.

On one trip Helen went specifically to see some women wrestlers. But on the way home, on a lonely road in northern Montana in 1949, 40 miles north of Shelby, another vehicle drove straight across their path. It was impossible to avoid a collision and Helen, in the front passenger seat, pregnant with Bruce, felt

Lord of the Ring

the brunt. Nearly every bone in her face was broken. Stu escaped with minor scrapes and bruises, and he marvelled at Helen's calm as she took out a notebook while they waited for the ambulance to arrive. She insisted on recording every detail about the accident for the personal injury claim she would later make.

Her recovery was slow and tedious. She required a series of major facial reconstructive surgeries, and these were done in Rochester, New York. While she recuperated with her parents in Long Beach, little Smith accompanied her. Harry and Ellie were so captivated by the blond, blue-eyed baby that they staked a substantial claim on him during the two years that he spent with them. Helen recalled that it was a little difficult ungluing Smith from his grandparents when it came time to re-join Stu in Great Falls — he had stayed, working to cover the costs of her medical treatments. It took a while for Ellie and Harry to understand that Smith wouldn't be staying with them for the long term.

Eileen Simpkins O'Neill of Ottawa, a close friend to Helen for many years, remembers being told how hard it was to detach little Smith from his grandparents. "They used to call him 'Shoey' because he had such dark brown eyes that looked like buttons on old fashioned shoes. Everyone knew it wasn't going to be easy when it came time for Stu and Helen to return to Montana. Gaga [the family's name for Ellie] was clearly upset. Finally, Stu in his pragmatic way just picked up little Smith under his arm and marched him off to the car as Smith screamed for his grandmother."

Smith remembers being in a high chair at his grandmother's house, all of his aunts gathered around him. They would put a bowl of spaghetti in front of him and watch to see what he would do. After a few seconds the toddler would throw it against the nearest wall. His aunts all laughed about how cute he was. When Smith tried this in front of Stu, when he returned to his parents, he met a very different reaction. Stu's wallop cured him of his errant ways immediately. Suddenly his mischief wasn't so cute.

Helen delivered a second blond, blue-eyed baby boy, Bruce Edward, in 1950. He was followed closely by Keith William, in 1951. A series of a dozen pregnancies in 17 years was well on its way.

On a trip to Edmonton in late 1950, Helen finally met Stu's father. She had been looking forward to the meeting and was confident her new baby boy would impress the man, or at least break the ice. Helen was a little startled by the crisp, no-nonsense manner of Edward Hart. When she held up little Bruce, her beautiful new baby, and asked Edward who he looked like, Edward eyed the child closely and gruffly declared: "He looks like himself."

During the summer months, wrestling shut down, so by the end of June each year Stu looked for something to occupy his time that paid enough to keep the larder full. Sometimes he'd join the side show in the Ringling Brothers Circus as a strongman or as a wrestler of "all comers" — for a dollar a round. It was rare that anyone came even close to beating him, but he earned reasonable money for the off season.

By early 1951, Stu was already planning to return to Canada. He had been up to Alberta regularly to wrestle, and finally a plum dropped into his lap — Mayor Fry and Police Chief Chute were pressing him to organize wrestling in Edmonton on a local basis. They were convinced that there was enough support, especially if the venture was promoted by a talented local athlete who had made it good in far-off New York. Plus, he still had a lingering following from his football and baseball days.

It didn't take Stu long to appreciate the opportunity he had been given. He jumped at the offer, promptly took out a licence in his own name, and set up the promotion. Things were humming in Edmonton and Stu engaged Al Oeming, his old neighbour from Bonnie Doone, to run the operation while he commuted from

Lord of the Ring

Great Falls. Soon Stu started keeping tabs on Calgary. He was convinced there could be a strong promotion there, too.

What wrestling there was in western Canada had been run out of the Great Falls booking office. Jerry Meeker and Larry Tillman had been in charge there for years and had never had a sleepless night about a competitor.

This was about to change. A buzz started to develop around Stu Hart, with his experience and personal connection to Edmonton and Calgary. Meeker and Tillman started watching the popular Canadian grappler closely. Sooner or later, they knew, Stu would realize he didn't need the Great Falls booking office at all. Still, they weren't clear on just how much interest there was in Alberta.

When Stu returned to Great Falls, Meeker quizzed him about his thoughts on Calgary's development as an urban centre. Stu, in his straightforward, sometimes naive way, told him it was the fastest growing city in Canada, and that they were selling out every match they booked there — whether he was wrestling or not.

On the strength of Stu's comments, Meeker dispatched Tillman to watch for a chance to get into Calgary to balance out Stu Hart's activities in Edmonton.

Darby Melnick was the Calgary connection to the Great Falls booking office. He was making a name for himself in dubious ways — certainly not for his skills as a promoter. He had been accused of getting far too physical with fans and had recently — behind the old Noble Hotel in Calgary — beaten a restaurant patron so badly that it was not clear whether he would have to be charged with manslaughter. Stu remembers Melnick as a very cocky guy, touchy and quick to anger.

Meeker did not miss the opportunity to manoeuver. He convinced Melnick that he had better lay low until the bad publicity blew over. He then arranged for Tillman to buy out Melnick for

Stu Hart

$5,000, which Tillman borrowed from wrestlers Dave Ruhl and Orville Brown, who had recently been the NWA champ. Not long after this, Melnick's victim rallied — but there was no longer room in the Calgary operation for Melnick. Tillman moved to Calgary.

Soon, however, Meeker and Tillman became even more uneasy about the success of Stu Hart's promotion in Edmonton. Stu recalls that Meeker and Tillman devised a plan to get him to work with Tillman in Edmonton, thereby giving Tillman some leverage and control. But Stu wasn't buying. Meeker and Tillman responded by refusing to book Stu on cards in Calgary, thereby depriving him of extensive exposure. None of it made sense to Stu, given his local popularity. Every time he wrestled, there were banner headlines in the *Calgary Albertan* sports pages and in the *Calgary Herald*. He was the Alberta-boy who had made good. His matches from Madison Square Garden, St. Nick's Arena, the Winter Garden, Jamaican Garden, and even his bouts in Oklahoma and Texas had been diligently followed up by the local press. By the time he returned to Edmonton, Stu was even more of a celebrity than when he left.

Despite the ink Stu received, Tillman and Meeker were determined to get rid of the competition. Tillman offered Stu a paltry sum for his rights in Edmonton. But Stu had the support of city officials, and nudging him out clearly was not going to work. Tillman's manner was so condescending and out of character (he was generally seen as a southern gentleman), that his words continued to ring in Stu's ears 50 years later: "Why don't we throw you a couple of thousand dollars and you go get lost?"

Stu told Tillman: "I'm not for sale."

He had just built a $1,500 ring for the new Edmonton Pavilion. He wasn't going anywhere.

By May 1951, the dispute came to a head, and Tillman finally invited Stu to buy him out of Calgary for $50,000 — a far cry from

Lord of the Ring

the pittance he had offered Stu for the Edmonton promotion.

Stu realized Calgary's potential, however, especially if he had the chance to develop the market properly, so he agreed to pay. He put $10,000 down, and made installments to cover the balance over the following six-month period.

Tillman used the money to open Dempsey Petroleum — with Jack Dempsey's blessing.

After Melnick was bought out, the Calgary promotion operated under the name Foothills Athletic Club. Stu kept the name for business purposes, but billed his new promotion as Big Time Wrestling. It later became Wildcat Wrestling — until the 1960s, when Stu finally settled on the Stampede Wrestling moniker, after he had established a close association with the Calgary Stampede and Exhibition. His gates were substantial from the outset. He did so well, in fact, that he had no trouble paying out the balance of the $50,000 in the agreed upon six months.

Plans for opening night in Calgary were made with the utmost of care. Stu chose the venue, the Corral Building on the Stampede grounds. Paul Baillargeon, whom Stu had met during matches in Columbus, Ohio, was brought in as a special draw. Burgeron's gimmick involved showing off his incredible leg strength. Before a sell-out audience, Burgeron set up a large tripod structure. He then placed a horse in a sling and suspended it halfway up the tripod. Eventually, he would pull the 1,800-pound horse up the rungs of the ladder with his legs. Although more of a circus trick than anything else, the gimmick helped establish Stu in Calgary.

Stu began looking at real estate, assessing the possibility of bringing his growing family to Canada. He and Helen had been discussing moving to Calgary, and were trying to decide upon the right kind of house. Helen favoured the long, low ranch style — the kind of place she had seen throughout Montana and the mid-West. A house with everything on one floor had its advantages, she figured. Especially when you're raising children.

Stu went house hunting while Helen was having final reconstructive surgery. When he called her in New York to tell her he had found the perfect place, she could hear the excitement in his voice.

"Is it a ranch-style house?" she asked.

Stu paused and replied slowly, "Well. . . . Not exactly."

Five

There may not have been a picture of a dream home fixed in his mind, but Stu Hart did have a good sense of what he wanted. A ranch-style bungalow wasn't it.

During his early years in Edmonton, Stu had long admired the McGrath Estate, a sprawling turn-of-the century mansion positioned in a well-treed area overlooking a golf course and country club in the west end of town. At the time, the McGrath place was the most prestigious in the city, and Stu would ride by on his bike to look at it, trying to imagine the sort of people who lived in such a grand house.

When he read in the real estate listings of the *Calgary Herald* that a stately home on 30 acres on the outskirts of the city was up for sale, he immediately called the realtor.

It was late summer 1951 when Stu drove the seven miles from downtown Calgary, up Old Banff Coach Road and over the hills to the house the aged Judge Patterson had decided to sell.

A sturdy red brick exterior indicated it was built to last. Three fireplace chimneys presided over the shingled roof, and two tiers of veranda, on the ground and second floors, ran the length of the house, front and back, to square off its rambling design. Multiple gables gave the place a sense of mystery. White railings set off the brick, and a complementary coach house out back was joined to the mansion by a small greenhouse with a trellis covered with climbing roses. The manicured lawns and many flowers were resplendent. The house was surrounded by open fields dotted with bushes and trees. The City of Calgary was clearly visible, settled as it was in a natural bowl. Stu felt like he was standing on the rim. He imagined that the distant city lights would make a pretty nightscape.

The setting exuded a kind of peace and serenity that Stu knew would be a welcome respite from days spent around rings and wrestlers. Little did he realize that the house would become a constant hub of wrestling activity for the next 50 years.

As he walked around the property that day a light breeze danced among the fall asters and goldenrod under a blue-amber sky. Stu felt as if he had just come home. It never occurred to him that Helen might feel differently.

As a boy, Stu had dreamed of this kind of place as he struggled to keep warm, cuddled with his dog in a frozen canvas tent. Even after the family had relocated to Bonnie Doone, Stu continued to dream about prosperity. He had come across a book in the school library, Dale Carnegie's *Power of Positive Thinking*, that he read again and again. Eventually he picked up a copy of his own from a bookstore remainder bin. He carried it around with him for years. Never a prolific reader, Stu became enchanted with true-life success stories. Later he would come across a copy of *Citizen Hearst*, a biography of William Randolph Hearst, the American newspaper baron. Stu checked it out of the Calgary Public Library and renewed it so many times over the course of years that the library finally just gave him the book. Stu reread it again and again and told Helen he wanted to take a trip to San Simeon, California, to see Hearst Castle, the estate left behind by Hearst and turned over to the State of California as a landmark

PROVINCE OF SASKATCHEWAN

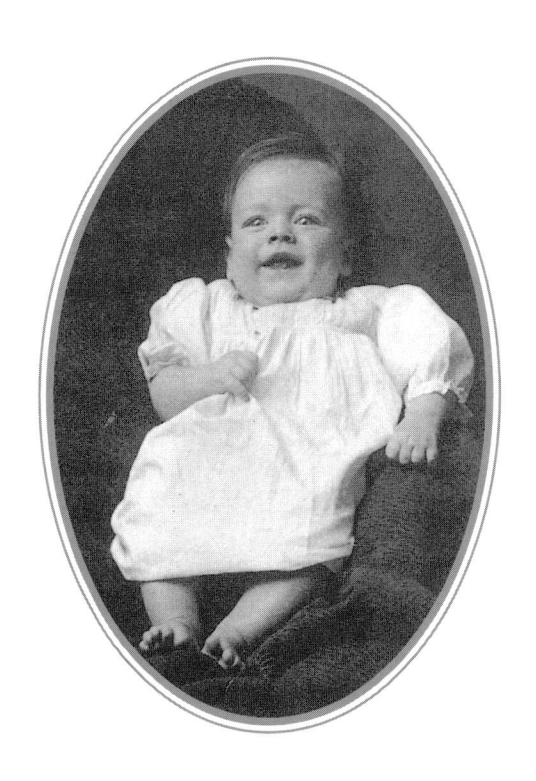

DIVISION OF VITAL STATISTICS

DEPARTMENT OF PUBLIC HEALTH

BIRTH DATE
May 3, 1915

REGISTRATION NO.
15-07-004397

NAME
Stewart Edward Hart

BIRTHPLACE
Sec.22, Tp.35, Rge.5, W.3, Saskatchewan

REGISTRATION DATE
May 11, 1915

SEX
Male

DATE ISSUED
May 13, 1970

CERTIFIED EXTRACT FROM REGISTRATION OF BIRTH
ISSUED AT
REGINA, SASKATCHEWAN, CANADA

DIRECTOR

CERTIFICATE OF BIRTH

Donald Stewart, Stu's maternal grandfather

John Hart (Stu's grandfather), Fannie Sargeant Hart (Stu's grandmother), and Emily Hart

Stu's parents, Edward and Elizabeth Hart

Charlie Sears

Ketchamoot School, 1925–26; *Back Row (left to right)* Kathleen Ingram, Eileen Sterritt, Maude Wildman, Edrie Hart, Ethel Brown, Margaret Mitchell, Miss Dickson, Janet Brown, Mildred Ingram, Sylvester Hart, Helen Schultz, unknown, unknown. *Front Row (left to right)* Unknown, Stu Hart, Toby Nomeland, Charlie Sears, Don Carlisle, unknown, Harold Coombes, Eugene Carlisle, Alvin Schultz, unknown, Harold Schultz, Art Williams, Jim Ingram *(Courtesy Tofield Museum and Archives)*

Helen with her parents,
Harry and Ellie

Back Row (left to right)
Helen and Harry; *Front Row
(left to right)* Betty and Patsy

Back Row (left to right) Patsy and Betty; *Front Row
(left to right)* Diana, Joanie and Helen, along with
Harry and Ellie Smith

Harry Smith, Smith Hart, and Harry's track trophies

Second Row from top, third from left,
Ken Frost; *Third Row from top, far left,*
Stu; *Bottom Row, far left,*
Jim Ingram, Dr. Koby McCallum,
Al Young. The All-Service
Championship Team.
(Courtesy Glenbow Archives)

Helen and Diana, about 1946

(left to right) Patsy, Helen, Sandor Kovacs,
(Lord) Jan Bleers

(All photos courtesy Glenbow Archives)

Hart House

(left to right) Ellie, Georgia, Stu (holding Bret), Smith, Wayne, Dean, Bruce, Keith, Helen (holding Alison)

Back Row (left to right) Wayne, Keith, Helen, Stu, Bruce, Smith; *Middle Row* Dean, Ellie, Georgia, Bret; *Bottom Row* Owen, Diana, Ross, Alison

Back Row (left to right) Smith, Bruce, Keith, Wayne; *Middle Row* Dean, Alison, Ellie, Georgia, Bret; *Bottom Row* Ross, Diana, Owen

Bruce, Stu, Smith, Helen and Keith

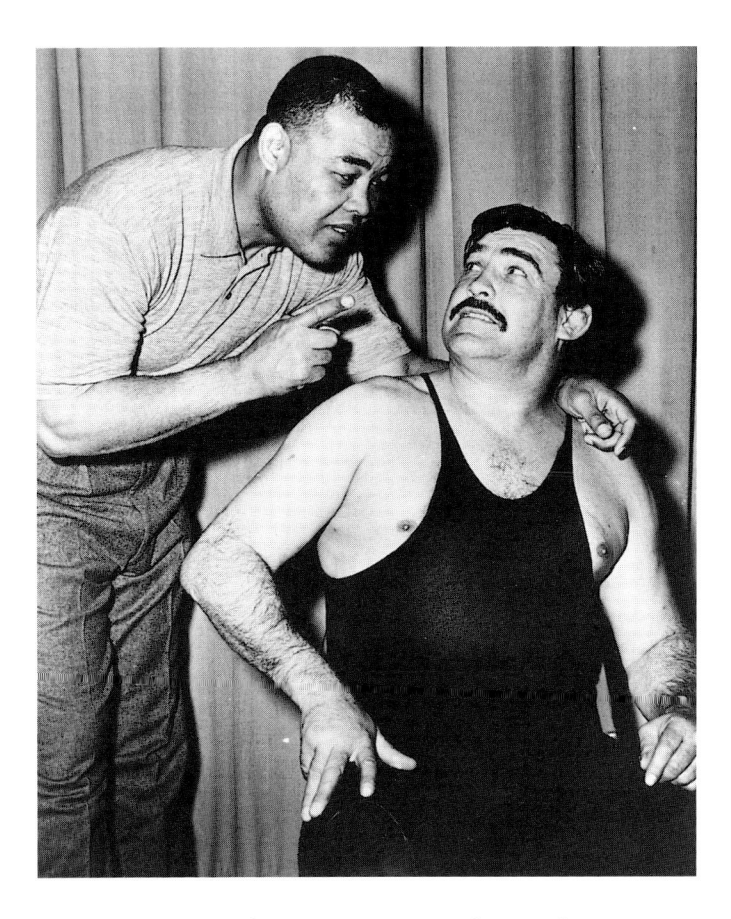

Guest referee Joe Louis with wrestler
Roberto Pico in Calgary in 1952

(left to right) Cyril Standen, Earl McCready, Tiger Joe
Marsh, Henry Viney, Dave Ruhl, Al (Mr. Murder) Mills
(wearing Canadian Heavyweight Championship belt),
Jack Dempsey, Les Watson, Stu Hart, Roland Meeker

Leo "the Lion" Newman wearing helmet; Stu was supposed to be handcuffed to Leo to keep Leo from interfering with his wrestlers

Stu has Abdullah the Butcher in a sleeper hold

MANHATTAN BOOKING AGENCY, INC.
INTERNATIONALLY AFFILIATED

JOE "TOOTS" MONDT
President and General Manager

IGNACIO "PEDRO" MARTINEZ
Chairman, Board of Directors

TELEPHONES
CIRCLE { 6-8174 - DAY
6-8175 - DAY
6-0700 - NIGHT

351 WEST 42ND STREET
NEW YORK 36, N. Y.

CABLE ADDRESS
MOMISTOOTS - NEW YORK

October 10, 1952

Stu Hart
Foothills Athletic Club
Room 103, Hotel Royal
Calgary, Alberta, Canada

Dear Stu:

Received your letter of October 6th inquiring regarding Rocky Marciano, the Heavyweight Champion of the World. We would be interested in booking Rocky into your large arenas for two or three dates only after the Election Day, the 4th of November. True, his engagement will have to be limited. Therefore I would suggest you follow the plans Mr. Weill, Rocky's manager, suggested to me: That you select three or four of your largest arenas and book Rocky as the wrestling referee of the main event. Due to the fact he requires no expenses, which is customary with boxing people, to make that trip, have your promoters guarantee him and Rocky $1500 for each engagement he appears as a referee in your territory with the privilege of 33-1/3% of the net monies taken in from the sale of tickets to see the World's Champion.

He is very popular and in big demand, Stu. To give you an idea; he gets $50,000 for two weeks in Las Vegas. Yet we know that's impossible for the wrestling promoters, but we believe wherever Rocky appears, he will jam pack the place at top prices. At these terms, we would be interested in going into Winnipeg if it is alright with Tony. However, Tony has been in touch with me regarding Rocky for his territory. On these terms you understand you would have to plan to do at least $4500 net, in order to break on the percentage deal. We are paying Rocky $2000 for his appearance in Baltimore with the privilege of 33-1/3%, Stu, and we feel we should draw $7000. It won't work in small clubs, and as I said before, Rocky won't have time for the small clubs anyway, so see if you can work out some high class promotional plans where you can invite us to come in.

Write or wire me about this.

Are you selling the book up there now? You should be in a position to handle a good many books now that you are in the driver's seat.

Congratulations and good luck.

Sincerely,

Joe "Toots" Mondt

jtm/em

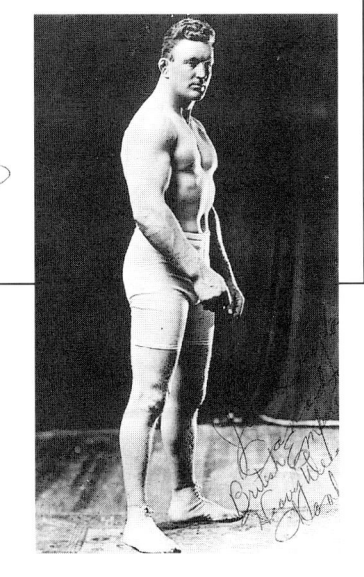

Jack Taylor

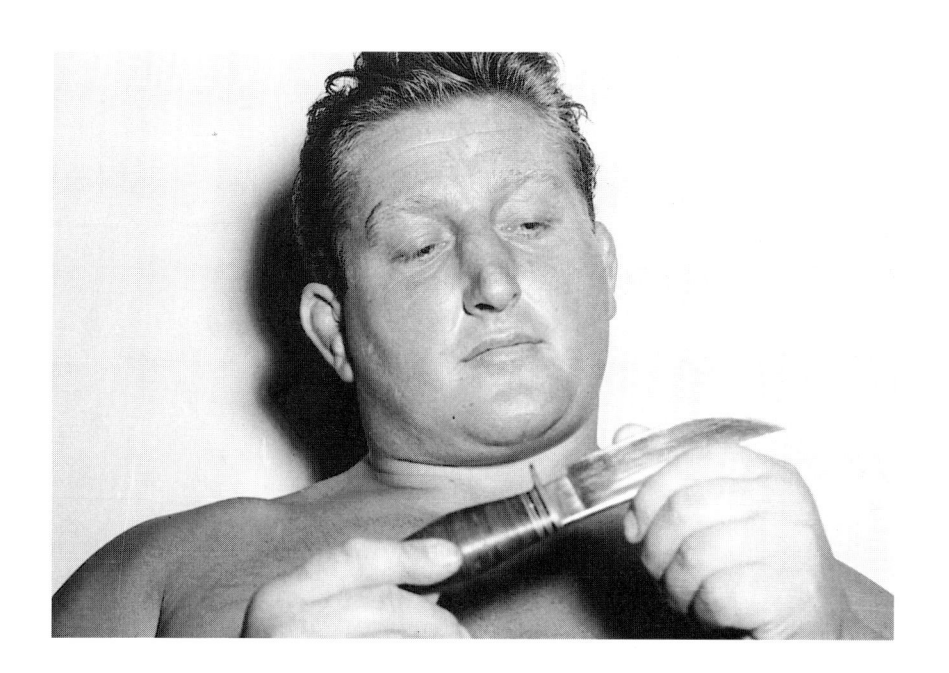

Yukon Eric

Walter "Killer" Kowalski

Gene Kiniski
(photo Padio Lanza)

Andre the Giant surrounded by *(left to right)* Harry Hays, Ellie Hart, Tommy Hays and Stu

Bret

Bret

Owen

Bruce, Bret, Keith
(Courtesy Glenbow Archives)

Bruce Hart, Dory Funk Jr., Dynamite Kid (Tom Billington)

Lord of the Ring

and tourist attraction after the magnate's death. He's never made that trip.

As far as the printed word went, in contrast, Helen was a voracious reader who kept many books close by. In later years, Bret would take part in promoting reading and sit as a celebrity chair for a national reading campaign. His interest may have been peaked by watching his mother devour book after book as he grew up.

Influenced by Carnegie, Stu firmly believed that you can have all that you want by believing you can have it and working hard. "Life is an oyster," he'd say. "You take what it is, polish it up and make the most of it." With the acquisition of his own prestigious home, one of his dreams became a reality.

The house had been owned by Judge H.S. Patterson, a former law partner of R.B. Bennett, later Prime Minister of Canada. It had been built in 1905 by Edward Henry Crandell, who had settled in Calgary in 1899 after moving west from Ontario. Crandell's brick and masonry concern provided the materials used to create a sturdy framework for the place in which the Crandell children were raised. Later, "Crandell House" became a refuge for orphans and convalescing children — the Red Cross occupying it until a hospital was built close to downtown Calgary. After the Red Cross gave up its lease, Crandell's son moved in with his own family. But when the brick business collapsed in the 1930s, the house became something of a white elephant, so Crandell turned it over to Judge Patterson. The judge raised his own children there, but put "Patterson House" on the market when they were grown and it became too much for him to handle.

As he listened to Patterson extol the virtues of a big place in the country, Stu caught sight of a large black cat. Following Stu's gaze, the judge said: "Oh, that's Bing."

The cat stretched and yawned in the sunshine.

Stu turned his attention back to the judge. He had made a

decision. "If you throw in that cat, we've got a deal."

Stu and Helen's names ultimately went on the property title in March 1954, after the $25,000 sale price was finally paid out. The house cost half what Stu had paid for the Calgary promotion.

After inking the deal that day in 1951, Stu called Helen in New York.

Helen first saw the house several weeks later. By that time, winter approached. It was cold and bleak; sleet hit the windshield as she and Stu drove up the hill.

Her face fell in dismay.

The glories of summer, in the fields and flower gardens, had long since faded. The Pattersons were gone, the house was bare and shabby without furniture to warm and brighten its spirit. Helen walked around with the baby in her arms and little Smith trailing behind. It went on and on, room after empty room. To Helen, it seemed more like a seedy hotel than the picture of country bliss Stu had painted. Yet her husband beamed. He had a sense of what Hart House would become, imagining furniture, drapes, rugs and new light fixtures.

A few weeks later Helen's mother arrived. She surveyed with her critical eye, seeing newspapers scattered on the floor and next to nothing for furniture. A few beds and chairs, that was it. The experience reaffirmed her ingrained belief that her daughter's marriage was totally hopeless. She continued to nurse the secret belief that Helen would, sooner or later, abandon her nonsense and return to civilization.

Resigned, Helen settled down with Stu and the kids and adapted to life in the country. A house with a history of being filled with children, it would fill up again over the next decade. Twenty-two rooms were spread over its 8,000 square feet, includ-

Lord of the Ring

ing two huge master bedrooms with fireplaces. White plaster walls were set off by oak wainscotting, vintage hardwood floors and high ceilings that Stu would later adorn with an elegant gold leaf trim. Hart House became the centre of Stu's world, and he furnished it with six massive chandeliers, most of them picked up for $500 each from Eaton's in the '50s. He also acquired some of the largest Persian carpets in the city, an eclectic collection of antiques, and oversized leather couches and chairs. Stu's antique, glassed-in bookcases would eventually display multiple sets of encyclopaedias and a collection of novels and books that ranged from Robert K. Massie's *Peter the Great* to a small blue volume by Bellamy Partridge published in 1941 entitled *Big Family*. The story, about the trials and tribulations of a family of eight children, would pale in comparison to what Stu and Helen Hart would experience.

An elegant staircase with oak railings, directly opposite the front door, led the way to the two upper storeys. Stu set up a small office on the second floor. Today, it still has a '50s look, with a battered oak office desk, aged gray steel filing cabinets and shelves that have acquired the clutter of decades in the wrestling business.

Stu and Helen occupied one of the master bedrooms, while their small sons shared the other. It would eventually be known as "the boys' room." The eight Hart sons born between 1948 and 1965 slept in two big beds. As the four Hart girls arrived, they would share a room as well. Eventually, the older children would move into the remaining bedrooms for peace and privacy.

Years later, Helen would muse, "I can't remember if we bought the house to justify the kids or had the kids to justify the house." The peace and serenity that Stu thought the house would offer, however, never materialized. As each new baby arrived, and pets were adopted, and wrestlers bunked in, it became more reminiscent of a three-ring circus.

All of the furnishings were symbols of prosperity for Stu,

representing his desire for the finer things in life. Helen, never inspired by domestic matters, left the decorating largely up to her husband, and he outfitted the place in a way that not only suited the structure itself but also created a comfortable environment for his family and friends. Once they'd moved in and set up their household, very little would change over the next 40 years.

Stu especially loved his chandeliers. He referred to them as his "girls" and gave each of them names like Maria Theresa and Josephine Marie. When one of his friends, gesturing to the chandelier in the dining room, asked in a mildly disapproving tone: "Doesn't that look kind of opulent?" Stu's eyes lit up.

"Yes!" he said, then paused to ponder the point of the question.

It wasn't long before Calgarians started driving up at night to look at the "house with the chandeliers." The frequency of rear-end collisions on the road outside escalated as drivers paid more attention to the house than their driving. When Stu found out what people were doing, he opened up all the drapes so the chandeliers could be seen from outside. He told his family, "It's my way of saying 'Hello Calgary.'"

The wrestling promotions in both Edmonton and Calgary were quite successful in the early '50s, and soon other western Canadian venues were added: Lethbridge, Red Deer, Saskatoon, and Regina all regularly held cards, as did a variety of whistle stops and Indian Reserves across the prairies.

Stu still had Al Oeming minding the store in Edmonton, but it wouldn't be long before the young zoologist would decide to leave and open a game farm. Stu employed Mike Bulat, then a student at the University of Alberta in Edmonton, for help with ticket sales. He moved to Calgary after graduating and picked up work with Stu again, managing tickets and doing other necessary chores. Bulat would work with Stu until 1956, when he moved to Victoria to promote wrestling there. His venture was not success-

Lord of the Ring

ful, however, and he returned to Edmonton to become a successful teacher and school principal, re-joining Stu's Edmonton operation as a sideline. Harold Sharlow, a close friend of Oeming and Bulat, was also involved, moonlighting in the wrestling biz to supplement his regular job as a teacher.

With hard work the promotion rapidly became lucrative, and Stu's lifestyle began showing the signs of his success. He was driving big shiny Cadillacs and adding to his collection of alligator cowboy boots. Everything around him had a stamp of well-being. He'd regularly cash-in gates of several thousand dollars a night.

Stu was still wrestling, as well as promoting, when he joined the National Wrestling Alliance in 1951. His activities were tracked in March 1952 in the NWA wrestling magazine:

[Stu Hart] loves to develop youngsters eager to wrestle. If they show any signs of promise, Stu teaches them the art of wrestling and gives them their start.

And in a report from *Ring* magazine in April 1952:

> Best match of the night from a real wrestling point of view was staged by Alabama football star, Tarzan White, and Stu Hart, pride and joy of Edmonton, Alberta. They wrestled in a 45-minute draw in a clean breaking, orthodox battle in which brute strength in breaking holds was the main factor.

Stu became closely aligned with the NWA and attended his first convention in Las Vegas in 1951. At these annual gatherings the promoters elected the new world champion; they spent much of the rest of their time figuring out where he would be introduced, where his championship bout would be staged. Once the title changed hands, the new world's champion would be paraded around the territories and used to attract healthy gates for everyone. To be a title-holder a wrestler had to be skilful, good on the microphone and able to capture the imagination of the fans. He also had to serve as a role model. No matter what, however, he had to have the ability to "put butts in seats."

Each promotion had a local or regional championship belt. Stu Hart's promotion was no exception. The NWA had the world championship belt, which usually remained in the United States, around the waists of wrestlers like Lou Thesz, who held the title for many years. Whipper Billy Watson managed to bring the belt to Canada, partly through his own prowess as a wrestler, and partly because of the influence of his promoter, Frank Tunney of Toronto.

During his New York years, Stu wrestled for the title on several occasions. He recalls challenging Thesz in Rochester, Minnesota, and having an incredible battle. Thesz was agile and baffling; he, like Stu, was naturally left handed. Like many southpaws at the time, Stu was forced to write with his right hand in his school days. It left him more or less ambidextrous. A left-hander can throw off an opponent, wrestlers often not expecting moves to be performed in the way men like Thesz would execute them. Thesz was a noted bodyslammer. "He'd throw you down very hard. It was fun wrestling him; you'd go into the ring wondering what this guy had for you," Stu recalls.

But in Stu's mind his most memorable title bid came in 1947, when he took on the great Frank Sexton of Ohio. "He was a big, powerful guy," Stu says of a man who stood six-foot-two and weighed 250 pounds to Stu's five-foot-ten and 230. The match was pure, unadulterated submission wrestling. Stu remembers how privileged he felt to enter the ring with the champ, three times, in and around New York.

Lord of the Ring

Stu also fought Bill Potts, better known as Whipper Billy Watson, for the title in Lethbridge, Alberta, in the early '50s.

"Whipper had a hold he liked to call 'the Avalanche.' He would grab his opponent by the leg, take him down, then somersault over him and roll him around the ring a few times, the opponent always getting the bumps and thumps. Whipper would then pin him when he least expected it. It was pretty hard avoiding that kind of leg lock.

"He was a very competent wrestler but he would take everything off you except your trunks," Stu says, explaining that in wrestling jargon, it means Whipper would not always work with his opponent. "Whipper tended to cut short on the returns."

Most wrestlers followed the practice of not hitting harder than necessary. Watson would take liberties.

With some guys, however, you had to hit hard or be pulverized yourself. Rube Wright was that kind of opponent. He was over 6'2", weighed 300 pounds, and an infamous shooter (a wrestler who made everything real). "You'd have to hit him hard enough to knock him down because if you didn't you'd better have a good pair of running shoes handy," Stu laughs.

In the early '50s, Stu's attention turned to television. He'd had some experience with it in New York as a performer, but as an Alberta promoter it posed many challenges. During the '50s and '60s, three major territories regularly exchanged their stars. Frank Tunney, in Toronto, had Watson; Sam Muchnick, of St. Louis, handled Thesz and Dick Hutton; and Stu Hart developed and promoted Gene Kiniski, all around the same time. Thesz, especially, would have an amazingly long career, wrestling until the early '80s.

Tunney's influence was vast, his huge territory including Ontario, Quebec and Atlantic Canada. He was televising matches nationally on the CBC and making household names out of men like Whipper Billy Watson — and even one of Stu's own wrestlers, Kiniski.

Because the Canadian Broadcasting Corporation was gradually coming into the homes of fans throughout Stu's territory, it wasn't long before Stu found himself negotiating to get Tunney's TV stars to appear on his cards.

Long a favourite of the print media because of his history and local connections, Stu knew he could not withstand the onslaught of Tunney's televised promotion. He set out to get his wrestlers on the air locally. After much negotiating, he struck a deal with CHCT, Channel 2, rather inconveniently located in the upscale residential area of Elbow Park. (The television station would later change its call letters to CFAC-TV.)

Shortly after he began broadcasting, Stu hired Sam Menacker — an American who had wrestled and played basketball, Stu met Menacker in New York — to be his ring announcer at the Pavilion, his television voice, and a general idea man.

Menacker was a colourful character, in appearance a cross between comic Steve Allen and a carnival huckster. Sam had thick, dark hair and wore large horned-rimmed, Harry Potter-style glasses. He had started out in New York and had worked for a time with Toots Mondt. Sam had developed a good microphone "jaw" and had some announcing experience. He could talk it up with the best of them, like a good used-car salesman. He made the most of this skill after leaving New York and migrating south to El Paso, Texas, where he established a reputation as the man who put Mitchell's Beer on the market with his sales pitches. His publicity-generating techniques would soon find their way to the wrestling ring.

Sam responded immediately to Stu's invitation to help his promotion on television. He arrived in Calgary with his wife, wrestling star June Byers. June was a compact, athletic woman,

Lord of the Ring

known more for her in-ring abilities than either her femininity or pleasantness. Around animals, she was a different person. Helen Hart believed June liked them more than people.

Sam was a chameleon — part wrestler, part actor, part hustler. No one knew what he would come up with next — he was always unconventional, but it seemed to work.

Everyone involved with wrestling in the '40s and '50s knew Menacker. He'd spent a lot of time kicking around rings in the United States and Australia and had a knack for hyping the fans. He also had an uncanny ability for predicting a gate. He'd wander around Hart House and use an old tube of his wife's lipstick to write his prognostication on mirrors. He was generally correct within a few dollars.

By the time Sam was hired, Stu's promotion had two separate television programs; a 15-minute spot called "Meet the Wrestlers" aired just before the news at dinner time on Fridays, as a lead-in to that night's Pavilion card; and a Sunday program, "Mat Time," which was filmed in the CFAC studios. Both programs were used to build up heat for action the following week in Calgary and in Edmonton. Wrestlers would grab the mic, hurl insults at their opponents, and generally put on a lively performance. Fans would race down to the Pavilion to see them follow up on their threats.

Among the most colourful was Killer Kowalski, who had a distinctive mic style. He would start out quietly, talking about what he would do to his opponents, then build to a crescendo, shouting and finger-punching at the TV audience. To make it, wrestlers had to perform well both in the ring and in front of a microphone. They developed colourful monikers and gimmicks to capture the imagination of the fans. Still, in those days things were strictly good versus evil, and sooner or later, good prevailed. Kowalski says he learned his microphone skills while travelling alone around the wrestling circuit, talking back to the radio.

Stu Hart

"No one would travel with me. I didn't smoke, I didn't drink and I'm a vegetarian. So I travelled by myself. When the radio announcer said 'It's going to be a beautiful day tomorrow,' I'd holler back at him — 'No it's not, it's going to the worst day of your life; there's a blizzard coming and you'll be up to your neck in it by five o'clock.'

"I stopped thinking about being asked a question and having to give an answer and just concentrated on giving an automatic response. I got so I could belt it out so fast. It helped my bookings a lot. Everybody wants a skilful wrestler with a mouth."

Kowalski, who retired from pro-wrestling in 1977, now runs a wrestling school in Boston and has passed on his skills to a new generation of stars like the WWF's Chyna and Triple H. He has spent a lot of time at Hart House, too.

"I just love them. All those kids running around. It's such a great family."

Kowalski never found the time to get married and have children of his own. But if he had, he says he would never allow his kids to watch today's WWF. He disapproves of the sexual references, crudeness and attacks on authority figures. "Kids start thinking it's okay to behave like the guys they see on TV. It's not a show for kids."

Calgary lawyer Jim Butlin recalls following the action on TV and at the Pavilion and the Corral as a teenager. He and his Dad enjoyed the humour, the nonsense and the atmosphere associated with the shows in the '50s and '60s. Butlin points out that at the time Stu's ring was the only place a sports-addicted teenager could see larger-than-life characters like boxers Primo Carnera and Jersey Joe Walcott because they were brought in as celebrity wrestlers or as referees.

He remembers seeing the looming Kowalski being interviewed, jabbing the air with his big fingers and using his

Lord of the Ring

belligerent, aggressive tone to say: "Look, Mr. Menacker, I came out here to wrestle some real wrestlers and all I'm getting is some second-rate competition." Stu Hart would then quietly interject in his calm, considered manner: "Well, no, no. We've got Timothy Goehagen and we've got the Mighty Ursus — these are very strong men. They will be all that the Killer will need."

One of the most memorable storylines of the time involved Kowalski and Bearcat Wright, a second-generation professional athlete whose father had been a celebrated boxer in the United States. Wright was a master of the Figure 4, a submission hold executed by a complicated threading of legs and twisting of feet, that can be both excruciating and virtually impossible to escape. In recent years the hold has become associated with the legendary Ric Flair. Wright was six-foot-six and 250 pounds — with long agile legs ideal for the executing his finishing move. Setting the bait on TV, Menacker asked Kowalski whether he could extricate himself from the dreaded Figure 4. Kowalski, pretending not to know what the move was all about, declared that no one could put the great Kowalski in a hold he could not escape. Then, again on TV, Kowalski allowed Wright to place him in the hold. Of course he could not extricate himself.

When he was finally freed, Kowalski erupted into an explosive verbal assault: "That's only one hold, Mr. Menacker, one hold. No wrestler can beat another wrestler with just one hold."

The stage had been set for a match between the two the following Friday night, and the fans came in droves. This time Kowalski avoided the Figure 4 and easily prevailed.

"Meet the Wrestlers" was complemented by a radio spot called "Dear Wrestler." Sponsored by Dad's Cookies, the short, comic segment posed fictional fan questions to a panel of wrestlers. A typical sequence might include:

"Dear Wrestler, when I'm out for dinner, should I eat my fried chicken with my fingers?"

"No, fingers should always be eaten separately."

"Dear Wrestler, my wife has flaky scalp, what should she do?"

"Tell her to go soak her head."

"Dear Wrestler, please tell me how to make lemon chiffon pie?"

"Take 30 yards of lemon yellow chiffon. . . ."

Both the letters and replies were written by Menacker and Helen Hart. Helen had fun with this, but it would offend her more refined sensibilities when Menacker would insist on a response too crude or blunt for her tastes. On those occasions she would just leave him to it.

By the mid '50s travel around Stu's huge territory was becoming tedious and time consuming. Menacker, a licensed pilot, talked Stu into purchasing a Comanche 250 for $25,000 from a friend of his, to ease their travel woes. At the time, matches were being held across the west every night of the week. Although Stu took matches to points as far flung as Alaska, the Northwest Territories, the Yukon, North Dakota, Montana, Oregon and Washington State, he concentrated his efforts in western Canada, primarily in Calgary, Edmonton, Saskatoon and Regina. The plane saved time for Stu and Sam, and allowed Stu to be home in the mornings when the kids woke up. Teams of wrestlers, however, still moved around on the ground.

In the early '50s the Victoria Pavilion on the Calgary Stampede and Exhibition grounds became the long-term home of Stu's wrestling enterprise. Periodically, larger venues like the Corral building were used to accommodate bigger cards. The Victoria Pavilion held 2,000 and Stu kept it packed. Often, line-ups ran down the street. The Corral would hold 7,000 or 8,000 when big names came to town.

Lord of the Ring

In the early days of the promotion, Stu realized he needed help with the financial side of things and he turned to Helen, who had some training and business experience. It wasn't long before she, too, was deeply involved, freeing Stu to work with the wrestlers and handle the matches.

Stu was notorious for neglecting to tie up loose ends with just about everyone he did business with. His carelessness about paying his accounts would lead to frantic calls from everyone from his advertising people to his lawyer, but Helen would always step in and sort things out. Stu was interested in the big picture, which he approached with broad brush strokes. It fell to Helen to pick up the bits and pieces her husband left behind — when she found out about them. Helen's graciousness had a way of smoothing everything over.

Stu acquired a heavy-duty, restaurant-quality juicer during those years, and used to make "athletic" health drinks for the wrestlers. Kowalski could drink a couple of quarts a day of Stu's orange juice. Stu made sure it was full of vitamins, adding celery and other fruits and vegetables. The drinks were not known for their taste, but their nutritional value was undeniable. Stu still has the giant-sized stainless steel salad bowl which Kowalski would drain in one sitting.

To keep Helen from domestic distractions, Stu took on as many of the household tasks as he could, including responsibility for their expanding brood. He became a familiar sight behind a Kirby vacuum cleaner, and kept the babies as snug in their diapers as little trussed turkeys. Stu got so handy around the house it became clear that he and Helen were both a great business team and on the cutting edge of equality issues. There was no division of labour along gender lines at Hart House. There were endless chores, yes, and they just got done.

Stu displayed a domestic self-sufficiency that eluded many of

Stu Hart

his contemporaries. When Helen came home from the beauty parlour complaining about the cost, Stu asked a friend whose wife was a hairdresser for instruction. Stu took over, and soon the sight of him wandering through the house with a hair roller stuck to his sweater became as familiar as seeing him in the ring. Rolling Helen's hair is something he would find himself still doing, more than 50 years after their marriage. It gave both Stu and Helen some time to themselves, and it was a shared intimacy they valued immensely.

Their daughters laugh now, unable to remember their mother without beautifully manicured nails, and acknowledging that she had no idea how to operate a single appliance in the place. The appliances were selected by Stu and of industrial quality, meant to last despite the wear and tear of a dozen kids. The kitchen, which Stu later renovated, would have suited a small hotel, with everything made of resilient stainless steel. As the children grew, Stu's morning ritual included getting the kids off and onto the school bus. They made sure they caught that bus. If they didn't, they knew they would have to deal with their annoyed father, something none of them would consider risking for a moment.

Stu would begin preparing a cauldron of porridge the night before and make sure the kids finished it before leaving the next morning. He made their lunches, too; and, not one to throw things away, tended to recycle their lunch bags. Ellie recalls: "We were the kids with the greasy lunch bags." When Stu was on the road, Helen prepared the lunches. She always wrote each child's name on a *new* bag; she would also cut the crusts off her sandwiches, and she included a note for each of them in their lunchbag.

Stu bought the kids' clothes and managed their young lives. His domestic management has become the stuff of Hart legend. When Ellie was born, it became clear that she was allergic to her

Lord of the Ring

formula. Stu researched the issue and discovered the benefits of goat's milk. It was next to impossible to find goat's milk in the grocery stores at that time. Undeterred, Stu bought a small herd of goats and milked them. After that, he put all of the children on goat's milk as soon as they were weaned.

The boys fared better than the girls in the wardrobe department unless Helen intervened. Stu tended to dress them all like little boys — especially during leaner times.

Ellie and Georgia particularly remember the time Stu — who was notorious for buying out the entire stock of a liquidating clothing store — got a "great deal" on winter coats. The red down-filled hunting jackets came in one size. Stu bought a dozen, and each of the children received one. The sleeves were fine on the older kids, but the younger children swam in them, their little arms finding their way out only after several rolls. The kids hated them. But their distaste abated when other kids at school started hounding their parents for a "Hart coat."

Stu was a stickler about attending classes, even in the worst kind of weather. If the kids missed the bus, he insisted on driving them. Stu had missed a lot of school himself before his family moved to Edmonton, and he would not allow his children to be absent under any circumstance. During one of Calgary's harshest cold snaps of the mid-'60s, the school bus could not make it up the hill to the Hart residence. Stu, determined to get all ten of his school age children to classes, decided to take them himself. Unfortunately, the -40 degree weather had taken its toll on the battery of his Cadillac. A determined Stu Hart walked across his yard, knocked on the door of the coach house he'd rented to Katie Ohe — a Calgary artist best known for a fossilized map of Canada that was commissioned for Expo '67 — and politely enquired if he might borrow her car. Katie, without pausing, handed over the keys to a little white Volkswagen beetle. She watched, bemused, as

Stu Hart

Stu proceeded to load all ten children into the vehicle. He then forced his sizeable frame behind the wheel and proceeded to work around the various arms, legs and other body parts obstructing the stick shift until he skidded down the hill to the three schools charged with educating his children. The kids were in knots by the time he reached his first stop, Wildwood Elementary. Stu went in to explain to the principal why his children were late. "The damn battery on my car wouldn't start," he blurted, only to be chastened by the principal's curt reply, "Mr. Hart, please do not use profanity here." An exasperated Stu abandoned the explanations and directed the vw in the direction of Vincent Massey Junior High and Ernest Manning High School.

The children grew up fiercely loyal to, and protective of, each other; they ran in packs and got themselves into typical youthful jams. They had few neighbours for most of their younger years, and only a very small number of outsiders penetrated the tight circle the Hart kids formed. But with so many children in the family, there was always someone to play with.

At age 12 Dean would come up with many clever, entertaining schemes. One day he decided that a tree fort should be built in the woods behind the house. He recruited Ellie, Georgia, Bret, Alison and Ross to help carry out the project with the help of a few of the neighbour kids. They hauled out boards and nails and anything they could get their hands on. The finished product was a sturdy little box; a rope ladder was used to haul goods, and the kids themselves, up and down. An old mattress and a battery-operated television set belonging to their father were quickly commandeered.

Eventually, Dean decided that a president of the fort should be elected. A campaign was organized and Bret and Ross were the contenders. Bret, at eight, took it for granted that he had the upper hand against his little brother, who was only five at the

Lord of the Ring

time; at least that's what Dean led him to believe. Unknown to Bret, Dean manipulated the situation from behind the scenes and made sure everyone voted for little Ross. Bret was taken aback when posters supporting Ross, handmade with crayons in a neighbour's garage, began to appear. When Ross won handily, Bret was furious, convinced that he had been sabotaged by the girls. Ross was elated with his win, and he was carted around in a red wagon in a parade of kids and dogs — all of which did nothing for Bret but get under his skin. When he found out the next day that Dean had been the mastermind, he accepted things better, according to Ellie. Bret was happier knowing he hadn't been bested by a bunch of girls.

The tree fort was well-used by the Hart children, who camped there and made it, to a large extent, the centre of their world. When Stu gave in to persistent pressure from the city and developers and sold the land behind the house, the little tree house — along with the trees — disappeared forever.

Stu dealt with domestic pressures more easily. At one point he brought home a commercial sewing machine he'd purchased along with four free sewing lessons. He thought it might interest Helen.

It didn't.

Typically, Stu decided to take the lessons himself and began stitching the kids' clothes when they needed repairs, his big sausage-like fingers guiding the material along, glasses perched on his nose, pins in his mouth. The sewing machine came in handy, and was even used for stitching up the wrestling mats. Stu made himself a button-up shirt, which Helen's sister Diana Osler said she couldn't help but admire.

Stu had picked up some sewing skills on his mother's 1910 Singer treadle when he was in high school. Back then he made himself a football jacket and some shirts. The football jackets

Stu Hart

some of his friends were sporting were too expensive, so Stu closely examined one, concluded that it was basically a simple garment, and decided to see if he could recreate it for himself. The jacket, with a little guidance from his mother, turned out well; at least Stu was satisfied with the results. He also learned a thing or two at Northwest Industries — sail silk was still used at that time on the skin of some airplanes.

Stu's daughter Georgia would say in later years that her father was so masculine he was feminine. He would take on tasks often attributed to women without batting an eye because there was never a moment's question about his manhood.

But while their father was engaged in domestic tasks, the kids lost no opportunity to torment him. They were intimately familiar with his predictable range of irritants. When he was down in the basement getting his workshop ready for a household project, Dean and Owen, who were, as children, perfect imitators of their mother's voice, would peek around the corner and, just as their father was about to start work, call out, seemingly from up stairs: "Stu, Stu!"

Up the stairs he would go like a trained bear, fuming at Helen's timing, only to discover that, each time, she had not called him. It took a few trips up and down before he realized what was going on.

"Those little bastards," he'd grumble, as the boys doubled with laughter, delighted with themselves and scurrying away before their father caught them in the act.

If he had caught them, they were likely to be led off by the ear to some penalty on the Dungeon's wrestling mat.

The boys loved to ring the outside fire buzzer, an alarm system that could be heard from distant corners of the Harts' acreage. They would wait until their father was as far away from the house as he could be, then they would set off the alarm and

Lord of the Ring

hide. They'd have to muffle their laughter as they watched their father's stormy reaction as he made his way back.

Stu also had an aversion to certain synthetic scents. He particularly loathed the smell of Thrills gum, the hard purple tablet that exuded such a pungent, soapy, sickly aroma when chewed. When the kids got in the car to drive down to the Pavilion for Friday night's matches, the boys made sure that they had enough Thrills to produce great wads and get their father growling about the horrible odour.

Ellie remembers a time when Owen chewed up a whole package and stuck it under the night stand by Stu's bed. He spent more than a sleepless night trying to figure out where the smell was coming from. After a few days Owen had to 'fess up. Somehow Stu managed to work up an exasperated grin over his youngest son's prank.

Later on, when Stu began worrying about what his older sons might get up to, and whether they might be experimenting with marijuana, Bruce and Dean invented a new prank.

Seeing Wayne napping in their father's car while waiting to be driven somewhere, they approached stealthily. Careful not to wake their brother, they slipped incense into the ashtray, where it slowly burned, emitting sandalwood or jasmine — both of which were unknown odours to their father. By the time Stu opened the door, the vehicle was filled with the scent. Stu, not having any idea what marijuana smelled like, jumped to conclusions, grabbed Wayne and hauled him out, accusing him of smoking up.

A bewildered Wayne didn't have any idea what was going on.

Rod Sykes, mayor of Calgary in the mid- to late '70s, admits to some parental concern about his son Henry, then 12 or 14, hanging out with the Hart kids. At one point Henry came home from playing at Hart House rather green around the gills. The boy eventually admitted he'd been siphoning gas out of a car. He'd managed to swallow some and got sick as a result. Dean Hart, a few years older than Henry, had a sports car he'd paid for working part-time at Russell Steele while still in high school. The trouble was, he didn't always have money for gas. To take care of this problem, the first thing he did in the morning was siphon gas out of his father's Cadillac before anyone got out of bed. There was nothing to it, he explained to Henry; but Sykes didn't get the knack right away.

But there was another adventure that Henry's father would not find out about for years.

In fact, it was Stu who startled the former Mayor with his seemingly out of the blue comment: "It was a good thing we managed to get young Henry out of that vault in the basement that time, wasn't it?"

Sykes didn't have a clue what Stu was talking about.

Henry and Dean had been hanging out in the basement. Dean showed Henry something interesting, an old vault, about the size of two telephone booths, which had been built into the foundation when the house was constructed just after the turn of the century. It still worked, and Dean encouraged Henry to step inside for a better look.

As soon as he did, Dean closed the door.

The problem was Dean couldn't get the door open again. After futile attempts to release his friend on his own, Dean finally panicked and ran upstairs to get help from one of his brothers. Eventually Stu found out, and he set to work to release the boy, who had been sitting alone in the dark, claustrophobic space for some time.

Stu had, in his words, "a devil of at time" getting him out, but Henry seems not to have been scarred by the escapade. He would later study law, become a partner in one of the largest firms in Calgary and follow up by becoming a vice president of Gulf Canada Resources Ltd.

Lord of the Ring

Stu Hart forged a close relationship with the Calgary Stampede Board in the early 1950s, and the Stampede started to rely on him to bring in some big name draws during their annual week-long rodeo and exhibition. The promotion became so closely entwined with the Calgary Stampede that changing the name to Stampede Wrestling in the late 1960s seemed a natural evolution.

Stu's wrestlers often stayed at Hart House and worked out in the small gym Stu set up in the basement of the house about a year after the family settled. He installed heavy wood panelling to protect the walls from the flying bodies of men in training. Stu started to train wrestlers the way he had been trained himself — painfully, on a thinly padded mat. The ceiling would forever be scarred, with holes that exposed the pipes, by the heads and feet that flew through. Stu also ordered custom-designed weights that had the Hart name imbedded into the iron. The basement became a kind of pain centre, and was eventually known as the Dungeon. No one recalls who christened the place, but it would become, in time, one of the most famous wrestling gyms in the world. All of Stu's sons remember how difficult it became to slip past the Dungeon's open doorway, even to get to the laundry room, without their father calling them in to "show them something." Before they knew what was happening, they'd be getting a "stretching," as Stu tried out moves on them.

Stu has always said that all of his sons had what it took to be wrestlers. He carefully avoids pointing out which one was tougher or better while they were growing up, however, or how he would have fared against the boys who wrestled professionally — Bruce, Keith, Bret and Owen — if he had been their contemporary. But, he maintains, emphatically: "I could take all my sons and squash them like maggots, give me five minutes with the whole crew."

Stu taught hundreds of wrestlers in the Dungeon, showing them how to inflict pain, and take it, while protecting an opponent from serious injury. His pupils learned how to fall and land with the soles of their feet flat, to protect their back by distributing the blow along a broader surface. They also learned to tuck in an opponent's head with a swift, unnoticeable movement before throwing him, as well as countless other tricks designed to decrease the likelihood of serious injury. These kinds of skills, for Stu, are an art form in and of themselves. He never wanted one of his wrestlers hurt, and he didn't want them seriously harming anyone else. Above all else, he wanted them to be skilful.

It wasn't long before Stu became known for his training techniques. Other promoters, seeing the ability of those who had passed through the Dungeon, encouraged their up and coming talent to spend time at Hart House, too.

Edmonton's Gene Kiniski, who went on to be one of the biggest heel draws in pro-wrestling, was trained by Stu Hart. Kiniski had approached Stu in the late 1930s about working out with him and learning some wrestling skills. They started out at the Edmonton YMCA when Kiniski was still only 15 or 16. Under Hart's tutelage, Kiniski learned the basic holds — how to get a man down on the mat, how to control and "monopolize" him once he was down, and how to take bumps. Ultimately, Kiniski learned how to handle himself in much the same way Stu had learned his own skills nearly a decade earlier.

Kiniski eventually won the provincial amateur championship in the heavyweight class, but missed out on the Canadian heavyweight championship when he was disqualified for being too aggressive. He later played football for the Edmonton Eskimos after spending time in Arizona State's wrestling program. He got clipped by Martin Ruby in a game against the Saskatchewan Roughriders, and it put him out of sports for nearly two years. After a lot of therapy he returned: to wrestling. By this time Stu Hart had established promotions in both Edmonton and Calgary,

Lord of the Ring

and Kiniski, a local celebrity like Stu, quickly became one of his first stars.

Stu's eyes catch fire when he talks about how good Kiniski was from the get-go.

"He was spectacular in the ring and a great talker. He could whip the fans up with his bragging, about how great an athlete he was. It turned the crowd against him, and all those grandiose claims made him a great heel." Kiniski would begin TV interviews by saying, "Hello out there in TV land, I'd like to welcome you as Canada's greatest athlete." He'd talk about his football days and his prowess as a wrestler.

On one occasion he was scheduled to take on Lou Thesz — who many argue was the greatest wrestler of all time — during Stampede Week. (Born in 1916, Thesz first became the NWA world champion at the age of 21. He continued to win world championships into his fifties. In the ring, Thesz was considered "catlike"; he also cut a handsome figure and had a knack for getting on well with people from all walks of life. And like Stu, he would wrestle into his sixth and seventh decades.) During the pre-match interviews, Kiniski told the television audience that he hadn't realized how much people in Calgary liked him. "When I arrived at the airport there was a band playing for me. I was overwhelmed by the hospitality Calgary showed to Gene Kiniski. I know I am the greatest athlete in Canada, but I didn't expect such a greeting here."

A few minutes later, Thesz grabbed the microphone and said he wanted the good people of Calgary to know that the band at the airport was paid for by the Calgary tourist bureau to welcome *all* of the Calgary Stampede visitors.

An early indication of how important television would be for wrestling came in 1955 after the CBC broadcast a Whipper Billy Watson–Gene Kiniski match that the two followed up with a tour of all the major Canadian wrestling centres. Because of the television exposure, every venue across the country was packed. Everyone wanted to see Kiniski, the wrestler everyone loved to hate, pitted against Whipper, who was their favourite "Easter Seal" good guy. Whipper earned the "Easter Seal" tag for his charity work with the Ontario Society for Crippled Children. For 37 years he was prominently involved in the annual Easter Seal campaign.

Stu recalls that when Kiniski first challenged Whipper Billy Watson, then the British Empire Champion, no one took him seriously. But by the time the two ended up in the squared circle, there wasn't a fan in either Edmonton or Toronto who didn't want to see Kiniski's butt kicked all over the ring. Whenever the two went at each other, whether it was in Edmonton or at Maple Leaf Gardens, thousands had to be turned away.

In the early 1960s Stu acquired the rights to use the Stampede grounds grandstand and scheduled a match between Killer Kowalski and Kiniski, who had been paired periodically as tag team partners. By this time they'd had a falling out — a clash of athletic egos. Kowalski launched into his usual pre-match rant about how he would destroy Kiniski. Kiniski countered with a blistering attack on his former partner, claiming he was a "cancerous influence" in Western Canada. The two were of comparable size, and the ensuing spectacle was a wondrous showdown of kneeing, kicking and yelling.

Earl McCready, a Saskatchewan-born wrestler who had been the British amateur champion and participated in the 1928 Olympics, became another of Stu's biggest crowd pleasers. Stu and McCready worked a one-hour match together in the late '40s, and Stu recalls being told by many fans that the battle was the best they'd ever seen.

Al "Mr. Murder" Mills from Camrose, Alberta, was also an early favourite. He had been trained by the great Jack Taylor, and was already in the promotion when Stu picked up the Calgary

Lord of the Ring

territory in 1951. Mills became a role model for Archie "the Stomper" Gouldie, a man described by Stu as one of the most acerbic wrestlers to have ever forced himself into a ring. Gouldie, who would fight Stu as his wrestling days waned, and Bret, in the years before the younger Hart hit it big, started out with Stu's promotion in 1952. He was stretched by Stu when still not much more than a youth, and then promptly vanished for about ten years. He later reappeared, training with Mike Sharpe, Hans Herman and other wrestlers in Stu's Dungeon. He spent some time in Kansas City as the Mongolian Stomper then returned to Stampede Wrestling in the fall of 1967.

Stu first met Gouldie while the wannabe was a junior football player. Gouldie would hang around the ring and challenge the wrestlers to take him on. Stu told him to get some experience first. But Gouldie persisted, to the point that he had to be removed from the Victoria Pavilion by the police after he leapt into the action. He put up quite a defence and managed to grab the microphone, still insisting that someone take him on.

Finally, Stu told him that if he wanted to wrestle that badly, he should come down to the house — that he'd put him through his paces in the Dungeon. Over time, after his various early collisions with pro-wrestling, Gouldie developed into a formidable talent.

Later in life Gouldie later took up sheriff and bailiff duties in Knoxville, Tennessee. His determined, no-nonsense stance, set off with a 10-gallon cowboy hat, guns and badge of office no doubt made him every bit as intimidating as he was in the squared circle.

One of the more explosive tag teams to work for Stu were the Kalmikoff brothers, Ivan and Karol. They arrived in Calgary on the heels of the launch of Sputnik, the first artificial satellite put into orbit on October 4, 1957 — an achievement the Soviets immediately turned into propaganda, proclaiming the technological superiority of communism.

Stu Hart

The Kalmikoff brothers milked the uneasiness which Sputnik created for the West, roaring into rings wearing Cossack hats and fur boots and shouting that they were better than the Canadians, better than the Americans, better than everyone in everything. Naturally, this did not sit well with fans in Calgary and Edmonton. The Kalmikoffs were actually Ukrainian immigrants. Stu had met them in Tulsa, Oklahoma, early in his career. The brothers caused such a stir they had to be escorted in and out of the Pavilion by moonlighting off-duty policemen.

Stu launched or propelled the careers of many other wrestlers: Maurice "Mad Dog" Vachon from Montreal; Dr. Bill Miller, a veterinarian from Ohio who had been an all-American football star at Ohio State University; Sweet Daddy Siki (born Reginald Siki, an American); Leo Burke (Leonce Cormier) and his brother the Beast (Yvan Cormier), the "Shediac Sensations" from New Brunswick; Paul and Joe Leduc, who wrestled as the "Leduc Brothers"; and "Abdullah the Butcher" (Larry Shreeve, a former janitor from Windsor, Ontario) were all featured on his cards. In more recent times, Stu's Dungeon became a breeding ground for a new generation of elite pro-wrestlers. Men like the "Dynamite Kid" (Tom Billington), Davey Boy Smith, Brian Pillman, Jim "the Anvil" Neidhart, Chris Jericho and Chris Benoit all benefited from his training principles. Legends like Greg "the Hammer" Valentine, Jake "the Snake" Roberts, and Sylvester "Big Daddy" Ritter, known in the WWF as the "Junkyard Dog," also improved with his tutelage. His influence has already created a remarkable legacy.

In the early years, however, most of Stu's wrestlers were ex-servicemen, boxers, football, hockey and baseball players looking for a way to continue a flagging athletic career. Primo Carnera, the Italian boxer who lost to Joe Louis in the 1930s, turned wrestler for a brief stint; as did Canada's Yvon Durrell, the boxer

Lord of the Ring

who twice lost to light-heavyweight champion Archie Moore in battles that mesmerized every Canadian with a black-and-white television. Durrell often wrestled Kowalski, who would generate heat by taunting his opponent as a punch-drunk has-been.

Stu brought in a parade of big names during his first two decades. Ex-champ boxers like Joe Louis, Jack Dempsey and Rocky Marciano peaked fan interest with their mere presence. Even American track star Jesse Owens did a stint as a referee on Stu's mats. Special guest referees were paid 10 per cent of the gate, which meant a healthy cut for minimal work. Dempsey would often pose with Stu Hart for publicity photos, the two of them sparring.

Stu was not above using gimmicks to draw crowds. Hypnotist Peter Raveen appeared in his ring, although his performance had nothing in common with the more typical appearances of celebrity referees, circus animals and midgets.

Raveen hypnotized one of the Stampede wrestlers.

Stu recalls the hypnotist telling his man: "Your body will become rigid like a bar of steel."

Once under, the grappler was picked up and placed between two chairs, his heels resting on one and his head on the other. The Mighty Ursus, a huge man with a head proportionally akin to that of a buffalo on a six-foot-six and 350-pound frame, then stood on the man's stomach. There wasn't as much as a murmur from the rigid, hypnotized crowbar.

Dr. Bill Miller, the Ohio veterinarian, and his younger, better-looking heartthrob brother Dan, wrestled as a heel tag team against the Scott Brothers, Sandy and George. The Scotts became so popular that a contest was created to give them a "name." Six months and thousands of entries later, the pair of babyfaces were christened "the Flying Scotts." When the Millers got wind of it they promptly announced, in menacing tones, that the pair would be the "Fleeing Scotts" as soon as they got them in the ring. At the time, the insult was pushing the envelope, Stu recalls with a laugh.

In those days, wrestlers-in-training were taught and expected to follow "kayfabe" — the sport's code of secrecy. They learned to reply to questions about whether the matches were contrived by saying: "If you think it's so fake, get into the ring with me."

Baby faces and heels were taught to keep their distance from each other, whenever they could be observed by the general public. They feigned anger and followed through with storylines even after the matches were over, and did not fraternize with each other anywhere fans might see them. All the wrestlers worked at keeping themselves in peak physical condition. Despite all the talk about connivance, absence of strong athletic skills made the credible work impossible.

Today, Stu recognizes that the showmanship and bravado of "sports entertainment" are necessary to keep arenas full: "Even in other sports, it's the colourful antics that keep people coming back. Great ability has never been enough to keep the crowds paying money to see the action. Money plays a big part in all sports. Without it a hockey player wouldn't be able to keep his skates sharpened, and a wrestler wouldn't be able to keep his boots in laces.

"But wrestling is a little like the big juicy steak you look forward to eating. Then you start experimenting with toppings which you keep on adding because you think it makes it so much better. Then one day you wonder what happened to that big juicy steak you used to enjoy so much."

Still, even if the combination of sport and showmanship was more balanced in the days of Stu's promotion, the actual in-ring work already differed greatly from the submission wrestling he had learned at the Edmonton YMCA.

Watching a submission bout can be tedious. It can take a long time for a wrestler to get an opponent into a hold and force him

Lord of the Ring

to quit. Olympic bouts, before matches were timed, could go on for hours before a wrestler would submit or the officials would declare a draw, awarding only silver medals to each participant.

Eventually, showmanship would become a bigger part of the equation. Stu Hart, though, was always careful to ensure that skill was emphasized.

Edmonton's Phil Klein, father of Alberta Premier Ralph Klein, wrestled as "Killer Klein" and refereed for Stu in the 1950s. Klein had a thriving concrete and cement concern and would eventually become too busy to continue working for Stu's Klondike Wrestling. Stu remembers him as capable and fearless, with hands like shovels and powerful forearms built up from years of working with cement. The two met through Stu's old hero, Jack Taylor, who had retired and settled in Edmonton. Klein remembers Stu as a "master at what he did, if not a tad sadistic."

Stu enjoyed taking would-be wrestlers down to his basement gym and forcing them into "the small package" — essentially a front face lock from which he would tuck the opponent's head under his arm and roll over. The pain that would shoot through the unfortunate wrestler's neck and back was profound. His forearm smash — delivered under the chin with sufficient force to knock an opponent off his feet — was another dreaded move. Klein says Stu would test guys to see how much pain they could endure. "If they could stand what he put them through for a couple of hours and then come back the next day, Stu figured they were tough enough for wrestling."

Stu's "sugar hold" was something he used to make sure someone was up to the task. It was a move that gave men like Klein the idea that he enjoyed inflicting pain more than he ever let on.

He'd work a man's head forward so that his chin touched his chest, pull his arms behind his head, and put his knee down behind the man's head and push. Then, he would force the man into a half-lying and half-sitting position. The pressure on the head and neck was unbearable. And then, when it was already more than anyone could be expected to tolerate, Stu would put his massive hand over the man's nose and mouth and cut off his breathing. He'd hold the guy there long enough for him to think he was going to black out. As the man struggled and howled through Stu's hand, Stu would pretend he couldn't hear and ask, "What's that, what's that?"

Stu explains: "I would get him on the mat, then cross over him and get his arms and legs tied up, then I'd bait him. You know the point where he's pretty much yours, and if you want to tease him a bit you put your hand over his mouth and nose to get a few squeaks out of him."

Stu has never injured anyone seriously in his stretching sessions — but wrestlers always left humbled and with new respect. Cocky rookies who thought wrestling was a piece of cake were in for a rude awakening. Given that he's basically a gentle person, these torture sessions present an incongruity that's not easily explained.

Calgarian Gordon Ivy survived Stu Hart's test in the '50s. Gordon, then in his twenties, approached Stu about getting into wrestling. Stu took him down to the Dungeon for a workout, and inevitably took him close to apoplexy. Gordon had a small birthmark, about the size of a quarter, just above his right brow. Because of the amount of pressure on his head and eyes during one of Stu's holds, Gordon's birthmark expanded three times its normal size and stayed that way, permanently. Luckily, he was good natured about it, and went on to wrestle as one of Stu's regulars for a few years.

Bruce Hart, who worked closely with his father in the promotion during the '80s and '90s, disagrees with any suggestion that Stu's stretching was about gratuitously inflicting pain: "Everything

Lord of the Ring

that was taught in the Dungeon was done for a rational purpose. The stretching was an initiation, a test. The lessons were very focussed. The guys who came out of Stampede Wrestling ended up on the cutting edge: Dynamite Kid, Bret and Owen, Brian Pillman, Chris Benoit, Chris Jericho, Jushin Liger, Konnan, Hiro Hasse, among others. The wrestlers were taught from square one to respect the business, not to sneer at it, not to divulge the inner sanctum. When you pay your dues through the hell you went through in the Dungeon, you acquired a sense of honour and expectation and you protected what you learned, you protected the business. That is missing today in the way training takes place.

"In teaching, Stu would stretch men half his age and test their staying power. Guys were drilled over and over in every move until they got it right. Then they gave the business their best because they had to earn their way into it through their own blood, sweat and tears. It is a complete misconception that Stu was cruel or sadistic."

Stu and Bruce agree that the methodology is important. Stu believes it's like any other learning process: "You have to learn the proper moves. It's like learning to throw a baseball properly or ballroom dancing. There are people who can take a broom stick and make it look like a great ballroom dancer, because they are that good themselves."

Chris Benoit, now a WWF star, started out in Stu Hart's Dungeon. He wrote about his experience in a column for WCW Online News in 1996:

> It was the most legendary training facility in wrestling history.... The first time I set foot in that place, I was petrified. I was 18 years old (early 1986) and I was in Stu Hart's Dungeon. It was a dream come true,

Stu Hart

something I'd been dreaming of since I was 12. I'd slept, ate and drank wrestling. Everything I did revolved around getting a chance to wrestle. And there I was facing off with Stu Hart in his Dungeon. It was a thrill but intimidating too. . . . Stu is one of the grandmasters of the world of wrestling. . . . When he talked, everyone listened. When he wrestled, people screamed. Many a cocky football player or bodybuilder descended into the Dungeon full of swagger, convinced he'd lick this wrestling thing in a day or two. Many left broken men. . . . I saw a lot of guys come down — big guys, like 6'4", 280, and they thought they could just walk into the ring and dominate. Well, it would take a minute with Stu and they'd realize how helpless they really were. Stu was in, what, his sixties then, and he'd just be killing these guys. Just killing them. They'd be screaming like little kids. It was an incredible sight, a guy his age doing that. Not so much what he could do, but the knowledge that enabled him to do it. It was all knowledge. . . . Stu Hart, you see, taught humility as well as wrestling. . . . But after Stu stretched you, he respected you. If you stayed. If you could survive the Dungeon, you were ready. . . . Being a graduate of the Dungeon means you have a certain style, a certain technique. But one of the things

Lord of the Ring

> that really stands out about anyone from the Dungeon is a certain attitude. Stu still has that air. It's a way of thinking, a way of life for him. We all have that attitude. If you're from the Dungeon, if you're from Stu Hart's territory, you have to succeed.

Over the years, Stu trained and then lost numerous fine wrestlers to other promotions. Phil Klein points out that Whipper Billy Watson took quite a few of Stu's better performers. "He'd come out and see a guy who looked promising and he'd say to Stu, 'What are you going to do with him?' Stu wouldn't say all that much and Whipper would add, 'You don't mind if I take him along with me do you?' Stu was always agreeable, even when it was to his own disadvantage." Often Stu's best pupils ended up in Eastern Canada with Whipper and Frank Tunney. Klein feels Hart's wrestlers should have been more loyal. "Whipper took them to Toronto and made a lot of money off their work. But the wrestlers made good money as well, and Stu Hart did not want to hold them back."

The promotion had its share of other troubles. Stu repeatedly locked horns with the Calgary Boxing and Wrestling Commission, which usually had members at every event. In early 1954 the Commission launched an investigation into reports that a large number of unsupervised children were attending the matches, and the Children's Aid Department was dispatched to carry out an assessment. In February two probation officers rendered their awkwardly worded report:

> A good portion of youngsters were accompanied by parents or were in the company of older persons who appeared to be

responsible for them. However, there was a large number of juveniles between the ages of eight and fifteen years who were unaccompanied and who congregated in groups of three to five, the largest group being about fourteen in number.

Apparently, these "juveniles" were engaged in "excessive heckling" and catcalls with the occasional use of bad language, throwing articles, cigarette boxes, chocolate bar wrappings, airplanes made out of programs in the crowd and on the ring, smoking, considerable moving about, congregating around the ring and talking to the wrestlers, following wrestlers from the ring to their dressing rooms seeking autographs....

It appears to the writers that wrestling as presented at the Victoria Pavilion cannot be called a clean, healthy sport and rather has its appeal to the crowd of spectators because of its lack of restrictions, unsportsmanlike practices (gouging, hair pulling, grudge matching, etc). It is the type of entertainment where the patrons feel themselves to be released from the restrictions of a binding code of conduct and freely give vent to their feelings verbally and gesture wildly, quite unrestrictedly, living enthusiastically for the moment what disciplined behaviours would prevent them from doing under different circumstances.

Lord of the Ring

> While such entertainment may provide a harmless outlet for feelings and hostilities in adults, it must be remembered that juveniles, to a large extent, pattern their actions and attitudes on what they observe in adult behaviour....
>
> We therefore recommend enforceable legislation that prohibits any juvenile under the age of fourteen years from attending these wrestling matches.

The legislation never materialized. In homage to his own youth, Stu often cast a blind eye to the kids who slipped into the arena to watch the action. While Stu's wrestlers were often told to clean up their act, these instructions were largely ignored. It wasn't long before wrestlers took to bringing "foreign objects" into the ring, forcing referees to spend a considerable amount of effort in "failing to see" what was so clearly evident to the crowd. Fan mail flooded the offices of the commission, complaining that the referees were blind or biased.

As the years passed, the Commission became more and more active. Fines were being handed out for infractions of all kinds by the mid-'50s. "Riot Call" Wright was fined $50 after a match with Stu himself. The Boxing and Wrestling Commission minutes for its meeting of March 27, 1956, record the following entry, under the heading "Business":

> The meeting was called for the purpose of discussing incidents which occurred during a wrestling match held March 26, 1956, between Jim "Riot Call" Wright and Stu Hart....

> It was felt that the actions of Jim Wright, particularly when he had Stu Hart apparently unconscious on the ring floor and after being awarded the match by the referee, were of a detrimental nature. . . .
>
> Stewart E. Hart was instructed to warn his wrestlers that the orders of the referees in charge must at all times be respected.

The Commission also attempted to intervene in Stu's television broadcasts, clearly looking for ways to control what the viewing audience was watching. On the strength of two complaints about salty language and wrestler behaviour, the Commission, spearheaded by one of its members, Pat Sullivan, assessed whether it had jurisdiction to enforce its rules in Stu Hart's TV programs "Mat Time" and "Meet the Wrestlers."

The Commission never settled the question of its jurisdiction, but it leaned on the television station as if it had. Sullivan, who lived across the street from CHCT on Rideau Road, hounded CHCT about the amount of traffic when the show was on the air. As many as 1,000 people would park their cars all over the neighbourhood every Sunday, trying to get into a studio that could only accommodate 150.

Sullivan produced a petition, signed by 11 other Rideau Road neighbours, which objected to the heavy traffic during Stu's broadcast. The problem was exacerbated by television executives who overreacted when an American heel attempted to draw heat by Canada-bashing. It was 1957 when Mike Dibiase, using his most belligerent villain posturing, told the Calgary audience that "If nickels were brains and ten cents could get you around the world, the average Canadian wouldn't be able to get across the street."

Lord of the Ring

CHCT executives reacted like Dibiase was claiming the Queen had lice. The traffic complaints added fuel to the out-of-control fire and "Mat Time" was moved to the Pavilion, where a single camera tried to catch the action in an empty arena. The ambiance of the studio, achieved with the use of multiple cameras, was entirely lost. To make matters worse, "Meet the Wrestlers," Stu's 15-minute Friday night promo show was dropped altogether.

Soon "Mat Time" was moved from its popular Saturday afternoon spot and aired on Saturday mornings. It lost viewers. Stu's "Big Time Wrestling," which had been doing so well, was about to take a downward spiral. It would take Stu Hart years to fully recover.

Six

Most western Canadian baby boomers grew up with televised wrestling. They either watched it themselves, or heard fathers and siblings howling in front of the set on weekend afternoons or evenings.

Its initial popularity can be partially attributed to the fact that it was one of the few televised sports, but it was always entertaining and unpredictable. Many early fans believed the storylines: it was *real*, the gospel truth. It did not occur to them that a significant part of what they watched was contrived.

The wrestlers, however, were given almost unlimited creative freedom. Stars emerged, the big names like "Killer" Kowalski, "Gorgeous George" Wagner, Gene Kiniski and Whipper Billy Watson — because of their wrestling skills, yes, but also because of their colourful personas and antics.

Gorgeous George was a dazzler who combined athletic prowess and showbiz glitz in an unique way. His ring entrance was remarkable. He'd breeze into the arena wearing a long, flowing cape. It would flutter behind him, setting off his shoulder-length golden curls, while he'd proclaim himself the best and most beautiful. His "valet," Geoffrey, would run ahead of him and sanitize the mat with an ostentatious spraying apparatus — cleansing it of the germs of previous wrestlers. George affected a disdain for being touched and would often throw red rose blossoms and gold "Georgie" hairpins to squealing female fans.

When George first worked Stu's territory, Helen, the keeper of the books and controller of the expenses, was presented with the bill for dozens of roses. She was horrified by what the wrestler did to them. Brandishing a pair of scissors, he mercilessly snipped off the soft red velvet blossoms. Helen would never have approved the purchase of the long-stemmed American beauties had she known what the wrestler had in mind.

It was actually Helen Hart who picked Gorgeous George's famous theme music. After observing his routine, her natural love of irreverence surfaced; she immediately decided that the only entrance music suitable was "Pomp and Circumstance." Years later Randy "Macho Man" Savage would make the song his own for similar reasons.

But for Stu the magic was dramatically diminished when his Big Time Wrestling broadcasts were dropped or forced to compete with Bugs Bunny, the Road Runner and other cartoons. Without prime time coverage his promotion started losing "Big Time" money. It wasn't long before Sam Menacker drifted back to the States and began working for promoter Johnnie Doyle. Abandoned, Stu was without an announcer.

During a card in Saskatoon, Stu had met an enthusiastic University of Saskatchewan student who was putting himself through school by picking up gigs as a radio and television announcer. Stu had him help out, getting him to announce matches in Saskatoon a few times, and he liked the young man's work. Eventually, degree in hand, the student was hired by CFQC in Saskatoon. By the mid-'50s, he had gravitated west to Calgary's CFAC-TV. Stu asked Ed Whalen to be his announcer, and a long and fruitful business relationship really began.

Lord of the Ring

Whalen was Saskatoon born and raised. After polishing off an Arts degree, he had originally planned to study medicine — which pleased his family. To help defray university expenses, Whalen took a job announcing for a local radio station. It wasn't long before he became completely enamoured with broadcasting. By the time television came to town in the early '50s he was so smitten that, much to his parents' chagrin, he unceremoniously dropped the idea of becoming *Dr.* Whalen. By 1957, he was working for Stu Hart to supplement his regular job at CFAC-TV.

In 1960 business was still lagging, and Stu embraced changes he hoped would improve things. A new television station, CFCN, had set up on Broadcast Hill, a grassy knoll not far from Hart House in west Calgary. But because Whalen worked for CFAC, he could not freelance for a competing station. Once again Stu was forced to look for a new announcer. He tracked down Sam Menacker, who agreed to return to Calgary and work on the new venture.

The new program was launched in 1961. Gone was the old name, "Mat Time," and the show known simply as "Big Time Wrestling" was born. It aired until 1963, with the Hart-Menacker combination working some of its old magic: the talent pool gradually improved, and interest began to pick up.

But a good thing doesn't always last. In '63, Menacker had a run-in with wrestler Mike Sharpe — Sharpe punched Sam in the face, breaking his nose.

Menacher's anger took on a life of its own. He decided to quit the promotion and return to the States.

Sam hated being challenged or embarrassed, and he didn't much like the man Stu intended as his replacement, Ernie Roth. His bruised ego took him to the offices of Gordon Carter, then Vice President of CFCN. He made a concerted attempt to discredit Roth, levying every disparaging remark he could think of, apparently to convince Carter to drop the show and promotion from

147

his television line up. He managed to instill some uneasiness in Carter, but the broadcasts continued. Why Menacker's anger with Sharpe would make him want to cause problems for Stu and Big Time Wrestling remains a mystery.

At the same time, Menacker discovered that the lawyer Stu had engaged to handle the purchase of the Comanche 250 had not done his job properly. The registration papers for the plane still recorded the original owner's name, despite the fact that Stu Hart had paid for it fully. The disgruntled announcer boarded the plane, fired up the engine and disappeared into the clouds. He would not to be heard from for another 25 years. Stu made attempts to locate Menacker and retrieve the plane, but without success. His lawyer escaped sanction from the Law Society of Alberta only because Stu never bothered to make a claim.

Ernie Roth was Stu's announcer until Henry Viney took over in 1964. But the promotion again showed signs of trouble. Stu's talent base thinned and fan interest waned. At the time, he'd cut the wrestlers loose at the end of a season, which culminated each year with the Calgary Stampede, then re-hire them in the fall. The approach had its risks. Employing wrestlers seasonally meant he was always competing with other promoters — and the wrestlers themselves would always shop around for the best offer. By 1965 the business was all but dead. The noise and excitement of wild and crazy nights at the Pavilion or Corral was gone. The houses were empty and the wrestlers who remained lost their inspiration. Performances suffered accordingly.

Stu worked hard to find ways to compensate for the failings of his local talent. He struck a deal with Kiniski, Sandor Kovacs and Rod Fenton, who were, by this time, promoting All-Star Wrestling in Vancouver. CFCN was already broadcasting All-Star matches. All-Star agreed to send wrestlers out to Calgary as long as Stu picked up the expense of flying them back and forth. But the pro-

Lord of the Ring

motion was pushed into the All-Star way of doing things, and that did not sit well with Stu. Arenas were still only half-full, expenses were astronomical, and there was a poor working relationship between the promotions. In the spring of 1966, Stu and All-Star parted company. CFCN decided it could not accommodate two promotions, and for eight months Stu broadcast nothing at all.

By the fall, Stu Hart's Big Time Wrestling was all but dormant.

Before the downturn of the early and mid-'60s, Hart House had glassed-in porches, lovely climbing roses which clung to picturesque trellises and flower beds with a wide variety of annuals and perennials. Bing, the cat that came with the house, and Basil the rooster presided. In the late fall and winter, when it was too cold outside, the boys played with their Matchbox toys in the warm, sun-capturing cocoon of the greenhouse.

Stu would come home from a tour through the northern States with Payday trousers and Pendelton shirts for the kids and Fanny Farmer Candy for their mother. It was the heyday of Wild Cat Wrestling, sponsored by Alberta White Trucks. Stu had 30 rings scattered around his territory. Many of them are still stashed in towns and cities across Western Canada and the Pacific Northwest of the United States.

It was in the small towns where the promotion really thrived. They were places where grain elevators presided over mile after mile of windswept fields. Towns in which Marshall Wells hardware stores were ever-present, always identifiable by a prominently displayed three-dimensional purple neon Jesus in the front window. Visitors would always wonder: "Who buys this stuff?"

Stu would take raw young talent out to prairie towns to let them cut their teeth in front of a real crowd, to discover what it was like to wrestle in front of over-excited, screaming fans who hovered close to the ring. He'd take a few popular, name draws to

149

make sure the venues filled up with the local farmers and townspeople. Fans in all the venues, whether located in large cities or small towns, reacted in much the same way: they'd scream, howl, threaten and unload frustrations of their own. They'd throw paper cups full of Coke and Pepsi, crumpled programs, candy bar wrappers and whatever else they could get their hands on. The smoke-filled arenas would be littered with debris by the end of the evening. Back then, the spectacle of a little old lady with perfectly set hair beating a heel with her purse or umbrella was not uncommon. Elderly men pointed their canes menacingly and shouted at the men in the ring. Wrestling revved up everyone, in the same way charismatic evangelists worked their tented Prairie pulpits before television came along.

Before his troubles started, Stu had cleared away the greenhouse, rose trellis and flower gardens from around the old mansion and hired a contractor to put in a swimming pool. The children were excited about the commotion and digging going on in the yard and, sad as it was to see things change, knew that with the swimming pool would come new flower gardens and underground sprinklers — plus all the summer fun a pool could offer.

Dwindling fortunes meant tightening belts, and the swimming pool had to be scrapped. All that was left was a big mound of dirt. It sat in the yard for years, until gradually overtaken by weeds. Old Cadillacs rusted in the yard, falling apart for want of servicing. It left the impression of a junkyard in the making. Keith Hart describes it as something out of Steinbeck's *Grapes of Wrath*. "We went from the family that had everything, to the Joads almost overnight." The hill of weedy dirt in the yard remained until after Keith finished his education degree at the University of Saskatchewan in the mid-'70s.

The house's appearance suffered in other ways, too. Stu had been in the process of upgrading the front windows. When the

Lord of the Ring

promotion went off the air, there was no longer money to finish the work, or even to restore things to their original condition. For two or three winters the windows had to be covered with plastic and cardboard. The house was cold and the children went around in stocking hats or earmuffs, wrapping themselves in heavy Hudson Bay blankets to keep warm.

During those years, Stu struggled to keep one of the old Caddies in working condition. Over time, tires inevitably grew so bald that the mechanics at the local service station refused to patch them. Keith recalls heated arguments between his father and mechanics — Stu insisting his tires could be patched because there was no money for new ones. In the end, they'd rummage out back for castaways that were in better shape than what was already on Stu's vehicle.

Stu could have closed shop and tried to preserve the assets he had left, but wrestling was like a mistress he couldn't resist. He stubbornly braced himself and carried on — again, it was not unlike his father's refusal to hand over the Tofield land, hoping against hope.

Stu's always had a way of accepting life's calamities with a calm that those around him find somewhat puzzling. It comes from his optimism, his confidence that things will, ultimately, improve. His attitude originated in a cold, damp canvas tent and was bolstered by a dog-eared copy of *The Power of Positive Thinking*.

Tom Walsh, who was Stu's lawyer in the '60s and '70s, still marvels at the way Stu persevered: "Times for him were so tough, and there wasn't much money in the bank, yet Stu struggled along somehow and kept wrestling alive, if only on life support. He had a good partner in Helen, and he loved and lived wrestling. He's the only reason pro-wrestling stayed in Calgary all those years."

Walsh fondly recalls the many times he'd run into Stu or meet with him up at the house. After they'd sort out the legal issue of the day, Tom would ask, "So Stu, how are the kids?" Stu would shake his head and say, exasperated, "They're aggravating, Tommy, they're aggravating."

Despite regularly seeking legal counsel, Stu generally did all his business on a handshake. "He didn't always take his lawyer's advice," Walsh says, and occasionally this would end up making tricky situations more difficult to resolve. From time to time his firm would get a call from Stu, and Walsh would dispatch one of his litigators to handle charges against some wrestler who'd kicked the headlights out of cars in one of the towns or villages around southern Alberta. Acting for Stu and his wrestlers, says Walsh, "was never dull."

No matter how lean the times got, Keith Hart says his parents made sure their children were well-fed and corralled into church. They would alternate between the Baptist Church, the faith of Stu's father, and the Catholic, the faith of Helen's parents. Sometimes, he says, they would attend the United Church as a way of meeting somewhere between the two. The kids would sit in a long row on the wooden pews, most of the boys out of Stu's corrective reach. When their boredom threshold was inevitably surpassed, they'd start shoving against each other, knocking hymn books to the floor and giggling. Stu's stage whisper was audible throughout the congregation: "Quit that, you little bastards."

Helen would shrink down in her seat, mortified, wishing she could disappear under the pews.

Stu knew all too well that if he did not get the promotion back on its feet quickly, a full recovery would be unlikely. He arranged a meeting with the station manager of CFAC-TV, which had once broadcast "Meet the Wrestlers" and "Mat Time" so successfully. The station had no wrestling interest at the time, and the opportunity they eventually presented was like manna from heaven. The

Lord of the Ring

station's Ron Chase agreed to provide the air time; Stu would only be required to pay a relatively modest set-up fee of $1,000. At that point, however, Stu simply did not have that kind of cash.

"I was broke, but determined to somehow raise the money," he recalls.

Stu Hart had plenty of high-roller friends in those years, but none came to his assistance. Even the banks were uncooperative, despite the fact that he had equity in his land. Instead, he borrowed the money from Harold Sharlow, then a vice principal at Viscount Bennett High School, who had moonlighted for him since 1952. Sharlow says he didn't think twice about lending Stu the money. "I earned it all from him anyway." Stu paid him back within the year. Without that loan, Stu is convinced, the promotion would have disappeared completely.

"That loan helped save our bacon," he says.

As "Wildcat Wrestling," the promotion returned to the air with a flurry. And Stu's association with Ed Whelan began anew.

Whalen was paid $25 a night at first, but the remuneration gradually increased. The new show debuted in late '65. Whalen appeared on screen with an urgent-sounding message for viewers: "Ladies and Gentlemen," he began, in his distinctive nasal twang, "do not adjust your sets. You are watching Wildcat Wrestling." On screen was fan-favourite Sweet Daddy Siki, also known as "Mr. Irresistible," sporting sunglasses, weird stage makeup and a cape, his snow-white hair a stark contrast to his ebony skin. That first broadcast set the tone for the excitement and showmanship that would distinguish the promotion for years to come.

By the late '60s the name "Wildcat" was shelved and the more familiar "Stampede Wrestling" was born. It took time to rebuild, but Stu was able to find the talent who would make the company a going concern once again. Luther Lindsay of West Virginia, and

Archie "the Stomper" Gouldie, of Carbon, Alberta, were back. Stan Stasiak from North Bay, Ontario, and Ox Baker, an Iowa potato farmer turned wrestler, shared cards with the "Shediac Sensations." Dave Ruhl also returned, along with Jerry and Bobby Christie and the Leduc Brothers.

Finally, in 1969, something occurred which would ensure the success of the promotion for the next several years.

To build up to the annual end-of-season card at the Calgary Stampede, "The Stomper" Gouldie was to take on Billy Robinson. The winner, expected to be Gouldie, would earn the right to face the new NWA champion, Dory Funk Jr., of Amarillo, Texas, who had pinned Edmonton's Gene Kiniski in Tampa, Florida, earlier in the year. The fight would be for Stampede Wrestling's North American Heavyweight Championship belt.

Robinson was an up-and-coming English wrestler who was keen on breaking into the business in North America. He was a charismatic and sound wrestler with a knack for building up crowds. He was a natural "babyface," clean cut and neatly groomed. Robinson had met Dave Ruhl in Japan. They hit it off and Robinson promptly packed his bags for North America. He signed on for a two-month stint with Stampede Wrestling in the spring of 1969. His run would culminate in the lead-up to the big Calgary Stampede match.

Archie Gouldie was by this time an experienced heel, just as adept at whipping up the fans in his own right. Stampede Wrestling built up the match between Robinson and Gouldie for weeks, but the results were unsatisfactory. No winner was declared: Gouldie was incensed, accusing Robinson of using "shooter" tactics and working stiff — failing to work with him in the spirit, or toward the storyline, of the match.

Bruce Hart, then 18, recalls Gouldie angrily throwing his boots against a wall and stomping out, leaving Stampede Wrestling in

Lord of the Ring

the lurch just before the big showdown with the NWA champ.

With Gouldie's dramatic exit, Stu had no choice but to put Robinson on the card to take on Funk. The Calgary Stampede featured two Friday night wrestling events during its 10-day run. The first match set up the excitement and anticipation for the big showdown on the last Friday night of the Stampede. The first Friday was a "broadway" (carny/wrestling talk for a draw or a fight that ends without a decision). It helped build anticipation for the end-of-season spectacular. But the chemistry between Robinson and Funk was as immediate as it was unmistakable. The two grappled for a full 60 minutes on that first Friday night and the fans were literally out of their seats, spellbound for the duration. When the final showdown came a week later, the place was packed. Dory Funk walked out with his title, but the action made even bigger names for both men — much to the annoyance of Archie Gouldie. Robinson and Funk returned to Stampede Wrestling at the beginning of the new season and continued to make visits to Calgary over the course of the next several years.

Ed Whalen took a liking to Billy Robinson because he was a clean, talented wrestler — the complete opposite of men like Abdullah the Butcher whose characters were rude, obnoxious and hard to control. Whalen appreciated the English wrestler's style and demeanor. When Robinson returned for another stint with Hart, the announcer was happy to see him return. Eventually a match between Abdullah and Robinson was booked.

Abdullah was billed as the maniacal bad boy from far-off, exotic Khartoum, but underneath he was Larry Shreeve, from Windsor, Ontario. His approach to arch-villainy was to go through Stu's stock of wrestlers systematically and make mincemeat out of them. One after another his opponents were carried out on stretchers. All of it, of course, was scripted, but to the fans it was still legit. Abdullah, the nastiest of the nasty, had to be stopped.

During an initial showdown, it looked like Abdullah was going to get the best of Robinson. Whalen was in the ring with them, trying to maintain an orderly interview, but at one point Abdullah looked like he was going to attack him, too. Whalen wasn't going to put up with that kind of thing and reacted instinctively. He hit Abdullah on the head with his microphone. Blood spewed from a seven-stitch gash in Abdullah's bald scalp, and it sent the crowd into a frenzy. Bleeding was nothing to Abdullah, who regularly wrapped his fingertips with Band-Aids which hid pieces of razor blades. He'd use them to get his own blood running himself, just to excite the fans — his scalp was permanently scarred from frequent bladings.

The Robinson and Abdullah run of the early '70s was so successful that for the first time Stu continued the promotion throughout the summer and kept his wrestlers busy year round. Stu says that wherever Abdullah went, he made the other wrestlers look good: "He was one of the biggest draws I ever had."

Minor blood-lettings and the staged violent rages of "King Curtis" Iaukea of Hawaii, Sweet Daddy Siki and others had the promotion humming and gates healthy. The reappearance of Kowalski, Dory Funk, his brother Terry and Andre the Giant kept the fans wanting more.

In one form or another, Stampede Wrestling had now been in living rooms all over Western Canada for years. By the early '70s the shows were picked up for syndication and names like Stu Hart and Ed Whalen would become synonymous with pro-wrestling in far flung regions of the world. Twenty years later pirated tapes from the '60s and '70s would show up in the most unexpected places — of course, without financially benefiting Stu Hart. Ed Whalen recalled a friend phoning him from Africa to say he had just watched him on local TV. He'd heard a familiar nasal twang and Whalen's trademark sign off, "until next time and in

Lord of the Ring

between time," and couldn't believe his ears. Stu once had a call from his doctor, Otto Spika, while the show played in the background in Japan.

Managing the promotion became an even bigger challenge. Stu was running Friday nights in Calgary, Saturday nights in Edmonton, Monday in Lethbridge and Tuesday in Red Deer. Wednesday and Thursday nights, wrestling came to Saskatoon and Regina. Periodically wrestlers would again visit remote outposts. The good times had returned. And it was the organizational skills of Helen which kept everything on track.

At venues outside Calgary and Edmonton, Stu usually had a local man helping with the set up, taking out the weekly licences, complying with the Boxing and Wrestling Commission requirements in the various locales. From 1963 to 1973 in Saskatoon, Stu worked with Ned Powers, Entertainment Editor for the *StarPhoenix* newspaper. He was recruited after he'd moved from the *Leader Post* in Regina. George "Porky" Jacobs had been running things in Regina, and he had introduced Powers to both Stu and the sport.

Powers describes Stu as "all business," although often careless about settling his advertising accounts from week to week. The Saskatoon man would have to engage in some wrestling of his own with his paper's advertising department — which insisted that previous accounts be settled before new ads were placed. Frantic calls to Helen would solve the problem before the promotion was deprived of local coverage. "She was always so sweet, so helpful," recalls Powers, who also wrote a weekly program and advance stories for the *StarPhoenix*, arranged commercials on TV and "engaged in a little ticket management" — all for about $25 a week.

Eric Knowles, the Editor-in-Chief of the *StarPhoenix* in the 1960s, hated wrestling with a passion and barely allowed the

157

sports pages to carry two or three paragraphs, even if a big event was taking place. When Gene Kiniski and Whipper Billy Watson did their cross-Canada tour, they attracted a sell-out crowd of 5,400 in the old Saskatoon arena. With a $6 ticket price, the gate was more than $30,000. Receipts in larger centres were much higher. The local norm, however, was gates of between $1,000 and $10,000. Still, coverage was lean. When Powers at one point wrote a column about Lou Thesz, one of the greatest wrestlers of all time, Knowles sent a terse note to the City Desk: another column on wrestling would cost Powers his job as entertainment editor.

Reporters could count on a colourful story when wrestling came to town. Dave White of Calgary, who was a young *Edmonton Journal* sports writer in the '60s, remembers being dispatched to interview a wrestler before a major event. White arranged to meet the man at his hotel. When he arrived, he knocked several times but got no response. Thinking this odd, given the specific arrangements, White continued to pound on the door. Just when he was about to give up, the door swung open. A burly, naked wrestler appeared, irate about having a mid-afternoon liaison interrupted by a scrawny reporter. White said, "I didn't have the impression that the woman between the sheets, clearly visible from the door, was the wrestler's wife." He ended up waiting in the lobby, wondering how he could work the incident into his story and whether it would pass his editor's scrutiny.

It didn't.

Wrestling became a crowd-pleasing feature of the Calgary Stampede. The celebrities who came in to hype the fans usually spent time with the Harts. Rocky Marciano, who retired as an undefeated heavyweight boxing champ, loved to entertain the children. In a photograph taken in 1964, two years before he died, Marciano posed with the then 11 Hart kids as they pretended to

Lord of the Ring

take each other on. The children loved the attention and lapped up these opportunities.

"Killer" Kowalski re-appeared many times in the showcase of wrestling stars. By the 1960s he had already earned notoriety, his reputation sealed when he ripped off part of "Yukon" Eric Holmbach's ear in a match at the Montreal Forum. Wrestling is hard on that particular body part, the pounding leaving many grapplers with "cauliflower ears" by the time their careers end. Stu Hart's are partially cauliflowered: a condition caused by calcification after a series of injuries which essentially began when he first grappled with Chick Garibaldi in 1946. Today, Stu's ears are rock hard. Inflexible, their outer edges curl slightly.

One of Kowalski's wildest matches was with Czaya Nandor; it took place in Calgary in 1964, in Stu Hart's ring. Animosity was built over a period of several weeks before the actual match. The two appeared on television, threatening and challenging each other. Nandor had been a freedom fighter during the 1956 Hungarian Revolution, a short-lived civil upheaval in which Hungarians tried to overthrow a communist government. The freedom fighters began with Molotov cocktails, bricks and rocks, then graduated to hand grenades and machine guns. A huge united front developed among the people as they got a slight glimpse of freedom. Many Hungarian refugees subsequently immigrated to North America, and Calgary welcomed a sizeable community. Nandor had made a dramatic escape from the post-revolution suppression of civil liberties. He had huge support from the local Hungarian expatriate community.

Compared to the massive Kowalski, the popular Nandor, even at 220 pounds and standing six feet, seemed diminutive. Nandor, however, claimed to have "a cast iron" stomach that could withstand the harshest punishment.

At the time Kowalski had been relying heavily on his infa-

159

mous "claw" hold, with which he would incapacitate an opponent by grabbing chunks of their flesh. In one interview after another Kowalski maintained that even a cast iron stomach could not withstand his claw hold — that he would rip Nandor to shreds. Pre-match hype featured episodes in which the huge Kowalski would climb the ropes and leap onto Nandor's "cast iron" stomach. The moves seemed only to send the Hungarian into fits of laughter.

But Kowalski laughed last. The next time Kowalski jumped him, he landed on Nandor's throat. The Hungarian began to choke and had to be rushed to nearby Holy Cross Hospital. It was feared that his neck had been broken. Luckily, he recovered in a few days — but not before the switchboard at CFCN lit up like a Christmas tree with calls from fans seeking information about their hero. Stu and station vice president Gordon Carter had to make an on-air announcement to explain that the Hungarian favourite was resting comfortably and would fully recover. Station brass were not amused.

When Nandor returned, the crowd lined up for blocks outside the Pavilion to witness the Hungarian take retribution. Fans were hysterical. Kowalski, the consummate heel, shouted back insults and was met with a hailstorm of used paper cups and rolled up newspapers. A loose script for the big match had been agreed upon. Nandor, the underdog, was to fight an uphill, losing battle, but in the final moments suddenly turn the hideous claw on the great Kowalski himself, reducing the monster to putty. It was, apparently, the only time Killer agreed to allow the claw to be used against him. Stu recalls that the script had to ensure Nandor beat Kowalski, because had he lost the fans would have rioted and ripped the place down timber by timber.

The wrestlers had fun improvising scripts, and they did not limit them to the ring. No one remembers exactly how the

Lord of the Ring

"Mabel" rib was born, but to Stu Hart its theme is as timeless as Shakespeare.

The notorious "Mabel" has been staged in countless wrestling promotions over the years, and has occurred within the ranks of other sportsmen as well. It was a favourite prank among seasoned wrestlers, especially when a highly suitable "candidate" came along. The perfect victim tended to have a particular swagger — he was generally a young wrestler who put off the vets with his bragging and boasting. A guy like this was an easy target.

In preparation for the actual prank, older wrestlers would make sure the guy-talk turned to tales of the incredible, voluptuous Mabel — a woman whose insatiable passions were the stuff of legend. The idea would be planted early in the week of a big show. Mabel, who was very discreet, had somehow, somewhere, seen the new wrestler and was anxious to meet him. She was built up as a woman addicted to young, virile grapplers. Once the young wrestler's interest was sufficiently piqued, he would be counselled about how and where a liaison might take place. It was explained that Mabel preferred remote locations, again insisting on discretion and privacy. Thus her choice of venue: a farmhouse in the middle of nowhere. Anticipation would often make the young victim half-crazed. Then, the veterans would feign reluctance about helping to make the rendezvous possible. It was too much for the young guy. Mabel had expectations and requirements, they'd say. Expensive tastes. She insisted her lovers bring caviar, champagne and stacks of Alberta prime rib steaks.

The response from the rookie was almost always the same: he could provide anything she wished. When he'd been whipped into a frenzy, the young wrestler would be told a rendezvous had been arranged. Part of the plan meant that the other wrestlers would arrive first and make small talk with Mabel; they were to make sure she was satisfied with the gifts. Then, the victim would be summoned. On his way in he would be told: "Oh, by the way, Mabel is married. But don't worry about it, her husband is out of town." While the other wrestlers congregated in another part of the house with the food and drink, the rookie waited to be "Mabeled."

After the young wrestler was left alone for a sufficiently anxiety-inducing period of time, a man playing the part of Mabel's husband would burst in with a shotgun and threaten violence. The would-be lover, naturally, went into a state of terrified shock. One of the veterans would then race into the room to "assist" the rookie — he'd be outfitted with a bag of blood, acquired from a local slaughterhouse, under his shirt. The "husband" would discharge the weapon, loaded with blanks. As the veteran fell to the floor, exploding the blood bag on the way down, he'd scream, "Run, run for your life!" The young wrestler, horrified, would disappear into the night, stumbling blindly across stubble fields, while the rest of the wrestlers feasted on caviar, champagne and steaks, howling over the latest "Mabeling."

The scenario played itself out in a variety of ways, sometimes incorporating the unexpected. When the Great Antonio was Mabeled, the script got re-routed. After the staged shooting, Antonio raced through the fields, got caught up on a barbed wire fence, and eventually reached a nearby highway, where he flagged down a passing police cruiser. The wrestler returned with the officers, who told him to stay in the cruiser while they investigated.

Once inside the officers got the whole story, enjoyed the prank and stayed for a bit of steak. An hour later they returned to the car and told Antonio that the situation was even worse than he had described. The terrified Antonio begged to be locked up overnight for his own safety. When he eventually discovered the truth, he was livid.

Sometimes a stand-in "Mabel" would be brought in, and she would get the wrestler bragging about how much better he was

Lord of the Ring

than the other wrestlers, not knowing that they were listening in the next room. He'd have a lot to live down the next day. Occasionally, a wrestler would refuse to run, insisting on staying to help his fallen comrade. The prank would then have to be revealed. However it went, the rib was never well received.

Stampede and Klondike Wrestling were about more than lucrative gates and pranks. Stu Hart sponsored many charity events each year, even when he could least afford to do so. Old *Calgary Herald* clippings include numerous articles about Hart lending a helping hand to a worthy cause. In 1964 Stu donated a crest bearing the Canadian Coat of Arms, presented to him when he won the Canadian Light Heavyweight Amateur Wrestling Championship in Vancouver in 1939, to the Petroleum Service League of Calgary to be used in a fund raiser for handicapped children. Periodically, he would hold a special event where wrestlers donated their services and he would turn over as much as the entire gate. Stu especially liked helping kids. "After all," he says, "we were all kids once." He could never refuse a charity call, especially if it was from Catholic Bishop Paul O'Byrne or Rabbi Lou Ginsberg, who had himself spent time in New York's boxing and wrestling rings. The trio liked to use sports events to support community programs for young people and those less fortunate. Stu's regular philanthropic projects ran the gamut, from Little League to churches of all denominations, the Cubs and Boy Scouts, Christmas toy campaigns, the Canadian National Institute for the Blind, amateur wrestling clubs and children's hospitals. The Bishop, the Rabbi and the Baptist wrestler made a curious team.

By the late 1960s Stu would lend charitable assistance to more than 35 different organizations in Calgary. Often the efforts came together spontaneously, or Stu would hand over a gate unannounced. The Calgary Olympic Development Committee of the

1950s was a frequent recipient of his support. The Committee toiled away, even though they wouldn't land the event until 1988.

But despite his work for the people of Calgary, Calgary did not always treat Stu Hart in kind.

In 1963, under pressure to hand over land to accommodate Sarcee Trail, a major freeway through the west end of the city, Stu Hart would find few friends in City Hall. He finally caved and allowed the expropriation; he was paid a mere $5,000. Stu acquiesced, believing political assurances: that in the future he would be able to develop the four acres cut off from the rest of his property and thereby maintain a retirement nest egg for himself and Helen. Thirty years later City Hall would let him down again, and the family was told they could not develop the land. Civic officials suggested that Stu turn the four-acre parcel over to the City so that they could be added to nearby Edworthy Park. In exchange he would receive an unspecified tax credit. Stu declined.

Even though Patterson Heights, a community constructed in the 1980s, now sits on what was once largely Hart land, the city named the new development after the previous owner of the house. Of the mansion's three owners, Patterson held title for the shortest period of time. Stu Hart's name appears nowhere on the hill, despite his long history of good works for his community. Stu eventually sold the balance of the acreage not already expropriated to Jack Singer and Abe Belzberg, wrestling fans who were also two of the wealthiest entrepreneurs in Calgary. According to Stu's eldest son, Smith, he was paid $850,000.

But Stu's problems with City officials have never detracted from his charitable impulses. Often he'd use touring specialty wrestlers and novelty acts to raise funds. He could always count on Jack Britton, a promoter of midget acts, to add to the circus-like atmosphere down at the Pavilion by bringing in crowd favourites Sky Low Low, Fuzzy Cupid and Mighty Atlas. Wild ani-

Lord of the Ring

mal acts also drew huge crowds. At one point, while still in his prime, the Fish and Wildlife Association asked Stu to wrestle both a tiger and a bear — "Terrible Teddy."

As a publicity stunt for the Calgary Stampede, Stu wrestled the tiger on the midway. Stu made sure to wear protective clothing instead of trunks, including a pair of black, tooled-leather cowboy boots. Stu recalls feeling lucky after his 10-minute tangle with the beast. He wasn't badly scratched: "You had to keep moving in the ring as the tiger liked to play a cat and mouse game." Needless to say its claws had been trimmed to reduce the potential of injury.

When the Fish and Wildlife Association suggested he wrestle a bear, Stu thought about it before he agreed. He knew that with bear wrestling the trick was to get behind the animal, grab it and jump on its back. The bear, instinctively, would toss you over its shoulder in a kind of "flying mare." Equally instinctively, the animal would then try to pounce on its "prey" and engage in a little not-so-playful mauling. If Stu was to live to tell the tale, he would have to get out of the way after the flying mare. Once the bear got on top, it would be quite a feat to get the 600-pound critter off — and there was always the serious risk of suffocation.

Stu agreed to wrestle Terrible Teddy. He followed his plan to the letter and had no problems keeping the animal out of pounce or maul position. To make the show more interesting, other wrestlers lined up to follow suit. Next on the card was Ron Starr. Starr was apprehensive about the exercise. He was able to get himself through the flying mare, but he lingered on the mat too long. The bear pounced and started to squeeze, nearly smothering him. Starr panicked under the weight. Stu quickly sent in Sweet Daddy Siki to distract the animal while Stu hauled Starr out from underneath. Siki took on the bear with such enthusiasm it was hard to decide whether he or Terrible Teddy enjoyed it more — or who got the better of the encounter.

Stu Hart

The Great Antonio was periodically assigned to wrestle a bear as well. He was a typical example of what Stu calls "an old crowbar" — a wrestler who was big and clumsy and would lock an opponent in a bear hug until he either passed out or gave up. Antonio seemed perfect for bear wrestling — he had a lot in common with the animals. But in the ring things don't always go as smoothly as planned. Once Antonio made the mistake of clipping a bear on the head. The bear winced and lost its humour. Nature took over, and it interpreted the shot as a cue to defend itself. The bear smacked Antonio back and got up on its haunches, a sure sign of trouble. Even though it was on a 20-foot leash, the bear fell off the stage and into the audience. Bedlam set in. People screamed and scrambled to get out of the way. A trainer had to haul mightily on the bear's chain to get it back into the ring. Next, he tried to pacify the animal with a can of Coke, a favourite treat. But the bear would have none of it. It swatted away the beverage and the trainer had to spend several tense minutes calming the animal before it could be safely taken from the Pavilion. Antonio lost his interest in bear wrestling after the episode.

At one point bear wrestling promoter Dave McKigney was making the rounds with a circus bear. It was an active wrestler, but by fall needed to hibernate. Stu agreed to find a place to put the bear for the winter. Stu stuffed it, cart and all, under the porch at Hart House. When Stu and the bear's trainer hauled him out the next spring, they walked him around to wake him and then proceeded to feed him as if it was a perfectly natural occurrence. To Helen, it was just another bizarre window into the world of wrestling. The kids, too, were well accustomed to such things. "What, doesn't everybody have a bear under their front porch?" Ellie remembers asking.

Every now and then an Australian wrestler would get in the ring with a kangaroo, another sure crowd pleaser. The kangaroos

Lord of the Ring

moved so fast there wasn't usually much of a match, just a lot of laughs. Alligators were recruited, too, but were used sparingly. The creatures were too sluggish in cold weather — Western Canada's bitter winter temperatures weren't inviting. In warmer weather, a trainer would prop open an alligator's mouth with a stick and put his head between the gaping jaws. The stick was the only thing keeping the creature from its snack.

All this time, Helen kept the business end of the promotion running. And despite the fact that she always played down her role, she definitely played an integral part in keeping everything on track. From time to time, however, she was pushed to the limit. Once, in the early '60s, a house full of small children, wrestlers, pets and the endless tasks finally took their toll. Eileen Simpkins-O'Neill recalls the Hart matriarch regaling dinner guests, a cast of journalists and photographers from the *Calgary Herald* introduced to the family by Jock Osler, Helen's brother-in-law, with the day she ran away from home.

Helen was just managing to keep things together when, uncharacteristically frazzled, she took a large load of dirty clothes downstairs to the laundry room. It was located near the Dungeon and when she heard a couple of grunts behind her she turned around, expecting to find wrestlers working out. Instead, she discovered a huge bear in its cage. Helen threw a tantrum, hauled out a suitcase and started packing. She stormed out, telling everyone that she was leaving. The driveway at the time was long and wound around the bluffs behind the house — a considerable distance to the main highway. The House itself was seven miles from the city. Helen walked and walked; and as she did, she found herself cooling down. After a while she sat by the side of the driveway on her suitcase, thinking about the fact she had nowhere to go. Soon a familiar Cadillac came down the road full of kids. Stu pulled over, picked up Helen's suitcase and put it in the car. Helen stepped in.

Stu Hart

Stu turned to her and said, "Well, Tiger, what will we do about dinner, should we pick up some chicken?" He completely ignored the tantrum and the incident was never spoken of again — except as a means of entertaining dinner guests. Helen would later say to friends: "I didn't even know if he had come after me or he was just going that way to get chicken."

In 1964 Stu took on a new off-season money-making venture: he purchased a 160-acre man-made sandbar called Clearwater Beach, near Twin Bridges, just west of Calgary along the winding Elbow River.

Stu operated hot dog stands, rented camping spots and took the kids out every day. The beach provided an income and kept the children in a healthy environment for many summers. The first guests were admitted free of charge: the Cub and Boy Scouts and YMCA kids' camps.

Something happened, however, which disrupted Stu's calm approach to every problem he faced. When his older kids came home from the beach one afternoon, they discovered that their youngest siblings, Diana and Owen, still pre-schoolers, were nowhere to be found. Stu had thought they were with their older brothers and sisters. They thought the little ones had left for home with their father. Stu jumped into his car and raced back to the beach, fearing the worst. He searched everywhere for the children but couldn't find them. When his desperation had finally peaked, out came Owen and Diana from behind a shed. They had been building a sand castle. It was the one and only time Helen or the older Hart children ever recalled Stu "losing it."

By the mid-'70s the idyllic beach would become a massive headache. Stu would face health department complaints after the water was deemed unsafe — Calgarians ignored the swimming-prohibited signs he'd posted and dove in anyway. It was just too

Lord of the Ring

much to handle with everything else going on.

For a while Stu enlisted an old school buddy, John Hopkins, a *Calgary Herald* columnist, to help. Hopkins, a colourful, witty character, loved to crack wise with tourists, especially when responding to questions he found irritating. If you asked, "Do you have any insects here?" he'd reply, "Just a few bar flies." Hopkins also wrote Stu's wrestling programs and gave him favourable ink in his columns whenever he got the chance.

John and Stu were another odd pair. Stu was the consummate athlete. John, in contrast, once described his own slight frame as "150 pounds of springy blue steel." After his untimely death, on Christmas Eve, 1978, Tom Moore, a *Calgary Albertan* sports columnist, took over responsibility for the programs. His purple prose made them a hot item.

In the early 1970s the older Hart sons, already in their 20s or late teens, also helped run the beach. Smith and Dean played the biggest role in convincing their father that the boys could handle the responsibility. Stu couldn't say no and he let his sons do their thing, deciding that it would be an opportunity for them to learn both responsibility and business skills. But the two brothers soon found that they could not work together: they both wanted to run the show. One weekend, Dean arranged a rock concert; Smith planned a similar event for the same time.

Smith apparently thought it was a good idea to let some local bikers show up; they, in Calgary's own small-scale version of Altamont, smashed the windows out of the vehicles of many of the attendees. Bottles were broken on the beach and the concession building caught fire and burned to the ground, all of which resulted in $30,000 in damages. The boys shrugged it off. It was at this point that Stu took to calling his eldest son Smith, already in his mid-twenties, "Shed." It took a while before anyone realized it was short for "Shithead."

Stu Hart

When the Calgary Board of Health finally closed it down as a health and safety hazard, as well as a general public nuisance, Stu was forced to unload Clearwater Beach in a buyer's market.

If Smith was "Shed," Dean was often not far behind. In his late teens he was particularly imaginative about making money at his father's expense. At one point he convinced his parents to let him have a New Year's Eve party at the house. He was in high school and the request seemed harmless enough. Unknown to Stu and Helen, their son charged admission. When word got out that a huge party was taking place at Hart House, crowds of people showed up. Dean made a killing. He had his sisters organizing food and refreshments. Unfortunately, people stole many of the crystals from Stu's chandeliers and it took him months to find replacements in antique shops around Calgary.

During the promotion's lean years, another investment caused him much expense and grief. In the mid '60s, Stu was advised to buy controlling interest in the Invalid Seat Company, which provided customized equipment for the disabled. He had Bert Moseley operating it for him. But Bert never let on how poor business had become, and Stu's investment quickly became a financial quagmire. The company went bankrupt, nearly taking the wrestling promotion with it. Later, he was able to sell some land in Edmonton and turn a profit; the sale buffered the effects of the Invalid Seat Company's drastic losses.

The early '70s were banner years for Stampede Wrestling after the haphazard '60s. Stu was promoting wrestling all over Western Canada and the northwestern United States, and strong gates meant he could operate all year. And even if he did shut down, he was invited to country rodeos (western Canada's answer to fall fairs) to add to the buzz and generally help increase profits. Promoters from all the NWA territories sent up their raw material and new stars for Stu and the boys to work with, and Stu

Lord of the Ring

responded in kind. Dory Funk, Jr., the NWA World Champion from 1969 to 1973, defended his title many times at Stampede Wrestling. Soon the Hart boys were making trips down to Amarillo to visit Dory and his younger brother Terry.

Funk fondly remembers meeting Stu Hart for the first time after hearing stories about him from his father, who operated a similar promotion in Amarillo. Dory was in Calgary for the Stampede and joined Stu and the family at the annual Hays Stampede Breakfast, which has been hosted by the Hays family since 1950. (Today, Senator Dan Hays carries on the tradition established by his late father, Senator Harry Hays.) A 6 a.m. start didn't guarantee a parking spot when a crowd of 1,400 were showing up for breakfast, but Stu managed to find a narrow space between two closely parked vehicles. He told his passengers to get out, then proceeded to squeeze into the not-quite-wide-enough space. Dory was puzzled about how Stu planned to get out himself. But wasn't left pondering for long. The driver's window came down and out came a pair of alligator cowboy boots.

Up until he effectively retired in 1984, Stu and Stampede Wrestling always had a wrestling float in the nationally televised Calgary Stampede parade. Something almost always broke down, however. It occurred so often, in fact, that the parade marshal finally decided to put Stu's float at the end of the parade, behind everyone else. Stu characteristically ignored the instruction and jammed his float into a gap in the line, right up front. Wrestler Dory Funk's brother Terry was in town for one such occasion. Bruce chronicled the events in a 1999 Christmas letter to Dory:

> . . . as usual, Stu had to butt in out-of-turn with his float, a ring full of wrestlers pulled by some contraption, followed by a couple of convertibles. Terry and some [women] on horses and the McGuire twins (750

pounds each) followed on mini-bikes. The parade marshal, as you can imagine was seething when he saw we were where a high school marching band was supposed to be. Stu had stretched one of the [wrestlers] on the float and was waving to the throngs of people. One of the McGuire twins had a flat on his mini-bike and had to waddle along after the float and nearly died. "Babette Bardot" on horseback was thrown off, shaken up and got hysterical. Near the most crowded part of the parade route, the shit-box pulling the wrestling float overheated or blew a gasket and limped to a stop, holding up the whole parade right in front of the live audience and the national television crew as well. Terry, who was on a horse, got an enormous kick out of all the wrestlers disembarking from the float and trudging along the rest of the route on foot while Stu berated the mechanic for the vehicle breaking down as the cops and parade marshal gnashed their teeth and made the usual threat that they'd never let us near the parade again.

There was always craziness associated with the name Stampede Wrestling — even the occasional lawsuit would add to the spectacle. A case filed by a wrestling fan before the (then) Alberta Supreme Court is a perfect example. The fan sued Stu Hart over a broken nose he'd suffered at the Pavilion. Stu dismissed the injury as "just another busted smeller."

According to court documents, one November evening in 1972 Calgarian Thomas Elendiuk walked into the Victoria Pavilion — by this time the recognized home of Stampede Wrestling — "in a spirit of adventure." He handed over his ticket and bought a program on the way to a seat located close to the ring. It was the first

Lord of the Ring

time he had ever attended, and he was excited.

Elendiuk settled into his seat. To his delight, he discovered there was to be a match between Japanese wrestler Kendo Nagasaki, managed by "Lord Sloan" — "a peer without peer" — against one of Hart's stock wrestlers.

The humour of what unfolded was not lost on lawyers John Fingarson (representing Elendiuk) and C.D. Evans (representing Stu). They used a great deal of creative licence in pleading the case.

Fingarson, in making Elendiuk's claim, states that the young patron "could scarcely contain his delight" when he heard that a representative of the "land of the rising sun" would "expose, for the greater glory and education of those in attendance, many of the mysteries, nuances and subtleties which distinguish the wrestling there from the more mundane Graeco-Roman form.

"As the evening progressed it gradually became apparent to the Plaintiff [Elendiuk] that someone had taken gross advantage of his childlike innocence and the absence of guile and sophistication which are hallmarks of his character.

"To his great disappointment the noble champion of Japanese tradition dropped his mask of Asiatic inscrutability, resorted to heinous and improper tactics to overcome his kindly but efficient opponent and was promptly disqualified."

Elendiuk, in his excitement, jumped out of his seat as Lord Sloan rushed to the ring and followed him to the action. Elendiuk's story, according to his lawyer, was that Sloan "incited the crowd to the extent that when he left the ring certain less restrained spectators fell upon him."

Lord Sloan, seemingly agitated by the disqualification of his wrestler, attempted a punch which missed its mark and landed full force in the face of the hapless Elendiuk, who was standing too close to the out-of-ring skirmish.

Fingarson's version of the facts continues: "When confronted by the obvious evidence of the effect of Lord Sloan's errant fist, Mr. Hart, with unwashed hands, and without benefit of anaesthesia, or even prior warning, seized the much maligned and misaligned sensor and thrust it back to the place from whence it had been so rudely removed."

Evans's response stated that Sloan's fist was struck by Elendiuk's nose and that Elendiuk should not have left his seat "saving and excepting necessary reply to the natural functions, humours and vapours of the body and stuck his big nose into an affair to which he was not privy or counsel and he got what he deserved."

The Statement of Defence continued: "If Lord Sloan's fist did come into contact with the Plaintiff's snivelling proboscis . . . the Plaintiff hit that Defendant on the latter's fist with the former's beak, causing that Defendant severe cramp to the knuckles of his duster, cauliflowers to his said mitt and quite of variety of related ailments. . . ."

Elendiuk appears to have been further irritated by the fact that Stu didn't take his predicament seriously. He sued for $5,000 in damages.

Despite the irreverence notable in the pleadings, the case proceeded to examinations for discovery — a pre-trial recording of evidence. But the suit was dropped shortly after Evans cross-examined Elendiuk. Stu recalls the man testifying under oath that the injury "impeded his sex life." Evans, never one to miss an opportunity or fail to recognize a gift horse, pounced on the admission with gusto. He proceeded to extract the details from Elendiuk of how this could be. Those in the hearing room, including Stu Hart, struggled to maintain the composure usually associated with such sombre proceedings.

There was much lightheartedness which marked these years, but there was sadness and tragedy, too. Stu's father came to live

Lord of the Ring

with the family in the '60s. To his grandchildren it was like he was from another world. Edward still quoted from the Bible and told stories based on moral lessons. He took a seven-mile walk, daily, to and from downtown Calgary with his dog, Zero. Edward Hart died at the age of 94, strong, physically and mentally, until nearly the very end.

Later, on a cold, blustery winter day in the 1970s four of Stu's wrestlers were travelling to a match in Lethbridge — a two-hour drive southeast — in a rented car. A blinding prairie snowstorm hit and the car skidded off the road. Yukihiro Sakedo, popularly known as "Tokyo Joe," was one of the passengers in the vehicle. He had stepped out to help the tow truck driver hitch up the disabled car when another vehicle came up the highway and ploughed directly into the tow truck. He was pinned between the two vehicles. Sakedo lost one leg above the knee and the other was badly mangled. The injured wrestler was bedridden for months. His in-ring career, of course, which had been on a steady rise, was destroyed.

Tokyo Joe had been a draw in his native Japan and had been touring Canada with International Wrestling Enterprises. He had been in Montreal for three weeks and was scheduled to do a few matches with Stampede Wrestling before heading back to Japan, where he'd be feted as a star who had excelled in North America. Although the accident irrevocably changed his life, he remained in the business as a talent scout for International Wrestling Enterprises. When IWE folded he joined New Japan Wrestling — which would also forge a close relationship with Stu's operation.

Seven

In early 1976 Muhammad Ali paced the concrete floor of Calgary's Stampede Corral, killing time during a training tour, preparing for an exhibition bout with Japanese wrestler Antonio Inoki at Tokyo's famed Budokan. He was told that local wrestling promoter Stu Hart had come down to watch him train. Ali asked to be introduced. He had heard of Hart, in much the same way that most of the athletes in boxing and wrestling rings hear about each other: reputation, infamy or a combination of both.

As the two greeted each other with a measuring handshake, Stu saw something in Ali's eyes he immediately recognized. He'd seen it in boxers many times before, the look that wondered: "Could a boxer take a wrestler?" Soon Ali was probing Stu for his thoughts on the relative merits of boxing and wrestling. He walked over to a speed bag and took a few swipes.

Ali had studied wrestlers before, many times in fact. His all-time favourite was "Gorgeous George" Wagner. Ali loved the ostentatious persona of the blonde-haired icon, learning from him in the '50s, when he was still just a kid dreaming of glory. George was the first wrestler of widespread recognition to turn wrestling into a sideshow. He never tired of winding up a crowd, teasing and baiting them into a frenzy. They loved or hated every bit of him — he knew it and he loved it.

Ali was fascinated by the reaction Gorgeous George "the Human Orchid" elicited, the way he made fans crazy when he sashayed into the ring, boasting he was the best and most beautiful. He told Stu how George had influenced him, planted the seeds that grew into the "Louisville Mouth." Ali took on the best and most beautiful act to new, profitable extremes.

Practising his own brand of self-adoration, Ali mesmerized fans as well: his verbal dexterity was at times as much of an asset as his physical prowess. That's where the "sweet science" of boxing, the "gentlemen's" sport, differed from wrestling. In the end a gimmick could never pass for the real thing.

Still, like many other boxers, Ali's curiosity about wrestlers was insatiable. He edged into a debate with Stu by asking how wrestlers punch a man without hurting him. He'd noticed that wrestlers look like they are tearing each other apart, and then often leave the arena without a scratch. "When I punch a guy, I hurt him, I hurt him bad," Ali said — which, of course, was no revelation to the wrestling promoter. Stu broke into one of his wide grins.

Ali accentuated the obvious again by jabbing at the speed bag. "If I was fighting a wrestler, this is how I would punch him." Finally Ali hit the bag with a solid right, sending it shaking, wildly, in every direction. Stu smiled again and told the champ: "Well, if you tried to hit a wrestler like that, he would hook your arm and move in close. He'd get a lock on you. You wouldn't be able to land a punch." Ali was not prepared to accept this or back away from his point.

"I'm so fast a wrestler wouldn't have time to do that. He'd have to be a sprinter to catch me. I'm so fast, I'm so courageous, he'd never get a chance to hook my arm, he'd never get a lock on

Lord of the Ring

me."

Stu replied as Ali danced around the speed bag, saying that once a wrestler is in close there's no chance for a boxer: "A good wrestler would have you down on the mat pretty quick."

Ali shook his head. No matter what Stu said, he had a comeback. He would not concede that a wrestler could get anywhere near a boxer — not a great boxer, like him. Ali was convinced he'd be able to handle anything a wrestler had to offer. Stu had a different view.

"A capable submission wrestler could give a good account of himself, even if he had a boxer or a karate expert on his hands. Size makes a difference."

Stu enjoyed the banter, as well as a bit of playful shoving as he and Ali measured each other. But they never got as deep into the Wrestler vs. Boxer debate as both may have wanted. Stu knew that Ali couldn't risk getting into a ring with a wrestler — at least not for real. He couldn't risk tarnishing his image, what it would mean to his career if a wrestler got him into a hold and kicked his butt. Ali was in great shape then, weighing, in Stu's estimation, 225; Stu was 61 but still not to be taken lightly. At the time he thought he'd hold his own with the world's champ. Stu would not wrestle his last match until 1985 — tag-teaming with his son Keith at the age of 70.

Ali's curiosity was something he'd seen in Louis, Dempsey, Marciano and even Jersey Joe Walcott. But to Stu, Ali was special. He began his boxing career the way Stu had wanted to start his — winning gold at the Olympics. Ali's star burned bright at the 1960 Rome games, igniting the dreams of many young American athletes. He became for America what Stu had so badly wanted to be in Canada. Only a war could have stopped him.

When Ali finally got into the ring with Inoki in June, 1976, there wasn't much to watch. Associated Press boxing writer Ed

179

Stu Hart

Schuyler, Jr. reported: "It was declared a draw after Inoki spent 15 rounds in a crab-like position on the mat kicking out at the circling Ali's legs. Ali was hospitalized for blood clots and muscle damage in his legs."

Ali's own comment?

"Nobody knew this was going to happen, so we had a dead show."

In the early 1970s Stu's children were a constant source of amazement. Clearly developing minds and opinions of their own, Smith, Bruce and Keith were all in university. Bret was taking an interest in film-making, using a home movie camera and a cast of friends to put together comical shorts by the time he was in his mid-teens. According to his university-educated brothers, Bret was not among the more academic of the Harts during his high school years, but he had the creativity that was as much a Hart trait as athletics. Later in life he would dabble quite successfully in acting. Owen also had potential. The brothers demonstrated this while working together, guest-starring in an episode of the Disney TV show *Honey I Shrunk the Kids* filmed in Calgary.

Classmates from Ernest Manning High School remember Bret Hart as the guy at the back of the room who occupied himself firing spit balls. Bret had taken up amateur wrestling and took the high school, city and provincial championships, as had his older brothers. But ironically, in his teens he showed little interest in joining the family business. He was too busy imagining himself either in front of a camera or behind one, directing. In time, the two worlds would meet in a very big way.

As he did with Owen, Stu attempted to guide Bret towards making a serious commitment to amateur wrestling. He was being groomed for the Olympics, but broke his collarbone just before the Canadian Amateur Championships. Bret needed a win

Lord of the Ring

to make it to the Olympic team, and that was it. After the bone healed, Stu started to use him in spot shows, hoping it would renew his interest. It didn't quite work out as Stu had planned.

The young Bret Hart and his father were different in many ways. Each had his own ideas about life, about how things worked and what he wanted. Stu recalls saying to Bret: "Don't you like the idea of walking down the street knowing you're so strong no one can touch you or bother you?" He still grins remembering Bret's reply.

"I'd rather drive down the street in a big limo and wave at everybody."

Stu taught his boys basic wrestling moves when they were still preschoolers. It was almost impossible for them not to take an interest — after all, the business was a part of their lives from the day they were born. Stu would have the four older boys, Smith, Bruce, Keith and Wayne, wrestling each other and learning together. Dean and Bret soon followed, and a few years later the youngest of the brothers, Ross and Owen, would join in. Working through the basic moves as children built up their self-confidence, but it made them quite bold on the playground. They became little scrappers, brothers who looked out for each other.

While Stu was physical and strict with his sons, he was protective of his daughters. They were all beautiful young girls. He wanted them to take their cue from their very feminine mother, and both he and Helen kept them away from the ring. In a pinch, however, they were there to help. From time to time they also caused their own brand of grief, and ladylike behaviour fell by the wayside.

It happened to Ellie once in Home Economics class — she was challenging a grade she had received. At first, telling the story herself, she sanitizes the event. But leaning over to ask Stu if he remembers the incident, another side of her character appears.

Stu Hart

Stu looks sideways at his eldest daughter and says: "You mean the day you kicked the teacher in the shins?"

Ellie had come home after the incident an exceedingly worried 15-year-old. Her friends were convinced she was in huge trouble, that there was no telling what might happen once her father found out. Almost worse, she knew that her chances of getting a pair of seal skin boots — which were all the rage at the time — now resided somewhere between slim and none. Ellie approached her father with some trepidation; the only way she would be allowed back into school was with parental — Stu's — intervention and assurances. Her mother would never be able to understand kicking a teacher.

Stu listened carefully to Ellie's story, extracting the full play-by-play. After the requisite scolding, he told Ellie that, together, they would meet with the principal. It was clear: Stu would do all the talking, and Ellie was to agree to whatever was suggested.

"If they tell you to stand on your head, you stand on your head," he said.

Ellie was allowed to return to school. Stu managed the situation typically — by simply agreeing with everything the principal said. Still, Ellie was worried about whether she'd irrevocably changed her close relationship with her father. She fretted about what lay ahead and imagined the punishment coming her way. Her worries lasted only until the school doors closed behind them.

Stu turned to his daughter and said: "So, what kind of seal skin boots did you say you wanted?"

In many ways, the Hart teenagers may have seemed out of control. But they responded well to their father's corrective techniques, generally without much prodding. Stu was an intimidating figure. His size alone was enough to keep the kids in line most of the time. As teenagers, Stu's way of dealing with unacceptable behaviours in the boys was to put them in painful wrestling holds and

Lord of the Ring

keep them there until they agreed to mend their ways. Once, Bruce caught his younger brothers, Wayne and Dean, sniffing model airplane glue behind Ernest Manning High School. A dangerous distraction, it was something a lot of kids were doing at the time. Bruce told his father about it and Stu sat the two down and gave them a stern "Hart to Hart" lecture on the harm they were doing to themselves. After the talking was done, Stu believed that the boys had seen the light.

A short while later, Helen went up to the attic to look for the pair. She smelled the glue before she found them. Helen pulled Wayne and Dean from between a wall partition and made them sit until their father returned from a card in Edmonton.

Stu was not impressed.

He put his sons into a hold called a "thread through." The other kids listened attentively. Time after time they heard him ask: "Are you going to sniff glue again?"

Dean and Wayne howled: "No! No!"

Finally Stu released them and sent them to bed. The next day he phoned the school principal and told him why his sons had bloodshot eyes. The principal told Stu he understood, and agreed that Stu should do whatever it took to keep the boys off drugs.

The "tough love" treatment kept Dean on the straight-and-narrow for the rest of his teenage years. Wayne, the older of the two, was harder to convince. Stu was terrified of drugs and the drug culture, and at times he went to extremes to keep his sons clean.

Stu kept a close watch on Wayne as he moved into his later teens. As he developed an alarming disregard for authority, Stu worried that he was becoming a hippie. Wayne began breaking the family curfew regularly. He had grown a long ponytail, and his father suspected he was once again dabbling with things he shouldn't. Coming home later and later, sneaking into the house,

Stu Hart

Wayne thought his movements went undetected. When he had reached his limit, Stu propped pots and pans over the doorway his son would have to pass through on his way to bed. The late-night crash and clang occurred as planned. Stu raced down the stairs like a gorilla, grabbed Wayne by the ponytail, hauled him into the kitchen and grabbed the biggest, sharpest knife. He then sliced off the offending thatch of hair. Wayne thought his neck was about to be severed, not just his locks, and, according to his siblings, for a long time harboured a deep resentment over the loss of his prized plumage.

Some of Wayne's resentment might have validity. In Smith's opinion, he'd typically absorb the blame for a wide range of his siblings's offences, and sometimes unfairly incur the punitive wrath of his father. Stu's child-rearing philosophy was firmly rooted in the first half of the twentieth century: expressions like taking the boys "out behind the barn" or into the "woodshed" were reinvented in his wrestling Dungeon, where he extracted promises of good behaviour under the threat of further unpleasant stretchings.

When Wayne was five or six, the family took a break from a road trip at a service station and restaurant. After they were finally on the way again, ten miles from where they had stopped, an RCMP vehicle, its lights blazing, stopped their car. Wayne was in the cruiser — he had been left behind. "The sad part," recalled Helen, "is that with all the kids and confusion, we didn't notice right away that Wayne was missing. He's never forgiven us for that."

Another time Wayne was accused of taking his grandfather Hart's teeth. Edward had lost some of his teeth to a flying ax handle and wore a dental bridge. Wayne had been seen by his bedroom and was cross-examined about the whereabouts of his grandfather's dentures. Wayne adamantly professed his innocence but became "the little goat." Later on, Edward found the

Lord of the Ring

teeth in his pocket. He immediately apologized and gave Wayne his pocketwatch to make amends. The name stuck, however, and to his siblings Wayne would be "Goat" for years to come.

While much of the blame for trouble in the house fell on Wayne, Smith or Bruce, Keith almost always managed to avoid scrutiny. And even when the younger kids were "aggravating" Stu, the punishment often still fell on their oldest brothers. Bruce remembers the time Dean was upstairs, playing with a toy barbecue, stuffing paper into the little machine and trying to light it. In the middle of his game, the dinner call came and he ran off to the dining room. He left the barbecue plugged in and the house caught fire. Because Bruce and Wayne had been caught a few days earlier holding a lighter under the outside thermometer, forcing the mercury up the gauge, Stu assumed the bad example led Dean to play with fire, too. In the course of the "discussion" about the incident, Stu clipped 13-year-old Bruce on the side of the head with a frying pan. Unfortunately, it sliced into his scalp, causing blood to flow and alarming the entire family.

Keith remembers being physically corrected by his father only once. As a young boy, he had been told to go to bed but kept watching the television show *Bonanza*, ignoring his father's request. Eventually, Stu struck him across the head with a loofah sponge. It was like being hit with a wet noodle and didn't hurt, he says. But he was so shocked he burst into tears and trotted off to bed.

Stu kept his sons in line. At one point he simply decided that he wasn't going to be outsmarted by a group of "snot-nosed teenagers who hadn't yet accomplished a thing outside the use of their father's name and connections." His sons eventually would do a fine job of writing their own résumés: as wrestlers, teachers, a champion pool player and a firefighter.

Ellie relates a tale of defiance, too. She wanted to see a band at a club Stu felt was inappropriate for his teenage daughter. She was forbidden to go. Ellie, of course, decided to sneak out while her father was at the Pavilion. Determined to get to the show, even if she had to walk, she set out on foot. Stu returned earlier than expected, discovered Ellie missing and got back into his Cadillac. He found her on the street, headed for the venue. He hauled her into the car and cuffed her ear. She never crossed wires with her father again.

By the mid '70s, the Harts saw many changes in their children. The older boys were all attending university and Ellie was in art school. Then, Georgia got married.

The first time a child is married, particularly a daughter, there's usually angst. That was definitely what occurred when Georgia Hart eloped with Bradley Joseph (B.J.) Annis. The two concealed their marriage from Stu and Helen for several months, and when the family finally discovered the truth, the situation was so volatile that B.J. would stay away from Hart House for a full year. In fact, he's never completely reconciled his place in the family.

In May 1976, Georgia and B.J. joined Stu, Helen and the rest of the Hart clan at a restaurant in downtown Calgary. They were there for Stu's 61st birthday dinner.

During the course of the evening, B.J. took Helen's hand and told her that someday he hoped to make her second eldest daughter his wife. Helen had high regard for the handsome, athletic American marine engineer. He was a graduate of King's Point, the famous military academy of the U.S. Marines located near Long Island, New York, where she had grown up. The school was as selective as it was famous: it took a congressional appointment to be allowed to walk the school's hallowed halls. As a young woman, Helen and her sisters had attended tea dances there.

Helen cautiously replied that she hoped that some day the 29-year-old would be married to Georgia, too. She made a point of

Lord of the Ring

emphasising "some day," making it clear she felt that, at 19, her daughter was far too young for marriage.

Georgia reacted immediately, kicking the left shin of a bemused B.J. under the table. Her parents still did not know that they had eloped the previous December, that they were wed before a justice of the peace in a fashion that Helen would have regarded with nothing short of the horror her own mother expressed when told she was engaged to Stu.

On December 4, 1975, with blood test and marriage licence in hand, B.J. and Georgia waited, in the living room of Justice of the Peace Vivian Miller, while another couple exchanged vows. Mrs. Miller was the only woman justice of the peace on the list provided by City Hall, and for that reason the young couple settled on her. Georgia was dressed in blue jeans and a pullover sweater, having skipped her commercial cooking class at the Southern Alberta Institute of Technology. The bride and groom ahead of them intrigued the young couple. Her pilled banlon sweater and missing teeth, along with his generally unkempt appearance made Georgia feel the whole scene was like something out of a hillbilly movie. She and B.J. laughed as they nervously waited their turn.

Georgia tried to picture her parent's reaction. She realized her mother would have wanted a big church wedding, with bouquets of fresh flowers and everyone wearing pretty dresses. That both her parents liked B.J. helped to calm her.

Eventually Mrs. Miller checked their paperwork and asked about their witness. The young couple had forgotten that detail. Mrs. Miller volunteered the services of her husband, who at the time was pulling a motor out of a truck across the street. He was brought in wearing unlaced, greasy boots, and had oil dripping from his overalls. Newspapers had to be arranged so he wouldn't soil the carpet.

Stu Hart

The whole ceremony, including the ring, cost $26.

The newlyweds returned to their usual routines. B.J. was in the process of putting the finishing touches on B.J.'s Gym Ltd., but it was no place to take a new wife. Unsure of how the Harts would react, the young couple decided against telling them and agreed to keep their marriage secret until the right moment presented itself.

Georgia tucked her ring away and continued to live at home while B.J. built his gym. He'd purchased the 7th Avenue property from Ralph Switzer after a year of haggling. Switzer really didn't want to go through with the sale, but the tenacious B.J. started bringing down walls so Switzer had to sign a deal before the place turned into a pile of rubble. Located a short distance south of City Hall, the gym was in a prime location.

At 19, Georgia was a tall, athletic, blue-eyed blonde with a sweet nature and a personality to match. None of this was lost on B.J., who had met Stu and Helen in July 1975, when the Hart kids were helping to set up a ring on a flat-bed truck for the Calgary Stampede in front of his property. B.J. spotted Georgia right away, and it wasn't long before he was making regular trips to Hart House in west Calgary.

His interest in bodybuilding endeared him to a family of athletes. As well, B.J. had an eye on Stu's barbells, made of pure steel and inscribed with the Hart name, specially ordered from a company which had since gone out of business. He offered to buy them. B.J. recalls eating endless cucumber sandwiches and drinking cup after cup of tea with Stu before he finally realized that Stu wasn't going to part with them. He also realized Stu would never give him a straight answer, one way or the other. Stu responded to questions like "Do you want to sell your barbells?" or "Do you want Smith to go to the Safeway store with you?" in the same way.

"Not necessarily."

What he meant, of course, was, "No."

Lord of the Ring

Getting nowhere with the weights, B.J. focussed on his real reason for spending so much time at Hart House — he set out to get rid of Georgia's boyfriend, a local hockey player, and win her for himself.

A native of Boston, B.J. acquired his nickname from his military name tag. "Annis, B.J.," served a tour of duty in Viet Nam, earned a degree in marine engineering at King's Point and spent time in the U.S. Army Corps of Engineers. He arrived in Hawaii and enrolled in graduate school at the University of Hawaii, where he started work on a master's degree in philosophy. He had also become a pilot and a line dealer for Cessna and opened a gym. One day, as fate would have it, he met a football player from Canada.

Ward Smith was a "bad boy" in both the CFL and NFL. B.J. relishes telling the story of how Smith distinguished himself after being dropped by the Winnipeg Blue Bombers. He slipped down to the football field before dawn the next morning and extracted his own payback — rototilling the turf on his way out of town. The bad boy of the gridiron and the good boy of the American Ivy League were intrigued by each other. The two could not have been more different.

B.J. soon found himself making trips to Calgary with Smith, even though the city in the early '70s had little to recommend itself to the ex-marine. At that time good gym facilities were few and far between and what existed had inadequate equipment. The local YMCA threw him out for bench pressing with Olympic barbells, which were prone to bending when dropped. As in Hawaii, he began thinking about opening a gym. In the interim, he and Smith enjoyed skiing in the Canadian Rockies, and the footballer's mother entertained the two voracious eaters in her Lakeview district kitchen regularly.

Several months after eloping, Georgia indulged Ellie in some serious girl talk in the room they still shared at Hart House. Ellie

189

was fishing for information — just how close was Georgia to B.J. anyway?

Feeling somewhat guilty for not confiding in her sister, Georgia told all. Ellie was not prepared for the bombshell. Irate, she demanded Georgia get an annulment — something not legal in Alberta once a marriage has been consummated. A heated argument ensued. The commotion was enough to make Helen shuffle down the hall in her slippers. The pair put off their mother and, after Helen's departure, Ellie insisted that Georgia confess to their parents the next day.

The following afternoon, B.J. and Georgia were working around the gym on 7th Avenue when Ellie pulled up in Stu's black Cadillac, her head barely visible above the steering wheel. The petite and fiery brunette was clearly on a mission. Like a drill sergeant, Ellie marched in and launched into an intense verbal assault. She demanded B.J. arrange for an annulment before Stu and Helen discovered what was going on. B.J. promptly ordered Ellie off his property. She retaliated by promising to drive straight home to tell her parents. B.J. would have to deal with Stu, she said.

In an attempt to control the damage, B.J. did the only thing he could. He phoned Georgia's father. Not realizing how difficult the truth would be, he spent several minutes beating around the bush, taxing Stu's patience. Stu, eventually fearing the worst, demanded B.J. get to the point.

"What are you trying to tell me? You had better not be telling me you've taken advantage of my daughter!"

The alarmed B.J. blurted out the whole story. He was met with a barrage of shocked obscenities.

"You pretend to be my friend and you come in here and elope with my daughter," Stu bellowed.

Helen heard everything.

Stu suddenly broke off the conversation. "Listen I can't talk to

Lord of the Ring

you anymore, my wife has just fainted."

The line went dead.

The stunned couple prepared for the worst as they drove to the house. They were met by an outraged Helen. In an instant, B.J. had metamorphosed from a nice King's Pointer into a fast-talking American sailor, who was not even from New York but, heaven forbid, Boston. He was the sneak who'd weaselled his way into the family home and made off with a prized jewel.

Saying that Helen Hart did not take the elopement well is an understatement. What particularly galled her was what B.J. had said at Stu's birthday. He'd already married her daughter yet lied, looking her straight in the eye.

Helen paced back and forth at the top of the oak staircase between the first and second floor, making a dramatic impression as she demanded Stu "do something." When she didn't get the desired response, the usually composed, gentle Helen shrieked her blunt solution: "Kill him, kill him!"

Stu went up and down the stairs liked a trained bear, trying to calm his hysterical wife while dealing with the young couple in the living room.

"Get him out. Get him out of this house!" Helen finally demanded.

Stu steered the reluctant B.J. out onto the verandah. Without either man's knowledge, Helen had positioned herself on the second tier, just above them. She was out of sight, but she could hear their conversation.

As he was pushed out the front door, B.J. expected some sort of physical assault and instinctively positioned himself sideways to avoid a leg sweep, one of Stu's favourite moves. His mind raced.

"This was no ordinary guy," B.J. recalls thinking of the man in his sixties. "I knew he was one tough son-of-a-bitch and if he took me on, I had no chance."

Stu Hart

B.J. quickly improvised a defence. "I thought that if he attacked me, I would grab him by the throat, which he wouldn't expect. Then while he was recovering, I'd have a second or two to run like the devil to my car and get the hell out of there, alive."

To his astonishment, Stu turned B.J. towards the beautiful panoramic view of downtown Calgary. Stu's habit of avoiding unpleasantness by talking about something else kicked in.

"You know this is one of the most beautiful pieces of property in the whole city," he said, going on to explain that a man he knew in Calgary's prestigious Mount Royal had actually offered to trade his property for Stu's hillside domain. Stu had turned him down flatly.

Suddenly, an unmistakable New York accent voice tore into the calm.

"Stu, Stu are you crazy? What are you doing talking to him? Kill him! Kill him!"

Taking B.J. by the arm, Stu turned his face upwards so Helen could hear better.

"You son of bitch. You come in here, pretend to be my friend, and like a thief in the night you steal my daughter."

He rounded this out with a creative combination of imprecations, hoping to appease his distraught wife. Then, whispering, he told Annis: "Look, I'm not sure what is the right way and what is the wrong way in these things, but I do appreciate that you did not take advantage of my daughter and that you two did get married."

A mutual respect was cemented at that moment, but even so, B.J. avoided the house and Helen's wrath for a year. He and Georgia moved in above the gym and five years later started a family. Helen eventually reconciled herself to the marriage and B.J. would eventually earn her affection as well. Both Harts would rely on B.J.'s honest, unbiased opinion. The first of his and Georgia's children, Ted, the oldest Hart grandchild, born in 1980,

Lord of the Ring

would inherit athletic ability of his own. Twenty years later he would try his hand at wrestling in a teenage promotion known as MatRats.

As his daughters entered their 20s, Stu eventually allowed them to participate in the Stampede promotion. Professional wrestling became a true Hart family business. At one point Stu was stuck out of town, unable to pick up his main attraction at the airport. He phoned the house. The only one at home with a licence was Ellie. He explained that he needed someone to take the Cadillac and greet Andre "the Giant," the massive wrestler from Grenoble, France.

Ellie liked the good-natured giant, who had appeared in Stu's rings on numerous occasions over the course of many years. But when she was ready to leave, there was no Cadillac in the yard. Her brothers had disappeared with it.

With no other option, she hopped into her own car — a rusty, 1959 Volkswagen beetle.

On the way to the airport she began worrying about how she'd fit Andre into her tiny bug — luckily it was a convertible. There was more than a double-take when Andre saw his transportation. Always agreeable, however, he squeezed into the back seat, his big body filling its width, and tried to centre himself, midway, over the axle. He then draped his legs over the front passenger seat. The little car chugged its way through the 35-minute drive back to Hart House.

Despite being sheltered from the wrestling world in their teenage years, each of the girls would fall for men who were either wrestlers themselves or involved with the business peripherally. (Ellie married Jim "the Anvil" Neidhart in 1982; Alison married Ben Bassarab, but later divorced him; Diana, the youngest, married Davey Boy Smith, but separated from him in the fall of 2000.)

193

Stu Hart

The young Jim Neidhart had already lived a colourful life when he arrived in Calgary. An All-American football and track star, he was raised in California where, like Stu Hart, he excelled in every sport he tried. He attended university on athletic scholarships, but excess eventually caught up with him and he careened out of control. After getting drunk and trashing a yacht club in San Francisco, he was convicted of vandalism. Still, the "big rhino" had charm and Stu Hart liked him.

When Neidhart was cut by the Dallas Cowboys in 1979, he hooked up with Mike LaBell, a Los Angeles wrestling promoter. LaBell suggested he try pro-wrestling, and sent him to Mallon Wilts, who had coached Neidhart with the San Diego Chargers. Wilts knew just the man to train him. He called Stu Hart.

Stu and Calgary represented a fresh start for a man who had a well-earned reputation for being hard to handle. In May of 1979 *Washington Post* staff writer Barry Lorge discussed Neidhart in the first of his series of articles about drug use in sports:

> In track and field, the classic case is that of Jim Neidhart, a Californian who became accustomed to popping a few uppers before every track meet in Long Beach, where he was the leading high school shot-putter in the country in 1973. He increased his drug intake during an ill-fated college career and went on several legendary drug-induced rampages.
>
> The most notorious came after the 1976 Pacific-Eight conference championships at Berkeley. Neidhart of UCLA, favoured to win the shot put, came in a disappointing second. Already fortified by

Lord of the Ring

a massive dose of amphetamine, he "unwound" with tranquillizers and alcohol and then, in the words of a witness, "just went berserk."

Neidhart, who weighed more than 300 pounds, practically dismantled his motel room, then tied four bed sheets together, strapped a fire extinguisher on his back and leapt Tarzan-style off a fourth floor balcony. Instead of swinging to another balcony, however, his arc sent him crashing through a plate glass window and into a first-floor room. UCLA wound up with a $5,500 bill.

When Neidhart arrived in Calgary he was shocked. Having spoken to Stu and Helen on the phone he had painted an erroneous picture of the couple. Stu's Saskatchewan drawl had evoked the image of a Vegas huckster/con-man. Helen hadn't fared much better. Her New York accent had convinced Jim he was talking to a former showgirl. Seeing them in the flesh he was confronted by the exact opposite of what he had imagined. Helen was a gentle, kind and very private woman who mothered everyone around her, while her husband came across like the home-spun country boy the huckster cons. And then Stu took the young athlete to the Dungeon. Neidhart is one of the very few wannabes who did not wither in the face of Stu's punishing training. A month after he'd started, Neidhart had already learned a great deal, and earned the legend's respect. He spent as much time as he could in the Dungeon, eventually learning to endure and cope with remarkable levels of pain.

Stu recalls working over Jim Neidhart for the first time. A

Stu Hart

cocky 24-year-old, ready to take on the world, the look on his face said everything: he was sceptical about combat with a man more than twice his age.

"I started out by telling Jim to try whatever he wanted. He immediately tried to grab me but that was not successful. I made him come to me, then I trapped him and got him down and put his head so he could have bitten his own bellybutton. I put his feet above his head, head on his chest, arms and elbow above his head. I twisted his head sideways. After a few minutes, Jim realized he had the real McCoy."

The two worked out regularly. The more Stu experimented, the more Jim wanted. "He yelled a lot. Sometimes, I had to revive him, walk him around the room if the holds were too hard. After two or three hours of this, he'd lay on a bench and sweat it out."

Bruce, by this time in his late 20s, was already developing into a next generation promoter. He saw potential fun in Jim's in-ring persona and convinced Neidhart to dye his brown hair blonde. The bathroom dye job didn't go well and Jim's hair turned a sickly green. Stu was livid; Bruce had turned his All-American track and football star, his "big butternut pig" — as Ellie describes him — into a green-haired clown.

Soon, Jim was smitten with Ellie; but Ellie, in her fourth year of studies at the Alberta College of Art, took little notice. She told her father, always her confidante, that she wasn't interested in Neidhart at all.

"How could I be, Dad? He takes up half the elevator," she said.

Eventually, Jim won her over. They married and had three beautiful, talented, daughters. He was picked up by the WWF and became "the Anvil" and, with Bret, one half of the original Hart Foundation.

Ellie and Jim had a tumultuous relationship and in 1999 they separated. Their most significant problem was Jim's substance

Lord of the Ring

abuse, which Ellie chronicled in court documents at the time of their dramatic split. Everything came to a head when Jim attempted to remove an antique piano from their house and Ellie had to acquire a court order to thwart his plans. Jim returned to the States to work as a talent scout and recruiter for the WWF but, according to Ellie, with his mother's death in the fall of 2000, he gravitated back to Calgary, reuniting his family after promising he had changed his ways. Stu was relieved when Jim finally decided to settle down and take some responsibility for his family, but it quickly became clear that Jim was not going to earn a living wrestling. In his mid-40s, past his athletic peak, he's found only sporadic opportunities in Australia and Europe.

Hart House has always been a magnet for fans and tourists. For years there have been calls and visits from complete strangers. Remarkably, the Harts have greeted each claim of friendship or association graciously. Completely unexpected drop-ins became expected. One summer day in the early '80s a big yellow chartered bus pulled up. A large group of Kenyan missionaries stepped out. They knew that Stu and Bret Hart lived in Calgary and their driver happened to know how to get to the house. Ellie remembers coming home and finding her father surrounded by a crowd of strangers, many of whom who spoke only Swahili. Still, Stu entertained the best he could.

Sometimes there would be just so many visitors that Helen would yearn for peace and privacy. Once, unable to deal with the thought of another drop-in and believing she was the only one who heard the doorbell, Helen ignored the ringing. When Stu wandered by and heard the door, he ushered the visitor in. Trapped in her own home and unable to face another awkward, protracted conversation, Helen dove under the burgundy-clothed dining room table. She thought she'd been undetected, and believed Stu would send the guest on his way in a few minutes. But then Stu and the man sat down at the table to talk; Helen could see their feet.

"Why doesn't Stu make some excuse and get rid of him?" she wondered.

The men talked endlessly. Worse, the troupe of family dogs discovered and joined her under the table. They licked her and wagged their tails in her face— she tried to discreetly push them away only to have them immediately return. Helen was trapped for at least an hour as the men droned on about what she considered nothing more than more sports drivel. When Stu's guest finally departed, Helen climbed out and told Stu what she thought about the quality of his conversation. Stu simply stared at her and asked, incredulous: "What were you doing under there?"

Stu has been described as "walking kindness," and he's always patiently entertained anyone who wandered into or called Hart House. To get a little peace, he and Helen developed a code. If she had reached her limit and needed to break up a chat or lengthy telephone call, she would walk up to her husband, put her hand on his shoulder or arm and say, "Boris K. Fabian is on the other line dear. He really needs to speak with you." Taking his cue, Stu would end the conversation.

Bruce finished his education degree at the University of Calgary in 1973 and began teaching as well as helping to run the promotion. When he married Andrea Redding, Stampede Wrestling was having its share of troubles. Eileen Simpkins O'Neill recalls helping to decorate the old mansion for the service. Everyone decided that baby's breath, tied with blue ribbon, would look pretty. Stu was dispatched to Edworthy Park with a large garbage bag to collect the flowers that grew there wild. But he had no idea what baby's breath was, and he didn't want to rock the boat by asking. He returned with several huge bags full of tumble weed and wild

Lord of the Ring

grasses — and managed to inadvertently pick up enough baby's breath to do the trick. The sorting of the baby's breath from the weeds was a chore for several pairs of hands, but Eileen recalls the stunning effect the tiny white blossoms had at the ceremony.

By '77, the promotion had become so sluggish and the talent trove so depleted that Stu toyed with the idea of selling out to Bud and Ray Osborne, two wrestlers who had turned to selling real estate. To show Stu they were serious, the Osbornes put up some land at Smoky Lake as a non-refundable deposit. The feeling was the last days of Stampede Wrestling had arrived.

Watching this unfold, Bruce decided to do something he had wanted to do for a long time: he went to Europe. He had always wanted to travel, and he made the most of the trip by taking on a wrestling gig with Joint Promotions in London, England. As "Bronco Bruce Hart," with a cowboy billing, fringed jacket, chaps and Stetson, he attracted a lot of overseas attention.

Bruce was intrigued by the weight-class divisions of European wrestling. The concept made sense: it gave smaller wrestlers a chance to participate and shine. The ones he watched and performed with were skilled, sophisticated and phenomenal actors.

In Chester he met a skinny kid named Tom Billington. Billed as the "Dynamite Kid," the 18-year-old wrestled like no one Bruce Hart had seen before. Part grappler, part acrobat, his high flying drove crowds wild. He bounced all over the ring, fast and clean. There was a lot more to his style than brute strength, but there was that, too. To Hart, Dynamite was revolutionizing pro-wrestling; at the same time, he was a low-key young man whose ego was definitely in check. Bruce made mental notes and on his return to Calgary quizzed his father about whether the promotion was going to continue. The real estate market had collapsed while he was away, which meant the Osbornes were no longer in a position to buy. Stu was simply carrying on, much to the disappointment of

Helen, who by this time, was sick of the business.

Bruce was elated. He immediately told his father about the young wrestler he'd met in England, arguing that he was just what they needed to revitalize the territory. Bringing over Tom Billington, he believed, would change everything. Stu resisted. Sometimes getting him to try something new was like trying to get him to buy a new Toyota instead of an old Cadillac: it wasn't necessarily going to happen. Terrible gates, however, bolstered Bruce's argument. The promotion was barely surviving with Stampede's stable of old crowbars.

In April 1978, Stu finally agreed to bring in Tom Billington. When Dynamite Kid joined the promotion, crowd reaction turned from ennui to enthusiasm almost overnight. The young wrestler was determined to make an impression, and he did just that by doing what he did best. A few years later his younger cousin, Davey Boy Smith, arrived as well, and together they would dazzle crowds in North America and become huge stars in Japan as the "British Bulldogs."

Bruce says that his brother Bret was influenced by both Billington's style and the reaction he was getting from fans. Bret wasn't taking wrestling seriously at the time, unable to identify with the rest of Stu's talent. They were boring; Dynamite was fresh, creative and electrifying. By the time Billington arrived Bret had dropped out of a journalism certificate program at Mount Royal College and was ready for something to fire his imagination.

Bruce recalls Bret and Smith heading off to Puerto Rico — they'd arranged a few matches to pay for their trip. When they returned, Bret started working out with Dynamite. Wrestling Billington was a revelation, like driving a turbo-charged Grand Am instead of a '59 Chevy.

And Dynamite was a true professional. He made everyone he worked with look good. Suddenly Bret Hart was shining. The

Lord of the Ring

change was not lost on Stu, and soon they were wrestling each other in front of Stampede crowds. Bret's maintained that he has always worked to make other wrestlers look just as good as Billington had made him appear in the those years.

Dynamite stood out for his size alone. Over time, however, he grew self-conscious about his gangly body and five-foot-nine stature and started to bulk up with pharmaceutical help, eventually reaching 210 pounds. He broke his chronically fragile back at the age of 27, ending his career bitter, regretful and wheelchair bound. His cousin, Davey Boy Smith, says Dynamite no longer even speaks of wrestling and has burned all his memorabilia.

By 1979 business had revived. Ed Whalen returned to the Stampede Wrestling fold after a three-year absence. Bruce was helping out with bookings and general operations. He was creative, if not, at times, a bit over the top, because he wanted to test the limits of the program. Bruce was also doing some serious wrestling.

In '79, Bruce Hart won the Commonwealth mid-heavyweight belt, and then in 1980 he followed up by taking the World mid-heavyweight title in a hometown match. He picked up the Open championship by besting Rocky Johnson, father of the WWF's "the Rock," in Hawaii, and the mid-heavyweight title, again, in Hanover, Germany, later the same year. In 1982 he shared the tag-team championship with Davey Boy Smith; he regained the Commonwealth title in 1983 in Antigua; and in 1984 he won the mid-heavyweight South Pacific title in Auckland, New Zealand. He won that belt in an arduous, hard-fought tournament, which took place over a two month period, in both Australia and New Zealand. Ric Flair and Harley Race were also contenders.

In 1980, Bruce worked with Peter Maivia, grandfather of "the Rock," in Hawaii, and got a chance to experiment. But things were unravelling again for Stampede Wrestling. Bret and Keith were wrestling in Japan and South East Asia, the Dynamite Kid had injured his knee and Helen was once more advocating that Stu shut everything down.

Stu called Bruce. After much stalling, he said, "Tiger wants to shut it down. Do you think we have enough to sustain the next few months?"

Bruce told Stu that if he shut it down, there may be nothing left to rebuild. He also assured his aging father that they had enough to carry on. Stu gave Bruce the go-ahead: "See what *you* can do." It was as much of an endorsement as Stu was able to give.

Bruce returned to Canada and quickly developed a plan to reinvigorate the lackluster promotion. Borrowing from the Europeans, he instituted a new weight-class and championship and built up the division until the title could be awarded at the 1982 Stampede. "The Mid-Heavyweight Title" would be contested in Calgary — Smith helped out by designing the new belt, having it made in the nearby bedroom community of Cochrane.

In June, Bruce started booking matches to lead up to the title confrontation. He convinced Dick Steinborn to defend the belt. They manufactured a little history: the "title" had been won, the story went, in a hard-fought battle in some obscure place overseas. The story was vague enough that the media never bothered to check it out.

Bruce planned to give Dynamite the win. The fans would love it, naturally, because he was already unbelievably popular. But Dynamite didn't want the belt. At the time he was trying to develop villain-persona possibilities, and taking a title that required a wrestler to be a role model/babyface wasn't appealing. Nothing could persuade him. Finally, Dynamite told Bruce it would be better for business if *he* fought Steinborn in the big showdown.

A world title had never changed hands in western Canada.

Lord of the Ring

The NWA still controlled the heavyweight belt and it was recognized all over the United States, Japan and Europe. And while the favourites in western Canada were allowed to get close, with very few exceptions the championship stayed in the States. The match was set up to look like Steinborn would win, and then at the last moment the little guy from western Canada prevailed. The David and Goliath story helped turn Stampede Wrestling back into a moneymaker. Other promoters started sending their talent up to wrestle again. All of a sudden, the attitude was: "Those guys have a world belt; they must be good."

Bruce's direction revitalized a promotion which had changed very little over the years. Then something else happened that created even more excitement.

Stu was sitting in his living room when a yellow taxi pulled into the drive. Three distinguished looking gentlemen stepped out. At the door, they introduced themselves as the Prime Minister of Antigua, a Senator and the Minister of Justice. Stu, not sure what the visit was all about, invited them inside.

The Antiguans were there to convince Stu to bring Stampede Wrestling to their island. They wanted his wrestlers to put on at least two shows over an eight-day period, in both Antigua and the nearby French Island of Guadeloupe. To help convince Stu that there was fan support in the Caribbean, they pulled out a cassette and played a Reggae song that was, at the time, a local radio hit. The tune's chorus — "We love Stampede Wrestling, We love Stampede Wrestling" — was convincing. They wanted the Harts. The Antiguans offered to pay the wrestlers' salaries, hotels and fares — the gate would be shared.

Stu rounded up his cast: Dynamite, Bret, Bruce, Rick Myers, Jim Neidhart, Kerry Brown, Danny Davis, David Shultz, Charles Buffong, The Great Gama and referee Cedric Hathaway. The ring announcer, of course, would be Ed Whalen.

Whalen recalled the huge crowd that greeted them as the plane arrived. Thousands of screaming fans jammed the runways. The announcer assumed there was a celebrity on board. When the troupe got off the plane, they quickly realized that the fans were there for them. They tried to act like it was an everyday occurrence. Whalen himself was mobbed and he said it gave him a taste of the what rock stars must experience. As the heels and babyfaces made their way into the arrivals area, they started shoving, throwing chairs and putting on a show. The Prime Minister, there to greet them, had to dodge flying objects as Stu Hart yelled for everyone take it easy.

The police had to break things up when the fans threatened to get in on the action. The Antiguan organizers loved the escapade and Stampede Wrestling sold out every show, bringing in gates of $100,000 a night on cards that featured only 10 wrestlers.

Events like the Antigua gig helped, but Bruce is convinced Stu couldn't fully appreciate what he had in his hand at the time. As a territory, the Caribbean was unmined, but then the U.S. invasion of Grenada made North Americans hesitate about travelling in the region.

Still, in 1982 the promotion was once again healthy. New challenges, however, were on the horizon. A name from Stu's past was about to resurface: Vince McMahon, Jr.

Eight

By 1982 Stampede Wrestling was feeling real pressure from Vince McMahon Jr.'s World Wrestling Federation. McMahon took over from his father, who eventually succumbed to cancer. Combining his experience as a rock promoter with a genetic understanding of pro-wrestling, he turned his promotion into a national concern. Independents like Stampede Wrestling grew more fragile by the year.

But there were pressures even before McMahon made his move. By the late '70s, Stu was carrying a large and growing payroll. Many of his own children — Smith, Bruce, Keith, Wayne (who had taken out a referee licence) and Bret — were employed by Stampede Wrestling, as were Stu's three sons-in-law: Ben Bassarab, Jim Neidhart and Davey Boy Smith. Ben was a strong, capable wrestler but once he and Alison were divorced he found himself out of the picture.

Bruce's ideas pushed scripts into new, creatively wild turns. Storylines became bloodier and even refereeing became a scripted part of the show. Fans were as enthusiastic as ever, but soon the Boxing and Wrestling Commission, renewing its desire to police wrestling, had real, meaty ammunition to work with.

Stu Hart

Despite Bruce's successes, Stu was reluctant to loosen his grip on a promotion he had shepherded for four decades. It wasn't a question of trust; Stu was simply happy with old, comfortable strategies. But by the early '80s, Bruce had established a working relationship with Vancouver-based agent Bruce Allen, who represented Canadian-based rock stars like Bryan Adams and Tom Cochrane. Later, he would also represent Bret Hart. Bruce Hart and Bruce Allen collaborated to create a blend of rock and wrestling that began to take off in Vancouver. The results for the younger Hart were exhilarating. Suddenly, there was hope that the big money would return.

Even with all the attempts to revive Stampede Wrestling and the constant search for new venues, Stu's roller coaster ride had lasted for years. The promotion was gradually eating up his real estate assets — Stu liquidated them to pay his wrestlers. Carrying a $10,000 a week payroll when arenas were only half full took its toll.

Stu began to seriously consider getting out. Helen truly hated the business by this time and was sick of watching the family nest egg shrink week by week.

While the promotion foundered, Stu also lost a good deal of money on an apartment building that Smith had talked him into buying. Stu had made the investment trusting Smith's assurances that he would be able to manage it and keep it profitable. The collapse of this venture could not have come at a worse time. Stu was forced to sell the property when it was overrun by squatters and drug dealers. The Calgary Police were watching the building closely and Stu, realizing that no one was actually supervising the apartments — or even collecting rent — sold and took heavy losses on his investment.

Worse, the Calgary Boxing and Wrestling Commission was making it very difficult for Stampede Wrestling to operate on any level. Gordon Grayston, who had been for many years one of Stu

Lord of the Ring

Hart's top referees, had become Commission chair. Grayston had won the Canadian light-heavyweight boxing title and fought professionally in New York. Like Stu, he had returned to Canada after finding success in America, but his attempt to make a boxing promotion a going concern failed. Grayston looked at Stampede Wrestling, especially in its heyday, with very green eyes. He seemed to believe Stu's successes should have been his own.

When Grayston couldn't find work after the collapse of his promotion in the early '60s, it was Stu who came to his aid, lent him money and hired him as both a wrestler and referee. But instead of appreciating the help Hart provided, Grayston became resentful.

Former Calgary Mayor Rod Sykes smiles and shakes his head when he remembers, from his own time as chairman of the Commission (a position traditionally held by the mayor until the early '80s), Grayston as a referee. Fan complaints still on file point to his failure to "see" foreign objects. Sykes, tongue-in-cheek, responded to the complaints by demanding that Grayston produce a certificate from an optometrist — to prove that he had adequate eyesight before returning to the ring. Grayston fumed, but produced the paperwork.

Later, after Grayston was appointed chair, the Commission became financially vindictive. Sykes attributes this to Grayston's thinly disguised attempts to even "old scores."

Stu agrees. He was shocked by Grayston's attitude, and his wrestlers began spending an inordinate amount of time appearing before the Commission. It got so bad, Stu became a familiar face at City Hall; his Monday mornings were spent there, clearing the fines levied on the previous Friday's Pavilion action.

At one point, Stu almost lost his licence. Calgary lawyer Ed Pipella recalls the controversy: it involved some phony daggers fashioned by a few wrestlers. They were a bit too convincing, pretending to knife each other. The media turned the storyline into a scandal, editorializing on the use of lethal "weapons" in the ring.

The Boxing and Wrestling Commission pounced.

Stu was summoned to City Hall and asked to explain himself. Sensing his licence might be in jeopardy, he had Pipella represent him. It was a kangaroo court and the charges were ludicrous. Pipella insisted that legal procedures be followed and for Hart to be given an opportunity to have a full and proper hearing. He also insisted that a court reporter be present because the accusations were being embellished almost by the minute. What he asked for was common to legal proceedings but foreign for the Commission. The lawyer finally refused to proceed unless a court reporter was present. When the penny-pinching body realized it might be on the hook for the court reporter's fee, they suggested the hearing be adjourned — so they could mull over the evidence more fully. A week later a letter arrived on Pipella's desk saying they'd dropped the case altogether.

By late 1983 Stampede Wrestling and the Commission were at war. Stu had paid a considerable amount in fines by this time, and he had to spend even more to battle other promoters who tried to move on his territory by applying to the Commission, in secret, for licences.

Stu Hart was not the only one who had to contend with interlopers. Dory Funk Sr. had to deal with similar things in Texas. Funk's direct and unmistakably blunt method of taking care of competitors has become legendary.

A would-be promoter named Al Lovelock wanted Funk to cut him into the action — he pushed and threatened until, finally, Funk had enough. The Amarillo promoter pulled Lovelock from his car and punched him out — in front of his wife. "Don't kill him, don't kill him!" she screamed. He stopped. Temporarily. Funk then jumped into his own car and attempted to run

Lord of the Ring

Lovelock down. After word spread, Funk no longer had to worry about anyone trying to move in.

Strong-arm tactics weren't Stu's style. When usurpers turned up, he invariably relied on his deep community roots and history of charitable work to solidify his place as the only licensed promoter in Alberta. An incident involving Bad News Allen and Archie "the Stomper" Gouldie, however, would all but cripple Stampede Wrestling.

Allen Coage, a big, good-looking African American wrestling under the name "Bad News Allen," took great pleasure in using his considerable talents to wind up the crowd. He was already established when he debuted for Stu in 1982, having earned a formidable reputation in America. Allen had instructed the New York Police Department in martial arts after winning a bronze medal in judo for the United States in 1976. A tough individual, he relished every minute in the ring.

In 1983, Bad News Allen was slated for a major grudge match with Gouldie. It was part of a plan to turn "the Stomper," a long-established heel, into a babyface. The idea was to show Gouldie being "victimized" by Allen, and the build-up would be slow but powerful.

During a bout that fall, Allen pulled a fork from his tights and appeared to dig into Gouldie. In truth, the tines had been bent back and the fork was incapable of harming anyone. The Boxing and Wrestling Commission did not examine the evidence closely and suspended Allen for three months. Stu Hart had to appeal the decision and then deal with one of his biggest stars being out of circulation. The Commission reduced the suspension after Stu's lawyer applied pressure, but the impact, on a program that developed week by week, was major.

A few months later, Gouldie, as scripted, was "knocked out" when Allen jumped him. While Gouldie was lying on the mat feigning unconsciousness, another wrestler, who was playing the part of Gouldie's fictional son "Jeff," ran into the ring to aid his "father." The storyline then had Allen "breaking" Jeff's neck — "paralysing" him in the ring. The spot was well executed. A phony ambulance arrived and a big deal was made about getting "Jeff" on a stretcher and off to hospital. It looked real and many bought it, hook, line and sinker. As soon as he was out of the building, however, the wrestler who played "Jeff" hailed a taxi and headed to the airport to catch a flight home to Missouri.

When Gouldie "regained consciousness," he picked himself up and, still groggy, discovered what had happened to his "son." And then he went berserk. The Stomper kicked over chairs and threw them wildly, although away from where fans were seated. He put on such a convincing performance that a number of people were truly terrified. They hurried for the exits because "Archie Gouldie's gone completely crazy." The frenzied crowd knocked a young female fan, who was standing on a chair to get a better view, to the floor. She panicked as the mob converged, sprained her ankle and required first aid treatment. *Real* paramedics attended to her.

By this point ring announcer Ed Whalen had already made it clear that he was not comfortable with Allen. The American was too aggressive, domineering, belligerent and hard to control. After what took place, Whalen again reached his boiling point. He grabbed the microphone and told the crowd that he was quitting. At the time no one thought anything of it — Whalen was capable of stirring up the fans in his own right, and had previously "quit" the promotion only to return. But by '83 the popular announcer had begun working with the Calgary Flames of the NHL, and was truly weary of the in-ring nastiness.

Grapplers had been taping razor blades to their fingers to draw blood and add to the appearance of carnage for years. In the old

Lord of the Ring

days, a little juice added to the "reality" of the match. In the early '80s, the violence escalated and the "injuries" became more severe. Some nights the bloodbath was starting to sicken the fans. Whalen felt it was unsavoury, not to mention unnecessary.

To Stu's dismay, when the videotape of the Allen-Gouldie incident was edited for Saturday afternoon television, Whalen insisted that his own resignation be included. He was serious. The timing couldn't have been worse. Actually, there would never really be a good time for Whalen to leave. Fans were accustomed to his affable hayseed twang and homespun phrases. His persona was such a big part of Stampede Wrestling that the promotion was bound to founder upon his departure — whether notice was given or not.

Some Calgarians actually believed that the wrestler who played Gouldie's son "Jeff" was really the Stomper's child, and that he'd had been paralysed. When no "Jeff" had been admitted to any of the Calgary-area hospitals, it was assumed that he had been spirited away. The events of that Friday night were the talk of the town. Years later, many still held the view that Stu Hart had hustled the boy out so he wouldn't die in his territory.

The build-up to the big grudge match had worked too well. The Boxing and Wrestling Commission pounced, as if everything was "real."

The re-match between Bad News Allen and Gouldie was slated for the following Friday. More than 2,000 people lined up outside the Victoria Pavilion. But the Boxing and Wrestling Commission padlocked the doors, turned the fans away, fined Bad News and Stu, and suspended the promotion's licence for six months. Stu eventually had it re-instated by court order, but by then the damage had been done.

While the suspension was in force, Stu tried to carry on at the Sarcee Seven Chiefs Sportplex on the Tsuu T'ina (Sarcee) Indian Reserve, adjacent to the City of Calgary. The reserve, as federal jurisdiction, was out of the reach of the City's Boxing and Wrestling Commission. But fans who were long accustomed to the Pavilion and Corral did not support the change of venue.

In one of the worst predicaments of his lengthy career, desperate, Stu brought back Sam Menacker to replace Whalen. It was a disaster. By this time, Menacker was elderly, completely out of touch with contemporary wrestling and unable to follow the spots. His commentary lagged behind in-ring action, and he had trouble remembering the names of the wrestlers.

When Menacker returned, Helen produced a cake decorated with the words "Play It Again Sam." Sam couldn't even remember the tune.

Bruce Hart grew impatient. He and some of his brothers argued with Sam about the way bookings were being handled. Creative control was at stake, and soon the Hart brothers were bickering among themselves. Sam, in Bruce's eyes, was a has-been. What was his father thinking? Stu, however, could only remember the Menacker of the golden days.

Handcuffed bureaucratically, even temporarily, Stu still had a payroll to meet. At least 25 wrestlers collected guaranteed salaries, plus there was transportation costs for them and expenses for additional wrestlers. Fans weren't sure how to get to the Sarcee Sport-plex. Stu chartered a bus or two, but the efforts weren't enough to keep the stands filled. Financially, Stampede Wrestling was bled dry. When his licence was re-instated, Stu returned to the Pavilion, but with a much diminished product.

The stress took its toll on the Harts. Stu was approaching 70 and Helen wanted out. Stu quietly pursued the possibility of selling and retiring. He and Helen knew that any open discussion of their plans would be met with strong opposition from Bruce. They decided to handle negotiations without him. In fact, most of the children were kept in the dark.

Lord of the Ring

In September 1984, Bruce Hart turned on the TV to catch the 6 p.m. news before he wandered down to the Pavilion. He was euphoric after a success he'd just manufactured in Vancouver's Pacific Coliseum. Stampede Wrestling had attracted a healthy gate, and he was trying to convince Stu that the promotion's slump was about to end. He was creating new audiences for wrestlers like his brothers, Dynamite Kid, Davey Boy Smith, Bad News Allen and Rotten Ron Starr.

Bruce eased into a chair, wondering if the local sportscast would promo that night's card. Instead, what he watched left him speechless. He leaned forward as the sportscaster said the night's match would be Stampede Wrestling's last. The promotion was shutting down after nearly 35 years of operation.

It had been sold to the World Wrestling Federation.

When the piece was over, Bruce, in shock, grabbed the telephone. He dialled Hart House, but there was no one home. He checked the time and hurried down to the Pavilion. The wrestlers were pacing, debating the news. Was it really true, had Stu Hart sold Stampede Wrestling to Vince McMahon Jr. and the WWF? Bruce was as confused as they were.

Stu did not arrive until halfway through the program and was braced for an angry barrage from his son. He calmly replied: "It's my promotion, I'll do what I want with it."

He had sold the promotion and Bruce had been kept out of the loop deliberately. Keith had handled the negotiations. A teacher and a firefighter, with his own long history in the business, Keith was realistic. He understood how his parents, especially his mother, felt about the struggling business. Both Stu and Helen knew they could rely on their third-oldest son to help them through deep waters. They also knew there would be strong opposition from within their brood, especially from Bruce, who had put in hundreds of hours trying to revitalize the operation. They recognized Bruce's successes in Vancouver and the B.C. interior, but they also knew there were never guarantees in wrestling. Stu and Helen were convinced that the time to retire was upon them.

Stu had analysed the situation carefully. Vince McMahon was lining up the TV time across North America and picking up talent from the NWA. Running a weekly television show out of the Garden wasn't enough; he wanted his product to be available to everyone. And as he had done with some of the other important NWA territories, he went after Stampede Wrestling and its potentially lucrative TV spots and audience. It wouldn't be long before he'd take the best of its talent into the WWF fold as well. Regional operations just wouldn't be able to compete. With the advent of satellite technologies, an international fan-base was inevitable.

Had Stampede Wrestling not overextended itself, put so many Harts and their spouses on the payroll or carried such a large stable of wrestlers, and if Stu had not suffered other financial pressures, he might have been able to withstand the Boxing and Wrestling Commission's devastating vendetta. He might have been able to hang onto his lucrative television spots, promotion material rights and faithful fans. But the events of late '83 and early '84 left him vulnerable. He made his decision hoping that his sons would make the big time with the WWF. Working for McMahon would be a smart career move for Bret, Davey Boy Smith and Jim Neidhart. Dynamite Kid (Tom Billington) was ready, too.

Stu was right, of course. They all succeeded.

In the aftermath of Stampede Wrestling's demise, Bruce reluctantly agreed to meet with Vince's people to discuss joining the WWF creative team. But Bruce wasn't comfortable with the attitude of McMahon's representatives. They didn't think Stampede Wrestling was up to speed. And, in his mind, the WWF had a "sorry set" of wrestlers at the time — nothing compared to

Lord of the Ring

the product Stampede Wrestling was regularly offering.

Stu says the deal he made with the WWF stipulated that he would be paid 10 per cent of the gate in any city within his old territory, and that he would receive $100,000 up front. It would amount to a million-dollar agreement over time. Stu and Helen would be able to retire and relax, travel as they had always planned. The only problem? Nothing was actually put on paper. After the fact, the two sides had very different ideas about what had been agreed upon.

Whatever the deal was, it left an unpleasant taste in Bruce's mouth. He couldn't believe that he had been shut out. It left him angry and bitter, and he couldn't understand why he was being treated like an unruly child. To his credit, Bruce did not allow what he saw as unfair treatment to alienate him from the family. He was man enough to accept his father's decision, and in time he let it go.

Bruce's initial concerns about the sale would prove to be justified. Stu says he was never remunerated. Over time, he and Helen were invited to participate in several Pay-Per-View angles involving Bret, Owen and the Hart Foundation, but it was a far cry from the deal he thought he had.

Stu says Vince phoned a year later and told him that fulfilling their bargain wasn't feasible, and that he would have no objections to Stampede renewing operations. But by this time, the WWF had all of Stu's top talent and television spots. There was nothing left to rebuild.

Stu did not mention their handshake arrangement. Perhaps Vince knew Stu Hart well enough to understand that he would not press the issue, especially because his sons and sons-in-law were rising WWF stars.

To ease the financial crunch, Stu pursued the possibility of developing the four-acre parcel of land isolated from the rest of his original property by the construction of Sarcee Trail. He recalls

Stu Hart

being told in the '60s, as he was being pressured to give up land to the city for the freeway, that he would not have any trouble developing the acreage when he was ready. Thirty years later, when he decided the time for development had come, he discovered that he did not hold water rights. The city refused to zone it for development. Stu has been pressed on numerous occasions to donate his nest egg to the city in exchange for a tax receipt. He'd been assured that the land would become part of Edworthy Park. Suspicions arose among the Hart siblings, however, given the family's history with local politicians and developers, that someone else wanted the four acres. If it ended up in the wrong hands, the land might find its way to developers who would slap up a condo complex. They knew Stu Hart wouldn't see a dime of that either.

To get around the restrictions, negotiations were initiated with Paul Funk, a developer who was interested in Hart House — by this time a heritage building — as a community centre in a condo community. If Stu sold the house and the five acres it commanded to the developer, he would then be able to share water rights on land Funk owned near Stu's property and development could then proceed.

Reluctantly, Stu gave Funk a legal option to purchase Hart House for $850,000. In 1998, when Funk tried to exercise his option, the family resisted. Stu was heartsick and wondered what would become of his "girls" — the six antique chandeliers. By mid-1999, Funk decided against proceeding and turned his attentions elsewhere. The option lapsed. Stu's four acres east of Sarcee Trail are among the few remaining undeveloped parcels in west Calgary.

Bored with quiet retirement, in 1985 Stu decided to join forces with Bruce and re-launch Stampede Wrestling. At the same time Bret and the "Hart Foundation" ascended towards WWF superstardom.

Lord of the Ring

Without the drawing power of their wrestling family, Stu and Bruce knew starting over meant facing seemingly insurmountable odds. The WWF had changed everything. The NWA had essentially become a single promotion in the Carolinas, and wrestlers worked exclusively. Few believed that the matches were real by this point, and in a few years time Vince would make this explicit by renaming his product "sports entertainment." Wrestling would become a dirty word.

Bruce started to scout talent again and trained potential wrestlers, keeping close watch, especially, on some of the guys who came up from the States to play in the CFL. Slowly, the talent base was replenished. Owen, too, began taking an interest in the family business. Being a Hart, he was already a relatively seasoned performer.

Sometime in 1987, Keith Hart took an interesting call from a football player named Brian Pillman.

Pillman had been trying to make it as a linebacker with the Calgary Stampeders. But things didn't work out and he was cut. He had heard about the Harts through another player, Stu Laird, who was quite familiar with the family's reputation in pro-wrestling. Pillman called Keith to talk wrestling and shortly after that he met Bruce. Bruce agreed to train him. Pillman thrived, and eventually became Bruce's tag team partner.

Pillman was a naturally strong, charismatic wrestler, with a penchant for the outrageous. The fans took to him easily. Pillman also liked to lecture to young people about staying in school and avoiding drugs: he had an endearing naivety, and it made him a prime candidate for elaborately contrived Hart family pranks. The ribs had grown in complexity since the boys' childhood, and by the late '80s there were few, if any, limits.

Bruce recalls a Saskatchewan junket in particular, heading for

Stu Hart

a match in the quiet, wholesome farming community of Tisdale. Travelling with him were Pillman and Owen. The youngest Hart loved pranks and was superb at both inventing and carrying them out. He knew how to nudge the rib along, anticipating what could potentially unfold, and then watching for the right opportunity to make it happen.

In Tisdale there was going to be the usual card — Pillman would then give his "Say No to Drugs and Stay in School" lecture to a community gathering.

As their vehicle approached Tisdale, located in a part of Saskatchewan known for harvesting huge quantities of the grain now known as Canola — but at the time referred to as "rapeseed" or "rape" — Pillman awoke from a sleep. Entering the town, he noticed a sign which read: "Welcome to Tisdale — The Land of Rape and Honey." Pillman, no farmer, asked: "What the hell does that mean?" The Hart brothers exchanged a knowing look and proceeded to concoct a story about Tisdale, Saskatchewan, being a place where men encouraged women to make themselves available to everyone. It didn't matter whether they were married or single, the expectations were the same. They pushed as far as they could, inspired by Pillman's incredulity. His reaction was explicit.

"That's just insane," he blurted, and then began an indignant rant about what kind of place Tisdale must be, questioning what they were they doing there in the first place.

Later, after wrestling and delivering his "Say No to Drugs" speech to a crowd of Tisdale fans, Pillman, in the gravelly, macho voice he'd developed after a series of throat surgeries he'd endured as a child fighting cancer, told the audience of men, women and children, that he had grave concerns about their cavalier attitude towards women. He went on for several minutes about the horror of allowing half their population to be so mistreated, saying that he found welcoming visitors to the land of

Lord of the Ring

"rape and honey" offensive, an insult to women everywhere. Anxious to provide as much helpful information as possible, he went on to caution his audience on the perils of multiple partner sexual relations and the diseases which could be contracted and spread throughout the community. When he finished with a carefully crafted explanation of the horrors of gonorrhea, every jaw in the audience was an inch from the floor.

It was all Bruce and Owen Hart could do to maintain their composure until they were outside. The people of Tisdale were left wondering what was wrong with Brian Pillman.

On another occasion, in Kelowna, B.C., Pillman wanted to see a woman he'd met on a previous visit. The two agreed to meet at a local club at a pre-arranged time. After checking in at the motel, Pillman, Owen, Ross Hart and a few other wrestlers piled into a van driven by Bruce. They headed for a venue in Salmon Arm, an hour's drive away. Pillman told his buddies that he wanted to cut the evening as short as possible to get back to his date. Later that night, Owen, nudging Bruce, told Pillman that he had to give his "Say No to Drugs" speech to a group of senior citizens. Owen, in his most sincere tone, said the old folks were really looking forward to it — that the wrestlers absolutely could not miss visiting them before heading back to Kelowna. Pillman, increasingly conscious of the passing time, was annoyed but agreed to make the stop, as long as they kept it short.

It never occurred to him to question why senior citizens would want to hear his anti-drug lecture.

After the match, they pulled up to a senior citizens lodge, only to find that all the lights were out. Bruce and Owen went to the door and summoned the caretaker, explaining that they had a wrestler with them who had been invited to give a talk to the seniors. The caretaker narrowed his eyes and shook his head in disbelief. Bruce using his best, innocent boy scout look, turned up the story a notch, saying that their colleague had come a long way and really needed to give his talk. The caretaker reluctantly agreed to let them in and disappeared to wake the residents. Old people shuffled down the hall to the foyer in their slippers and bathrobes, some of them pushing walkers. Pillman gave his speech to the puzzled, tired gathering, who listened politely. Owen checked his watch and, seeing that not enough time had passed, asked the caretaker: "Don't you have some tea and cookies or something around here?"

The caretaker jumped up. "Oh yes, there is some carrot cake in the refrigerator."

Out came the refreshments and the wrestlers had to stay for tea. Bruce and Owen stretched things out as much as possible. Pillman finally insisted that they head back to Kelowna, worrying about his rendezvous and repeatedly checking his watch.

Rain had set in, making the drive back slower-than-usual. When they finally arrived, Pillman ran to his room, dumped his travel bag and returned to the parking lot — only to find that the van had left without him. Bruce and Owen had gone for a pizza, leaving Ross and manager Bob Johnson at the motel to deal with Pillman. Pillman raced off in the rain on foot. By the time he got to the club, it had closed. When Bruce and Owen returned with the food they found a mangy, wet dog that looked like it hadn't eaten for a while in the parking lot. They took the animal to Pillman's room and fed it pizza while rummaging through Pillman's clothes. Before securing Pillman's sunglasses to the dog's face, they outfitted it in one of his T-shirts and draped it with his sports jacket. They then settled the dog in Pillman's bed and removed all the light bulbs from the room.

When Pillman finally returned he couldn't find the light. Finally, he propped open the door to illuminate the room from the hallway. The commotion, of course, startled the sleeping dog,

Lord of the Ring

which immediately tried to attack the intruder. Pillman ran down the hall shrieking that a dog wearing sun glasses and a sports jacket was chasing him.

Bruce says Ross, who organized the trip and was supervising the wrestler's activities, got wind of Pillman's late night adventures and reamed him out at breakfast — accusing him of "obviously doing drugs." Pillman's actions, he maintained, were totally reprehensible — especially when he was so vocal about their dangers. That Pillman stuck with his story did not help his cause.

Sadly, the man who preached the evils of addictive substances fell prey to addiction himself. Seriously injured in a motor vehicle accident in his mid-30s, Pillman developed a prescription drug habit. In his last days his behaviour became extreme and erratic. He died, overdosing on painkillers.

Bruce took on much of the leg work in the reborn promotion. Ross, who had been editing Stampede Wrestling film footage since the early 1980s, again involved himself and worked with Bruce to both promote and train new talent. Rebuilding was slow and arduous. McMahon, to his credit, allowed Bret, Davey Boy and Dynamite to appear in Stampede rings from time to time. Their presence injected enough excitement to keep things going until 1990.

At that time a conflict arose among Bruce, Keith and Bret, and the British Bulldogs. To keep the peace, Stu allowed Tom Billington to do the bookings — hoping he would be as good at running the promotion as he was at actually wrestling. He wasn't. Crowds grew thinner by the week. A serious back injury caused Dynamite to experience seizures, and he too became increasingly dependant upon pain killers.

When the bickering could not be resolved, Stu gave up. At the age of 75 he decided to shut down, again, permanently. He would participate in special events from time to time, but it would not

Stu Hart

be until May 1999, that an attempt to re-ignite interest in Stampede Wrestling would occur.

(Bruce and Ross now combine their energies. The brothers reopened Stampede Wrestling to some fanfare, and have once again put the Hart name in a promotion spotlight. The shows ran twice monthly, initially, with Friday night cards offered to modest crowds at an Ogden legion hall in southeast Calgary. It's now a weekly event. With Keith, they also opened the Hart Brothers Wrestling camp, which operates out of the infamous Dungeon.)

When Stampede Wrestling shut down for the second time, Owen, Pillman, Steve Blackman and Chris Benoit all moved on to stardom with WCW — and later with McMahon's WWF. Chris Jericho and Lance Storm, who also benefitted from the Harts' training, followed similar paths.

While the in-ring success of Bret, Owen and the Hart Foundation would make the '80s the decade in which the Hart family name known world-wide, the '90s would burden the family with multiple tragedies. The last ten years of the millennium brought Stu enough pain to last a lifetime. It all began on November 21, 1990, with the death of his son.

Dean Hart had been a source of worry for his parents since the day in 1978 when a City of Calgary Transit bus struck him. He had been waiting at a stop on 8th Avenue, by the Eaton's department store in downtown Calgary, his body positioned half on and half off the curb. Regular traffic ran one way, but buses were permitted to travel against the flow. Dean, confused by the discrepancy, was looking the wrong way when a bus hit some ice and slid into him. The accident was eerily reminiscent of his father's run-in with the fire truck in 1941. Dean was rushed to the Holy Cross Hospital, but stubbornly checked himself out before he could be thoroughly examined and treated. He arrived at Hart House with

Lord of the Ring

a terrible headache. Dean had a trip to Hawaii planned in a few days time, and nothing was going to keep him in the Canadian cold. He told his family little about the accident. His headaches persisted and he began smoking marijuana medicinally. It only masked his pain, keeping him from dealing with his injury. Later on, he went to the Foothills Hospital in Calgary. Ellie says tests showed that the accident had damaged his kidneys. She also recalled that about 18 months later, Dean, who was helping clean up after a fire, fell through the upper floor of the coach house and landed on his back. He brushed off the incident, but Ellie believes he may have further injured himself at that time.

For the next ten years, Dean lived in Hawaii. He loved the beach, warm weather and ocean. He avoided returning to Calgary, and during those years a number of fights and minor accidents further compromised his condition.

Born in 1954, Dean was an "individual" from the start. He never lacked confidence, and that sometimes landed him in trouble. Struggling through high school with help from his older brother Bruce, he loved to provoke the teaching staff at Ernest Manning, and drove around in a new cherry red '72 Eldorado Cadillac, its white top down in summer. He, too, had the Hart good looks and, with the car, was like a magnet for high school girls. Dean paid for the Caddy by saving every dime he made working night shifts at Russell Steel — which in part accounted for his less than satisfactory academic performance. He simply slept through most of his classes. Ellie says her brother — who was only one year older — was "not vain in the slightest, but oh so confident. He wouldn't blink at taking on the world."

Like his brothers, Dean had been a good amateur wrestler. He had his share of high school honours, despite his slim five-foot-eight, 160-pound frame. Too small to make wrestling a career, in the real world he never shied away from challenging bigger men.

Stu Hart

Dean's dreams did not involve wrestling, but living in paradise. He thought his desires had been granted when some Hawaiian Asians offered to let him stay in their beach house, rent free. But soon "the deal too good to be true" turned out to be just that. Somewhere along the way he discovered, to his dismay, that some of the boxes his benefactors had had him moving around in lieu of rent were full of ammunition.

The next thing he knew, the Asians were being charged with the death of the Honolulu District Attorney's son, who had been found buried on a beach, his feet protruding from the sand. The Asians thought their house guest might be persuaded to testify against them, about the ammo they had stashed and whatever other information he might have unwittingly picked up. Dean sensed what might be coming and headed for cover.

Back in Calgary, Stu and Helen started receiving strange, threatening calls from the men who were indeed looking for their son. Ugly threats poured in, with graphic details of what would happen if Dean dared to testify.

Keith remembers driving to a card in Edmonton with his father, when the RCMP pulled them over. There was a "family emergency" and Stu was asked to follow the police cruiser to a nearby detachment to phone home. Immediately, Stu thought of Dean in Hawaii.

When Stu called home, Helen told him Dean was in protective custody. A Honolulu newspaper had phoned, asking for a statement from Dean's parents about their son being a witness against the Asians. The chief of police there wanted Dean out of town for his own safety. He felt comfortable enough with the Harts to phone Stu. The police chief's son had wrestled for Stu as "King Curtis" Iaukea.

Dean returned to Calgary with a pregnant dog, Lana Keela. She had been given to him by Peter Maivia, grandfather of "the

Lord of the Ring

Rock," currently one of the WWF's biggest and most celebrated stars. Maivia had a promotion of his own and Dean had been helping out. Dean "assisted" by calling wrestlers like "Bad News" Allan Coage and convincing them to head to Hawaii. He imitated his father's voice so well the wrestlers assumed they were talking to Stu. They would travel to the island at their own expense, with "Stu's" assurances that they'd be fully reimbursed. Dean, as "Stu," promised them $1,000 a night, with return airfare and all expenses paid. The Maivias were not aware of any of this, and ultimately had to contend with outraged wrestlers who demanded everything they'd been promised. They were even angrier after learning that Stu Hart had nothing to do with it. Dean's approach had always been "the end justifies the means" — just get it done, then worry about the consequences tomorrow.

Stu was relieved when Dean was safely back in Canada, but his son couldn't be pinned down for long. After the dust settled and those who had been stalking him were safely in prison, he headed back to the islands.

Dean's health deteriorated and soon he was suffering from serious kidney dysfunction. He returned to Canada for medical care and spent the last years of his life on dialysis, waiting for a transplant. At one point, returning to his vehicle after paying a string of parking tickets, he saw his car in the process of being towed away. He ran after the tow truck, managed to get in its way, and was run over. Two broken legs only worsened his already precarious condition.

In November 1990, he was running a bath in the second-floor bathroom at Hart House. His sister Georgia, who had just arrived with Helen from a jazzercise class, heard a loud thump. Georgia and brother Smith ran upstairs and found Dean collapsed on the bathroom floor. He died at the age of 36 from a heart attack brought on by kidney failure.

Stu Hart

On July 1, 1996, a second tragedy devastated the Harts. Georgia's son, Matthew — a lively 13-year-old who loved wrestling — had been out in the yard with some of his cousins and a few other children. It was a beautiful, early summer day. The ring was set up in the yard and the kids were practising their moves. They were gearing up for the Rockyford Rodeo, which held matches featuring children, and they were excited about participating. Matthew was going to be on the card with some of his cousins.

He had already started wrestling at school, and he was becoming a strong, athletic young man. His mother and father were both physically gifted, and he came by his wrestling ability honestly as a member of both the Hart and Annis families. That day, playing, Matthew had the wind knocked out of him. Over the next several hours, he seemed slow to recover, so his mother took him to a local medical clinic. He was diagnosed with a groin injury.

Matthew's dad, B.J., was working his shift as a firefighter that night. The next day Matthew told him he had pains in his leg and that he couldn't walk. His father took his temperature and became alarmed. They immediately took him to the Alberta Children's Hospital in Calgary.

The tests taken showed that a virus had been triggered by the injury. Matthew was suffering from flesh eating disease.

The boy's condition deteriorated rapidly. His uncle Owen sat with him in the hospital, talking to him, trying to encourage him to find the strength to beat the disease spreading rapidly through his young body. He'd always loved the vintage 1967 maroon Mustang Owen kept stored in his garage. Owen promised Matthew that when he got better, the Mustang would be his.

Friends of the family tried to assist, offering prayers for the once lively youngster. Close family friend Danny McCullough, owner of Maclin Ford in Calgary, enlisted the prayers of Mother Teresa and her Sisters of Charity in Calcutta.

Lord of the Ring

On July 14, Matthew lost his battle with the devastating disease. It was a crushing blow for Georgia, B.J. and the whole family. One of the last school assignments Matthew had handed in was an essay. The theme, ironically, was "What would you do if you had three weeks left to live?" In the paper Matthew wrote that he would want his ashes sprinkled over the wrestling ring in his grandfather's yard.

Uncle Owen made sure his wishes were granted.

Nine

Montreal Gazette sports columnist Dave Stubbs was speechless. Bret Hart was one of the WWF's biggest superstars, ever, and in Stubbs view, one of pro-wrestling's greatest athletes. Now, he'd been set up.

Why?

Stubbs hadn't been following the WWF as closely since he'd given up refereeing after a six-year stint. The sideline had been a lot of fun: he'd even managed to shock his wife and friends when a wrestler dragged him into the action. It was part of the script, but those out of the loop didn't know that the sports columnist had spent several hours the day before learning how to react convincingly.

Stubbs had taken out a referee licence for his newspaper column. He planned to get the credentials, referee a couple matches for the WWF and then write a colourful piece. Getting the licence was easier than he anticipated — nothing more than a one-day training session and a written test any junior high school student could pass.

The columnist paid the $25 fee and made a mental note about the process being a sham, a way to augment fines penalizing wrestlers for "improper conduct." Few other sports have licensing requirements, but wrestling and boxing have submitted to bureaucracy, at least in Canada.

A fan as well as a columnist, Stubbs liked the circus atmosphere of wrestling, the colourful characters who showed up both inside and outside the ring. He enjoyed the bravado, the camaraderie and the macho storylines. Lately, even referees and promoters were getting in on the act. But despite the nonsense, Stubbs understood that wrestlers were also top athletes, men and women who had both the physical and artistic ability to make complicated storylines believable.

In the old days it was the Forum crowd that saw Killer Kowalski brutalizing Yukon Eric's ear. Now, the Molson Centre was the venue of choice for big house-shows and WWF Pay-Per-View events. A part of it all, Stubbs enjoyed being privy to pre-match huddles, where scripts were discussed. Including the referees had become crucial. A ref had to be in on the pre-arranged finish: he had to watch for it and know when to signal the wrestlers to "go home" — finish things up.

After filing his *Gazette* piece, Stubbs stayed on for the fun of it. Eventually his editors forced him to stop moonlighting — but that didn't stop him from sitting in the bleachers.

That's where he was on November 9, 1997. At the Molson Centre for the Survivor Series, watching five-time WWF champ Bret Hart defend his title against arch rival, Shawn Michaels.

That Bret was leaving the WWF to join WCW at the end of the year had just been made public. The Montreal event would be his penultimate Canadian WWF performance. Bret was fiercely loyal to McMahon's promotion, but was left with no alternative. Caught in the middle of a WWF/WCW bidding war, the Hitman was under considerable pressure.

He'd been offered a three-year, nine million dollar contract by Ted Turner's rival promotion, enough, certainly, to turn any

Lord of the Ring

wrestling superstar's head. Bret weighed his options and then turned the offer down, opting instead to stay with the WWF — to earn considerably less per year — for a guaranteed 20-year term. When he could no longer perform, he would be given a high profile front office position. Still, McMahon had upped the ante significantly. And either way, financially, he was in a far better position than before WCW had come calling.

Bret knew McMahon had given him his big break. Stu had secured Bret's position in the WWF, but it was Vince who pulled him out of the pack to replace the WWF's main attraction, Hulk Hogan. Bret's star ascended rapidly — helped along, of course, by his charisma, skill and good fortune.

Hogan left the WWF wounded, with a huge void to fill. He jumped ship to WCW when his relationship with McMahon soured, almost overnight, after testifying about steroid use in proceedings in which McMahon and the WWF were defendants. Hogan damaged McMahon's case and undermined his image — even though McMahon was eventually acquitted. Bret was pushed into the spotlight. Adept at making that opportunity work for both himself and the WWF, he rolled with the punches and focussed his energies on what would become a long-term project — the business of being the Hitman.

Despite his split with McMahon and Bret's newfound superstardom, the Hulkster's star never really lost its lustre. He had top billing in WCW and was popular with fans and fellow wrestlers alike. Killer Kowalski recalls being interviewed at the peak of Hogan's career. The reporter wanted to know if Kowalski could have "taken" Hogan — if the two were both in their prime. Kowalski said he would never have had a chance. One of Kowalski's friends heard the interview and challenged him, suggesting Killer had not been shooting straight, insisting that the retired legend's skills were far superior. Kowalski said there was no reason to answer the question differently: "He's at the height of his career, mine is long over. Why should I detract from his work?"

Some time later, in one of his forgettable Hollywood movies, Hogan appeared wearing an eye patch. When asked about the injury, instead of delivering his response as scripted, Hogan said: "Killer Kowalski did it."

Kowalski appreciated the classy display of "professional courtesy and camaraderie."

As the end of his long, loyal WWF career approached, Bret Hart would receive no such courtesy from McMahon. That night at the Molson Centre, Vince would "screw" Bret, spitting in the face of the deal the two had made to allow Hart to leave a company he'd literally bled for with grace and dignity.

McMahon had offered the long-term contract that would keep Bret in the WWF just as his corporation would experience a serious financial crunch. In fact, the timing couldn't have been worse. Battered in the ratings war with Turner's WCW, his number one product had slipped to number two. Then came a costly legal battle with Jesse "the Body" Ventura. Now Minnesota's flamboyant governor, the former wrestling superstar sued McMahon and Titan Sports for unpaid royalties on products bearing his likeness. Ventura won. McMahon had to pay a substantial settlement, not to mention expensive legal fees. As 1997 drew to a close he was both saddled with the Hitman's large salary and strapped for cash; Ross Hart speculates that he may also have been worried about the precedent he was setting, that he had unwittingly raised the salary bar for other superstars like Shawn Michaels and the Undertaker (Mark Calloway).

McMahon tried to renegotiate Bret's deal; the Hitman stood firm, insisting that McMahon live up to his part of the bargain — especially when he had just turned down WCW's generous offer.

Lord of the Ring

Having just won at Summer Slam, Bret was poised for another long title reign. With all this in play, McMahon may have been calling Bret's bluff, banking on both Hart's loyalty and the promise of top billing, when he encouraged him to reopen negotiations with WCW. McMahon was wrong; Bret stuck to his guns and signed with Turner. McMahon, says Ross Hart, offered to renegotiate with Bret after the new WCW deal was inked. But, having already turned them down once, and with his confidence in the future of the WWF shaken, Bret's decision to leave was final.

As the Survivor Series pay-per-vew approached, it was no secret, especially within the industry, that there was both a personal and professional rivalry between Bret and HBK — "the Heartbreak Kid," Shawn Michaels. Eight months earlier, the two had engaged in a dressing room brawl when Bret called Michaels on a personal jab. Michaels had threatened to quit WWF after the incident, irate with what he perceived as McMahon's inaction and claiming that Bret had assaulted him. The incident caused wrestlers to take sides, but everyone knew that Bret, who had the right to approve storylines written into his contract, would never have readily accepted losing his belt to Michaels, especially not "at home," in front of Canadian fans.

Whether McMahon wanted to strip Bret of the title to ensure he would join the competition as a diminished product is the stuff of speculation. But the fact is: Bret rose to the top of the WCW in no time, leaving questions about his marketability on the soles of his wrestling boots.

Strapped for cash and about to lose his biggest draw, heading towards Montreal McMahon had another problem. What do you do with a wrestler who has been a universally adored superstar for a long time but shows no sign of waning? Bret was the squeaky clean good guy, a role model for most of his career. McMahon decided that the hero persona was wearing thin — in fact, he'd argue, heels were "in." He convinced Bret to play the villain, knowing there was more leeway to vary scripts when a character was no longer a babyface.

McMahon decided that Bret, a proud Canadian, would become an America basher. Back in his early Hart Foundation days, Bret had poked some playful jabs at the United States, but cracking wise about gun control and medicare was the extent of it. At the idea of hardcore insults, Bret bristled. He was reluctant to alter his Hitman character and agonized about the ramifications, especially because his mother had been born and raised in New York and still had strong ties there. He had three aunts who lived in the States, too, and his three eldest brothers were all born while his parents were still there. The truth was, Bret liked Americans. But, the show must go on.

He compromised with McMahon, agreeing to slag Americans during matches south of the 49th parallel. In Canada, however, he would continue to play the clean-cut babyface.

Stu did not disapprove of the Hitman's new direction. From the old school, he believes the relationship between a promoter and a wrestler should be one of respect and obedience. Wrestlers were employees, and they should do what they're told. The "promoter knows best" approach was a part of the storied history of the sport. "When a promoter tells one of his wrestlers to sit on a hot stone, he is expected to do it without question," he says.

The fact that promoters like to keep the wrestlers under their thumb is also a part of the sport's legacy. Stu himself did this with his mere presence — he was that physically imposing. He also used the time-honoured technique of keeping wrestlers insecure by telling them as little as possible about long-term plans. His ace in the hole, however, was Helen. Whenever someone called in to find out about where they were going or what they would be doing, they would talk to her first. She had a way of softening

Stu and Chati Yaguchi

FOR YOUR EYES ONLY
BY STU HART

A lot of fans have wondered, and asked, if Don Gagne is any relation to Vern Gagne, one of wrestling's greats. The answer is no. There is certainly no relationship in the styles used by the two.

★

Tony Marino, normally a friendly guy, is going to be in a pretty bad humor until he gets a match with Karl Shotz and or Gil Hayes. He's aware of the remarks the two have made, saying that he wouldn't come to these parts because he was afraid to meet them. The truth, of course, is that Marino was injured in an automobile accident. This delayed his arrival for a couple of months. But the former Mr. Universe is recovered and more that anxious to prove that the likes of Shotz and Hayes don't frighten him a bit.

★

Shotz is pleased that he has the North American belt back in his possession, but can't understand why people are surprised. His reasoning is that he's the best man around, hat he's the only proper person to hold the belt and that he lost it briefly only because of some bad luck.

★

When it comes to championship thoughts, few have more than Moose Moroski. As he announced before, he pans to win both the North American and the International tag team belts According to him, it's just a case of when he makes his move. He ponts out, too, that he once fought Archie Gouldie for the North American belt and lost it only because of a "hometown decison." Says the giant Moroski: "I had him beat all the way, but there was no way that anyone was going to let Gouldie lose at home.. So they really outdecked me."

★

One of the new faces around here is a man known only as Tapu. And about all that is known about him is that he is from Figi.

★

As mentioned elsewhere, there's quite a fight coming in Japan - Muhammad Ali against Inoki, a legend in his own time even though he's only 24. I have not seen Inoki n action but many wrestlers here have been in Japan and they say that he is a superb fighter. I really wouldn't want to try to predict a winner, but in other matches where wrestlers and boxers have tangled it has always been the wrestler who has won. But then again, no wrestler has ever had to fight a boxer like Muhammad Ali.

★

Lumberjack Luke once thought of becoming a professional guide in the north. He is an experienced hunter and woodsman and enjoys being in the outdoors. But his partner backed out because of personal problems and Luke just couldn't go it alone. He is, however, still hoping.

Stu's column from *Body Press*, Official Wrestling Program,
Foothills Athletic Club

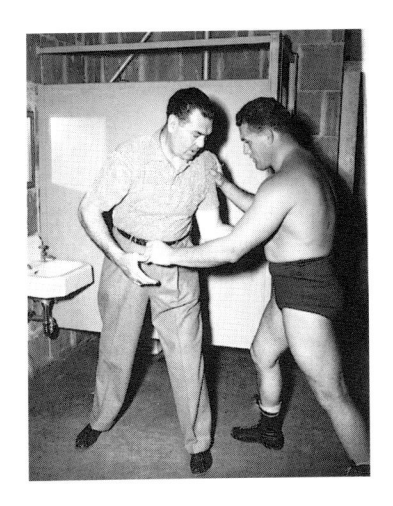

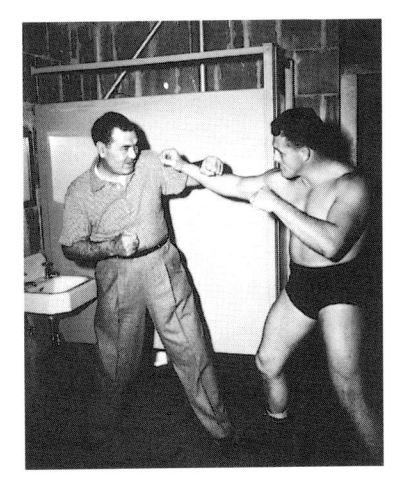

Boxer vs wrestler: Jack Dempsey and Stu Hart

Muhammad Ali and Stu Hart

Davey Boy Smith and rocker Bryan Adams

Ring official James Baker examines Owen's eye

Bulldog Bob Brown being interviewed by Ed Whalen

Stu, Ed Whalen, Archie "the Stomper" Gouldie

Bruce, Owen, Bret, Georgia, with Stu waving his hat

Stu wrestles a 600-pound tiger

Dave McKigney takes on a bear

Jim "the Anvil" Neidhart

DAVEY BOY SMITH
"THE BRITISH BULLDOG"

Bruce Hart

Bruce Hart and Brian Pillman

Ben Bassarab and Owen Hart

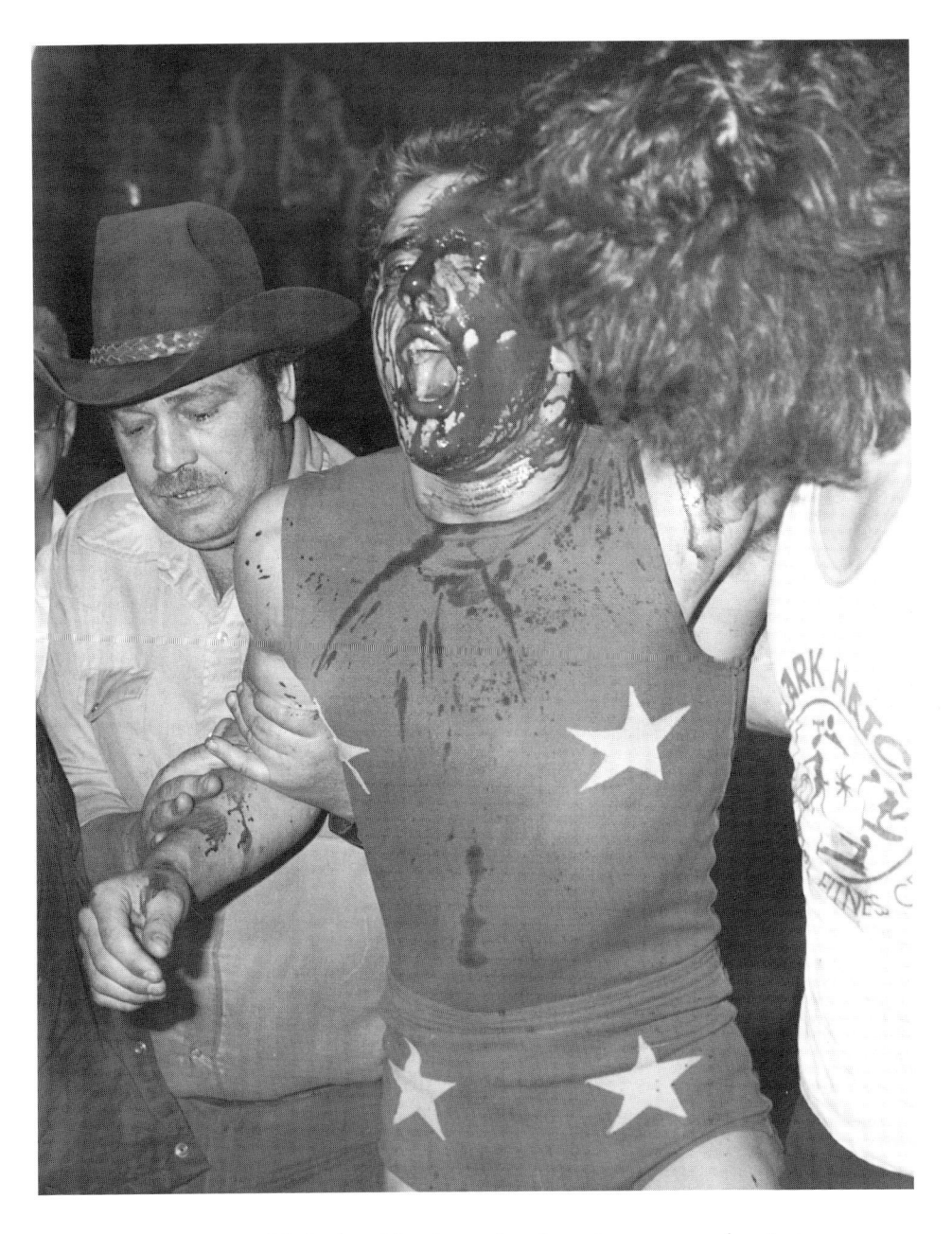

Davey Boy Smith helped back to the dressing room after intense Texas Death Match with Bad News Alan

The Hart Foundation, Bret Hart and Jim Neidhart

Stu and Helen

Helen, Stu and Penzi (Bruce's dog)

Stu stretching Greg Everett

Martha, Athena, Owen James Hart and Oje

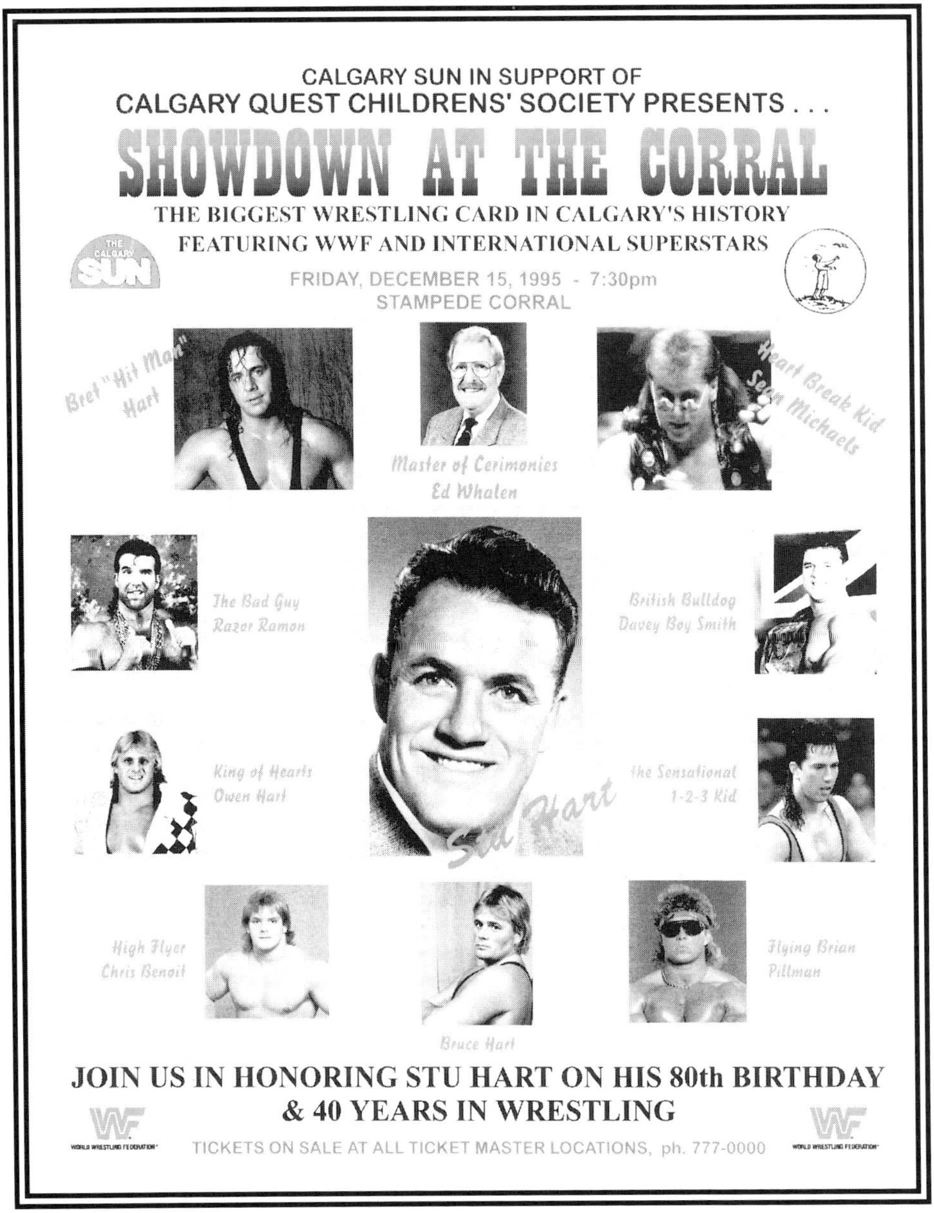

CALGARY SUN IN SUPPORT OF
CALGARY QUEST CHILDRENS' SOCIETY PRESENTS . . .

SHOWDOWN AT THE CORRAL

THE BIGGEST WRESTLING CARD IN CALGARY'S HISTORY
FEATURING WWF AND INTERNATIONAL SUPERSTARS

FRIDAY, DECEMBER 15, 1995 - 7:30pm
STAMPEDE CORRAL

Bret "Hit Man" Hart

Master of Cerimonies
Ed Whalen

Heart Break Kid
Sean Michaels

The Bad Guy
Razor Ramon

British Bulldog
Davey Boy Smith

King of Hearts
Owen Hart

the Sensational
1-2-3 Kid

High Flyer
Chris Benoit

Bruce Hart

Flying Brian
Pillman

JOIN US IN HONORING STU HART ON HIS 80th BIRTHDAY
& 40 YEARS IN WRESTLING

TICKETS ON SALE AT ALL TICKET MASTER LOCATIONS, ph. 777-0000

Cedric Hathaway (referee), Bret with the mic and Stu

(left to right) Brooke (Alison's daughter), Annie, Alison, Stu, Georgia, Helen

(left to right) Dan Kroffat, Marty Funk, Georgia, Dory Funk, Alison, John Kosman, Brian Blair, Hulk Hogan, Stu (with Molly at his feet), Rick Bognar, Bruce Hart Jr., Georgia Hart Jr., Diana, Chris Benoit, Chris Jericho, Shane Douglas, Sean Waltman, Terry Funk, Vicki Funk, Don Kolov, Bret, Bob Johnson

Stu receiving the Order of Canada from Governor General
Adrienne Clarkson, May 31, 2001
(Courtesy Sgt. Julien Dupuis)

Lord of the Ring

them up before Stu got on the line to deliver hard news. Finally, Stu and Helen instituted a double signature policy to keep wrestlers from harassing Stu on the road for paycheque advances. He could always simply refuse, because Helen wasn't there to sign a cheque, too.

Vince McMahon had other means of keeping the talent in control, but the job became more difficult as a wrestler achieved superstar status in the eyes of the fans. In Bret's case, McMahon would break one of the cardinal rules of being a pro-wrestling promoter — the Hitman wriggled out from under his thumb.

Even though he agreed to take the Hitman in a new direction, Bret Hart was not a man to be toyed with. Superstars like Ventura, Hogan and, now, Bret Hart had had back-up plans and options — they'd invested their earnings and were comfortable no matter what the future might bring.

Hulk Hogan made dizzying amounts of money during the Hulkamania years, and he still drew a healthy take at wcw. His film appearances only added to his mystique and marketability. And while control had not really been at issue with Jesse Ventura, his impressive post-wrestling political career kept him in the spotlight.

Bret was a street smart, but sophisticated athlete. No matter what, he'd land on his feet.

When Vince called Bret in and said he was unable to honour their contract, naturally, Bret was shocked. Suddenly, he understood what his father went through when Stampede Wrestling shut down. Stu's nest egg never materialized because Vince turned his back on their agreement. Now, Bret's contract was worthless, too, because although Bret may have been in a position to sue, negotiations with wcw may have prejudiced the outcome.

Bret exercised his other options. He quickly made arrangements to join McMahon's rivals, even though the nine million dollar deal was no longer on the table.

Loose ends would have to be tied up. Bret's title had to be passed along to another superstar. Storyline discussions began in earnest.

By the fall of 1997, it was decided that Bret would be succeeded by Shawn Michaels. But since there was plenty of time to pass on the belt, Bret made it clear he wanted one more big win in Canada.

When he realized the WWF wanted him to drop the title to Michaels in Montreal, Bret balked. McMahon had promised he wouldn't have to lose at home, and the Hitman forced the issue. On the afternoon of the Survivor Series, McMahon finally relented, agreeing to a "schmoz," a disqualification finish. Bret would retain the title for a few more days before losing it in the U.S.

At least that's what Vince told the Hitman.

In reality, the WWF boss set up a very different scenario.

Behind the scenes at the WWF some debated about whether a disgruntled Bret Hart would willingly give up the title. But McMahon and the WWF should have known better. Any suggestion that the Hitman might not cooperate was simply unfounded. For the more than dozen years that Bret wrestled for the WWF he had displayed nothing but professionalism and the kind of fierce loyalty that led him to turn down Turner's lucrative offer only a year earlier. And although McMahon had recently suffered the indignity of watching a former employee dumping a WWF title belt into a WCW trashcan, he surely knew he could trust a Hart to do the right thing. Perhaps he was unable to be anything but sceptical, however, considering his own tendency to ignore promises.

Bret's trust in McMahon may seem a little naive, considering his father's experience. But Bret had other reasons for believing the Montreal bout would go as planned. A man he respected and felt he could count on, Earl Hebner, was refereeing. And even though his own family warned him to be cautious, Bret walked into the

Lord of the Ring

Molson Centre ring confident, despite the fact that his signature "Sharpshooter" finish was to be used on him by Michaels. According to the script, the Hitman would work himself out of the submission hold and then turn it back on his opponent.

What followed, on November 9, 1997, transpired before a packed arena. The fans were pumped. And so was Dave Stubbs.

Bret gave what Stubbs calls a "stunning performance." But the truth, the sports columnist says, is that Bret Hart "has never given a poor performance. He has always been totally professional in his matches."

Stubbs had a great view of the action, and as the match progressed he began to see how it would unfold, right down to the finish. But just as Michaels applied the sharpshooter, and before he even had Bret fully locked into the hold, Hebner signalled that Bret had submitted. He clearly had not. Vince ordered the bell to be rung from his position at the commentator's table.

It was over. Pandemonium set in. Even Michaels looked shocked; it was as clear to him as everyone else that the Hitman had not submitted.

Still, the Heartbreak Kid was the new WWF champion.

Reportedly, referee Earl Hebner immediately disappeared into a vehicle idling outside. He was spirited away, into the darkness of a November Montreal night.

Everyone involved in wrestling knew immediately that Bret had been set up. Not only that, he'd been disrespected. That he was double-crossed with his own finishing hold was, in industry terms, an unconscionable slap in the face.

Reality began to set in. It was the Hitman's last WWF Pay-Per-View match in his own country and he'd lost to a wrestler he held in little regard, in the worst way imaginable. It was the lowest point of Bret's otherwise stellar career.

He reacted.

Bret approached McMahon and spat in his face. Vince wiped his brow as the Hitman destroyed TV monitors and fans screamed approval of every outraged move. Finally, Bret stormed towards the dressing room. A few minutes later, McMahon followed. Vince tried to approach Bret, but Bret warned him to leave. He was going to shower, he said, and expected McMahon to be gone when he got back. He wasn't. Vince tried to launch into an explanation, but the Hitman cut him off, again demanding he leave the room. When he didn't, Bret's strong, well-placed fist met Vince McMahon's face. As this happened, Davey Boy Smith and Jim Neidhart were restraining Vince's son, Shane, partly to keep him from getting into the fray and partly to ensure Vince would receive his just desserts. Split seconds later McMahon was out on the floor. Bret would nurse the bones he broke in his hand for some time later, but he's never regretted his actions. Former NWA champ Dory Funk Jr. later told Bret that "it was a good hit." The Hitman, he said, needed to get it out of his system.

Days later, in Calgary, Stu and Helen mulled over what had happened in Montreal. It seemed so unbelievably devious — even for Vince — so calculated and lacking in integrity and honour towards a wrestler who had always been a real team player. A saddened Stu was faced with the realization that this was the second time a Hart had made a monumental mistake in placing his trust in Vince McMahon. The Stampede Wrestling fiasco was bad enough, but to set up his son like this, on his own turf, was disgraceful.

"Vince was like a girl with two boyfriends [Bret Hart and Shawn Michaels]," Stu says. "And he didn't know what to do." When he finally figured out what he wanted, wrestling's patriarch maintains, McMahon handled the matter in the worst way imaginable.

"Vince had a lot of pressure on him, but because of how he

handled things a lot of people have lost faith in him."

Ellie says that in similar circumstances there's no question her father would have honoured his promise and found another way to pass the title.

Just two years later Vince McMahon would have another confrontation with the Hart family. His inability to gracefully handle difficult situations would again play a role. But this time, his shortcomings would go far beyond the shocking betrayal of one of his most loyal employees. One of wrestling's great family relationships, an association that began more than five decades earlier when a fresh faced Stu Hart walked into a 42nd Street wrestling office and met Jesse McMahon, would shatter, forever, in Kansas City's Kemper Arena.

It would be the most painful episode of the Hart/McMahon saga. The families would meet again, but nowhere near the squared circle. Instead, they would face off across a boardroom table in a Kansas City law office to examine and re-examine the tragic circumstances of Owen Hart's needless death.

The proceedings were scheduled for February 2001. A sombre, panelled courtroom in Jackson County, Missouri, would hear the multi-million dollar lawsuit: Hart v. McMahon, the WWF, Titan Sports Inc., and a string of other companies.

For the Harts, the courtroom represented a place where honour and integrity still meant what they were supposed to mean. Still, Stu was torn by the decision to sue. He was not a vengeful man and he did not believe that Vince Jr., the son of a friend and the grandson of a man he respected, could have deliberately scripted a scenario so dangerous that someone might die. Keith Hart, however, has consistently adhered to the belief that the stunt was so poorly planned, and had so few safeguards in place, that the accident was inevitable. His experiences as a fireman inform his

Stu Hart

opinion. "I just can't see it any other way," he has said repeatedly.

Stu and Helen both understood that Owen's widow Martha had to protect the financial future of their grandchildren — the lawsuit, therefore, was all but a foregone conclusion from the beginning. If Martha had other reasons for forcing the issue, that was her own business. To support Owen's family, Stu and Helen allowed their names to be added to the lawsuit.

Everyone said it would take years for a trial date to be secured or for an out-of-court settlement to be reached — and that there was always the spectre of long term appeals after the fact. Some speculated that Bret secretly hoped a judgement in the family's favour would cripple McMahon and bring the WWF to its knees.

Stu was 84 when Owen died, and couldn't reasonably expect the matter to be resolved in his lifetime. The prospect of spending the rest of his life with the spectre of litigation hanging over his head loomed larger every day.

He was also somewhat uncomfortable with the decision to sign over all the control of the proceedings to Martha. The "Contract for Employment of Attorneys" signed by Martha, Stu and Helen Hart in Calgary on June 5, 1999, less than a week after Owen's funeral, retained lawyers in Kansas City and Calgary. It read:

"We hereby agree to join Martha Hart individually and on behalf of her two (2) minor children as claimants with respect to the wrongful death of our son, Owen Hart and, as befits her proper role as widow of Owen Hart and the mother of his two surviving children, hereby defer to and grant to her sole authority and discretion as to all tactical and strategic matters in consultation with counsel including, but not limited to, identity of all defendants, identity of legal theories and claims, full settlement authority including authority to extend or reject offers and authority to accept any offers from a particular defendant or defendants where we as parents of the deceased would be a formal party to those claims and/or attend trial...."

Lord of the Ring

Months later, when he was receiving no information about the progress of the lawsuit, Stu bristled, feeling hamstrung.

Ross recalls that there was also division among the siblings from the start. Bret was appalled by Diana's decision to pose with McMahon, on the day of Owen's funeral, for a newspaper photograph, questioning her timing and judgement. Ellie and Diana encouraged considering offers from Vince's lawyers for a quick financial settlement — health issues and the age of their parents were behind their opinions. They were also concerned about their husbands' careers. Jim Neidhart wanted to return to the WWF and Davey Boy Smith had been rehired just before Owen's tragic accident. Bret viewed this as a betrayal of Owen and Martha. Ross also says Bruce was very supportive of Martha, initially, and strongly condemned the WWF.

Later, when it appeared that Bret was not overly supportive of his brothers' attempt to revitalize Stampede Wrestling, Bruce took it as a personal slight. Bruce also became upset with Martha — for not allowing him to speak at Owen's funeral, even though he had been especially close to Owen when his youngest brother was still a child. Martha was adamant: she, Bret and Ross, only, would speak.

According to Ross, almost immediately Martha began to alienate the family. At the premiere for the Highroad Production's film about Owen's career, in the Roxbury restaurant, she introduced several of the guests — but did not acknowledge members of the Hart family, despite the fact that Stu and Helen, as well as Ross, Alison, Bruce and Keith, were in attendance. Other family members, again including Bruce, were excluded from the film's production.

There were clearly many contentious issues.

Still, the lawsuit proceeded to resolution. The internal familial tension, however, remained.

Because of Stu's advanced age and fragile health, a Jackson

County, Missouri, judge set an early trial date — for February 2001. Proceedings were delayed, however, when lawyers for the McMahons and the WWF, Jerry McDevitt and Craig O'Dear, complained about an Allocation Agreement between the Harts and their lawyers. The document had been drafted to cover the possibility of the lawsuit surviving both Stu and Helen. It was signed by each of the Harts, except Ellie, Diana and Bruce. The document called for the cooperation of all of Owen's siblings, and allowed them an interest in the proceeds if they cooperated with the Plaintiff's case. A sibling who cooperated with the defendants would not share in any recovery. It also sought to prevent any of the siblings from communicating with the defendants. Ellie had remained close with the WWF and Vince and Linda McMahon. She, Diana and Bruce were accused of taking a position against the agreement as an attempt to press for a settlement in which there would have been proceeds for themselves. Ellie faxed a copy of the Allocation Agreement to McMahon's lawyers.

Bret accused his sisters of wanting to secure WWF jobs for themselves or their husbands. But logically, had Diana, Ellie or Bruce been attempting to secure something for themselves in the lawsuit, it would have made more sense for them to have supported the Agreement.

The WWF lawyers argued that the Allocation Agreement amounted to witness tampering, that it gave potential witnesses a financial interest in the outcome of the lawsuit.

Martha's Missouri lawyers, Gary and Anita Robb, countered that the document merely attempted to secure family unity, but agreed to rescind the agreement as soon as the controversy arose.

On July 29, 2000, *Kansas City Star* reporter Dan Margolies argued that the agreement "raised ethical questions" and then put the issue to Cornell University law professor Charles Wolfram, who said: "I have never heard of anything like it — perhaps for

Lord of the Ring

good reasons." The article went on to say that other legal experts believed the result, if the allegation had been proved, could have been disciplinary action against the lawyers and, possibly, their removal from the case.

The controversy, however, may have inadvertently facilitated the settlement discussions which opened in September 2000.

A meeting took place at the offices of their lawyers, Robb & Robb, in Kansas City. Looking back a few months later, Helen Hart recalled the embarrassment she felt over the way everything was handled.

When Robb & Robb came to Calgary to meet with the Harts, they booked expensive suites in the best hotels, dined at the finest restaurants and made their way around town in a limousine. Helen fretted about the cost and wondered why it was necessary. Prior to one meeting, Stu had prepared a huge meal, but when the lawyers arrived, they insisted on going to a downtown restaurant.

A potential witness, who would testify about the equipment used on the night of Owen's fall, was in Europe. Helen said four lawyers travelled to Europe for the deposition. She questioned why it took four to do the straightforward work, she believed, of one.

When depositions were being taken in Kansas City, each of the Hart children were lodged in separate suites in an upscale hotel. When Helen protested, saying that the brothers and sisters would be more comfortable sharing rooms, her concerns were brushed aside. "They acted like we were hillbillies who had never stayed in a hotel before, and they were giving us this opportunity."

Ellie recalls that just before her testimony was taken, Gary Robb passed Owen's wedding ring to Martha, saying it was time she had it back. No one asked why Robb had the ring in the first place. Ellie believes the whole scene was an attempt to intimidate her.

Helen also said that during the September negotiating session, Stu was not permitted to be in the room at all. The fear was that he would shake hands with Vince, someone he'd known for decades — in fact, virtually all of the younger man's life. Helen and Stu were such well-mannered, gracious people, everyone believed they'd have great difficulty being cold or rude to anyone — even the man whose carelessness cost them a son. To them, Vince's real mistake came with hiring the wrong people to put the stunt together.

Helen was also uncomfortable with the way she was forced to dress for the settlement meeting. She was told that the clothes she intended to wear were "not suitable." Instead, she was given a dowdy, matronly outfit, and shoes that were just as bad.

"They were trying to make us look pathetic," recalled a woman known around Calgary for being impeccably well-groomed. "We couldn't understand it. Vince McMahon knew very well what we looked like."

Helen also said that she was told to snub the McMahons at the settlement meeting — to make absolutely no eye contact with them. She loathed the posturing, but felt helpless to do anything about it.

When the day arrived, the settlement meeting opened as planned with a statement from Martha Hart, denouncing, in no uncertain terms, the McMahons and the WWF. As Helen listened to Martha's speech, her head began to spin. She wondered when it would all end. But as soon as Vince McMahon spoke she began to feel encouraged. Perhaps there was a light, finally, at the end of a long and painful tunnel.

His crisp reply cut through the air, piercing the tactical balloon the lawyers had inflated with Martha's predictably angry words.

Helen recalled McMahon's speech as a breath of fresh air. "Vince made it clear right away where he stood. He said: 'I am responsible for Owen Hart's death. I want to do right by his family.

Lord of the Ring

I know that nothing can ever bring him back.'" She struggled not to collapse into her chair, feeling the weight about to be lifted.

A final meeting occurred in early November 2000. The actual settlement was hammered out beforehand and the meeting would simply confirm the offer and the acceptance. Vince and Linda did not attend. The case was settled for $18 million USD. Martha would receive $10 million, less her lawyer's fees; her children would receive $3 million each; and Stu and Helen Hart would receive $1 million each, less their share of the legal fees.

Those fees were set out in the "Contract for Employ-ment of Attorneys," and included a provision for 25 per cent of the total recovery in addition to the expenses of the lawsuit. Helen was shocked by how high the combined fees and expenses were.

Once the lawsuit had been settled, Martha transferred some of her anger to her in-laws. She went on televison to say that except for Stu, Helen, Bret and Keith she was cutting ties with Owen's family.

And while this came as no surprise to the Harts, the fact that she found it necessary to make such an announcement publicly was puzzling, given the history of her attitude towards the family. From the time she and Owen were married, many of the Harts believed that Martha had made a concerted effort to keep him from their influence. Martha was the youngest of many children herself — she had ten siblings. In her view Owen's own family was dysfunctional, and she made it clear that she wanted her life with her husband to be radically different. The Harts had been a favourite of the Calgary media for many years. Everyday events in their lives seemed like a WWF storyline, and there was always a ready and willing audience. Internal divisions made for good copy. And the media, inevitably, became a tool that one Hart faction could use against another. Yet despite Martha's stated desire for a more ordinary life, she still bought into the Hart family penchant for airing personal business publicly and then thriving in the wake of the drama.

The divide created by Owen's tragic death grew wider and the siblings divided into camps — one dominated by Bret and another led by Bruce, Ellie and Diana. The famous Sunday night Hart House dinners changed. If Bret attended, Ellie and Diana did not.

In the pre-settlement period, Bruce's wife Andrea left home, apparently with the encouragement of her brother-in-law Davey Boy Smith, whose own marriage to Diana had been on life-support for months. It, too, abruptly ended. Intense and messy separations for both erupted over child custody issues. Diana had Davey Boy arrested for threatening herself, Ellie and Bruce, and Davey's photo appeared on the front page of the *Calgary Sun*. His crudely worded insults were carefully recorded on answering machines. The charges were eventually dropped, but newspaper headlines, for the next several weeks, dismayed Stu and Helen and left them wondering what would go wrong next.

Ellie renewed her relationship with Jim Neidhart, who she had been separated from for more than a year, shortly after the Anvil's mother died. The event, according to Ellie, caused him to reassess his values. But then Jim, in an apparent attempt to pay Ellie back for having him removed from their house in the summer of 1999, had Ellie committed to a hospital, claiming that she was suicidal. While family and friends figured out how to secure her release, she fumed about Jim's audacity in attending provincial court to swear out a mental health warrant just as he was leaving town, in the spring of 2001, for an independent promoter's European wrestling tour. Despite this, the two reconciled again later that summer. Their relationship, however, remains somewhat tentative.

Smith, the oldest of the eight Hart sons, had been engaged in a battle over the custody of his youngest child, whose young mother had died two years previously. Her family wanted to raise the five year old. Smith sat in court with his parents and watched as Bret and Keith testified against his ability to raise the boy. Smith was denied custody, although he was given some access rights. He launched an appeal. The fact his brothers chose to testify against him added to the already strained relationship among Stu's children.

After Owen's death, Stu's health became increasingly fragile. He spent a week at Rockyview Hospital battling pneumonia in the summer of 2000 and his ability to hear steadily diminished. The closure the settlement brought rallied his spirits, but the 18-month ordeal had taken its toll. Still, he began working out semi-regularly with a young local wrestler, Adrian Gilmore, who wrestles for the new Stampede promotion as Crazy Horse Eddie Mustang. The workouts put colour back into his cheeks and renewed his gusto. In the early spring of 2000, Stu and his family were presented with a long overdue recognition of civic contribution by the City of Calgary. Ellie, in one of her more cynical moments, called it the "Sorry We Screwed You on the Land Deal Award." In her view, a plaque wasn't nearly enough.

In February, 2001, Stu was honoured by the wrestling world when he was presented with the Iron Mike Mazurki Award, the Cauliflower Alley Club's highest honour, in Las Vegas. The award came as a complete surprise. He thanked peers and fans for a "wonderful life" that had provided a "pretty good" living for his family over the years. It was not the first of such honours: he had already been inducted into the Edmonton Sports Hall of Fame in 1984, just after shutting down his promotion.

Stu's spirits were further lifted in May 2001, when he and Helen and their daughter Georgia travelled to Ottawa. There, at Rideau Hall, the official residence of the Governor General of Canada, Stu stood among others from across the country to receive the Order of Canada for lifetime achievement.

Stu Hart

The Office of the Governor General confirmed the award in a telephone call to Hart House on February 14, 2001. Typical of Stu's humility, he did not believe the news. On December 21, 2000, he'd received a letter from the Advisory Council to the Order of Canada saying that he was being recommended for one of his country's greatest honours. Stu thought that meant someone had simply nominated him, and though he was flattered by the recognition he felt it unlikely that he would be given the award.

When the phone rang on Valentine's Day morning, neither Stu nor Helen believed they were actually speaking with a representative of Her Excellency, the Governor General. Whenever someone called Hart House, which was often, it was usually one of the children, grandchildren, young athletes wanting to become wrestlers or some old crowbar wanting to reminisce about the old days.

Helen was searching for a document needed by the family accountant that morning and was too busy to take the call. Stu was not quite out of bed, enjoying the chance to sleep in while Helen rummaged. When she asked Stu to answer the phone, his reply was, "You answer it."

The phone kept ringing, and finally Stu reached for the receiver. There was a soft voice on the other end, out of Stu's range — he wasn't wearing his hearing aid. Curious, Helen reached for the receiver.

"The sweetest voice came on the line with a lovely French accent," Helen said. "I couldn't believe what she was saying — I got tears in my eyes. She was telling us that Stu had been awarded the Order of Canada. We were stunned."

They immediately shared the information with the rest of the family, but Helen and Stu were still sceptical. By late afternoon, when no one from the media had called, they both thought the whole thing was some sort of practical joke. In a conversation with her son-in-law B.J., Helen questioned the validity of the news.

Lord of the Ring

Using his pet name for his mother-in-law, B.J. said: "Yes, Lou Lou, it's the real thing, I assure you."

Later in the day a reporter from the *Calgary Sun* called and wanted to drop by with a photographer. When the reporter did not arrive at the agreed upon time, Helen decided that the award was, in fact, someone's idea of a prank. Family ribs had become so elaborate in their orchestration that every event was weighed against the possibility of it being a set-up.

Stu had a theory: "I thought it was some wrestler paying me back for all those Mabel parties."

But when *Calgary Sun* reporter Cameron Maxwell and photographer Mike Drew finally arrived, it sunk in: the of pro-wrestling legend had indeed been recognized for his contribution to his country.

Established in 1967, the Order of Canada recognizes outstanding achievement and service in various fields of human endeavour. Appointments are made on the recommendation of an Advisory Council chaired by the Chief Justice of the Supreme Court. The Order of Canada specifically honours those who have made a difference in the lives of their fellow Canadians and therefore deserve national recognition.

It would be a few more months before Stu Hart would walk into Rideau Hall for the formal investiture. The Harts would be treated with great deference. Georgia recalled driving around Ottawa in taxis, the drivers telling her father what an honour it was to have the man who created Stampede Wresting in their cabs.

The time between the announcement and the actual ceremony gave Stu a chance to reflect on a life lived to the fullest. As he sat at the dining room table of a friend the day after his appointment, Stu flipped through the pages of a photo album. He smiled at a picture of himself and his two sisters sitting on the grass with other students outside Ketchamoot School in 1926.

Stu Hart

Memories of his boyhood returned — the open prairie, the slingshot he had used to bring down partridge and gophers for his mother's cooking pot. A sudden chill coursed through his bones when the damp canvas tents came back to him.

"You can never forget an ordeal like that," he said, turning a page of the album, stopping at photos of Helen from 1946, when they first dated. He leaned closer to his wife, carried back in time. Still more photos — Stu in his Navy uniform, standing with Emile Van Velzen in Edmonton. And there was Hart House, as it was 30 years before, providing the background to an image of Stu, Helen and their 12 children. Helen held one of five young boys, smiled and handed it to Stu.

Stu also examined some old publicity shots. Other memories returned — there was the string of boxing greats, Primo Carnera, Jersey Joe Walcott, Jack Dempsey, Joe Louis and Muhammad Ali. He picked up a yellowed newspaper clipping and read about his own days with the Edmonton Eskimos; another talked about the match in 1939 that made him the Canadian Amateur Wrestling Champion. Stu thought about all of the mats he'd grappled on. He remembered the pained faces of dozens of young wrestlers, including his own sons, intent on learning the skills they needed to survive wrestling's squared circle.

It had been 72 years since he had his first taste of wrestling. More than a lifetime, for some.

Stu picked up a photo of a grinning, toothy Abdullah the Butcher. The curled edges betrayed the years that had passed. He listened to Helen recall writing pay cheques and wondering how many of the names she had been given were legal. Helen smiled, remembering the colourful parade of characters, but her expression still said: I'm so glad it's all over.

Finally, Stu picked up a childhood picture of Owen. He was sitting with a monkey on his lap, the two looking like the best of

Lord of the Ring

friends. He handed the photo to Helen, who took it gently, with an expression of deep sorrow which, at that very moment, was shared by them both.

Now, despite the honours and the passing of time, the family's divisions remain a source of sadness. It may be up to Bret "the Hitman" Hart to take the lead and heal the family's wounds. Whether Bret has enough of his father's great gift of conciliation to provide that leadership remains to be seen.

Ten

May 28, 2001.

It is early afternoon and Calgary's Pengrowth Saddle-dome, near the city's downtown core, is filled with activity. In three days Stu Hart will receive his Order of Canada in Ottawa. A team of technicians and labourers is setting up a wrestling ring and connecting audio and video equipment while internationally known wrestlers mill around, watching and listening as systems are checked and re-checked, killing time talking to each other in hushed voices.

The person responsible for all of this activity, Vince McMahon, stands with his hands in his pockets. His thoughts are anyone's guess. The WWF's Raw is War has arrived in Calgary; the live Monday night broadcast put hundreds of thousands of dollars into the promotion's coffers. McMahon is in a good mood. The 18,000-seat Saddledome sold out in 40 minutes after tickets first went on sale, a record for Calgary. Despite the buoyant spirits of the motley crew, few could ignore the fact that this city was home to the late Owen Hart.

The lawsuit had been settled seven months earlier and some of the wounds were beginning to heal. Vince and Linda McMahon, reacting to friendly overtures from Stu and Helen, had invited the

Stu Hart

living legend and his family to the event and they had accepted. But whether *any* of the Harts would actually show up was still unclear.

That morning Bruce drove to his parents' house. He knew his sister Ellie would be there already. They had heard rumblings from their brother Bret and they were worried that their father would be persuaded to snub the broadcast. Stu had battled pneumonia and heart trouble at the Rockyview Hospital for much of the previous month and they certainly didn't want to see him stressed about deciding to attend. The pair had self-interested reasons, too, for wanting a reconciliation between the Harts and McMahons to take place. Wrestling was the only game they really knew and both still wanted to be involved in the big leagues.

Bruce had put together a detailed proposal about operating a training camp, and he wanted to formalize a deal with the WWF. With their backing and the Hart history and know-how, it was sure to be a success. He had already missed numerous opportunities to land with the WWF — bad timing or bad blood always kept him out of the action. Now, it appeared Bret would do everything he could to ensure that Stu stayed home, while Bruce was anxious to see Stu stay the course. Ellie had proven to be a reliable organizational asset and the pair desperately wanted another crack at restoring the old Stampede lustre. Ross, as well, supported the endeavour; all three recognized that life must go on — even without Owen.

That Bret was still angry at McMahon and the WWF was clearly justified. And despite Owen's death and the fact that more than three years had passed since the Montreal incident, Vince didn't miss many opportunities to take a dig at his former superstar. Recently, he'd named one of his ill-fated XFL football teams the "New York Hitmen" — and it was interpreted by some wrestling observers as a shot at Bret. Still alive in the Hitman's thoughts after the Kansas City tragedy, perhaps, was the old

Lord of the Ring

adage: *There but for the grace of God go I.* Other wrestlers of his calibre must have thought about it, too.

When they arrived at Hart House, Bruce and Ellie knew how far Bret would go to prevent his parents and the family from attending Raw. It was difficult to accept, however, when just a year earlier Bret himself had attended WWF house shows. He had visited his old buddies and chatted up Benoit and Jericho — though McMahon had not been present. As far as Bruce was concerned there was no substantial difference to what the family now planned. Did TV and the fact that the WWF boss would be present really matter all that much in the spring of 2001?

Bruce pulled into the yard and parked by some massive lilac bushes. In full bloom, they framed the newly renovated coach house, now the residence of Ellie's daughter Natalie, the co-host of MatRats — a wrestling forum for younger performers which had attracted several of the third generation of Harts. Natalie, a stunning, petite blonde teen, had been considering a career in modelling, but MatRats had captured her imagination in the same way it had her talented cousins, Georgia's son Ted, and Diana's son, Harry.

Bruce was relieved when he found neither Bret's Jaguar nor his Durango four-by-four in the yard. Knowing his mother would be at her Jazzercise class, he went in through the kitchen door to find Stu. His optimism quickly faded. Stu was sitting on the stairwell between the kitchen and the dining room, talking on the phone with Keith, who was closely allied with Bret. His father's frustration was obvious, and the words he carefully chose to respond to Keith told Bruce everything. He exchanged a meaningful glance with Ellie as they heard their father's raspy, insistent words: "Keith, I'm not disrespecting anyone. I'm looking forward to talking to Vince."

Stu was also excited about seeing the wrestlers, many of whom

Stu Hart

he'd helped train in the basement Dungeon, especially Benoit and Jericho, international stars who never forgot where they got their start.

When he finally put down the receiver, Stu was visibly angry.

"I can't speak or do anything without my kids telling me how high to jump," he barked, assuming Bruce and Ellie were there to give him more grief about his decision. "I don't want to be told by anyone what to do."

"Let's get some lunch, Dad," Bruce said, knowing it was just a matter of time before Bret would walk through the door. It was a confrontation he wanted to avoid.

Luckily, a few minutes later, Mike Davidson, a friend of Bruce's, dropped in and invited Stu, Bruce and Ellie to join him at Forbes' Restaurant in the Northland Shopping Centre for lunch. They loaded Stu's wheelchair into the vehicle and left.

Bruce and Ellie felt justifiably worried that Bret would try to intervene in their father's plans. Just a year before, on May 31, Bruce and Ross had organized a celebration with the reborn Stampede Wrestling for their father's 85th birthday. They invited everyone, from the wrestling legends of Stu's heyday, to the young talent recently trained in the Dungeon, to join them. They were overwhelmed by the response. Bruce recalls: "31 guys signed up in half an hour" — at their own expense. Among them were Terry and Dory Funk, Hulk Hogan, Sabu, Rob Van Dam, Stone Cold Steve Austin, Mick Foley and a number of Japanese superstars. When the event was announced publicly Stu sat ringside, at a Stampede event. A TV camera captured everything.

The next morning, Bret arrived at his father's house. Bruce was sitting in the kitchen with Stu and Helen when Bret walked in carrying a printout of the Stampede Wrestling website page that announced the event.

"Stu is not going, do you understand?" Bruce recalls his

Lord of the Ring

brother saying as he waved the computer paper. "He's not doing it."

As a result, family members marked Stu's 85th birthday by taking him out to dinner.

Stu and Helen had been enthusiastic about the plans at first, but because of the sensitivity of the proposed date — the first anniversary of Owen's funeral — and because of the negative comments which appeared in the *Calgary Sun* and the *Calgary Herald* condemning the organizers for working with WWF wrestlers when the lawsuit was still unresolved, the show was cancelled. Many fans were disappointed, as were the stars who had eagerly looked forward to honouring Stu.

During lunch Stu relaxed, especially when he realized that Bruce and Ellie were going to respect his decision and not try to talk him out of seeing "Vincent." The trio lingered until Bruce suggested that they go to the Saddledome to see how the set-up was going and have a pre-match visit with whoever was around. They arrived at one. As the old man was wheeled in, every wrestler who saw him stopped to shake his hand and wish him well. Bruce recalled Stu looking around anxiously, as if he was half-expecting Bret or Keith to charge in and drag him away. But he was soon distracted from such thoughts: Stu began demonstrating head holds on Kurt Angle, the American 1996 Olympic gold medal winner.

The three also spent time with Vince and his children, Shane and Stephanie, talking about the old days in the Saddledome office Vince had taken over for the night.

Unknown to any of them, Bret *had* gone to Hart House looking for his father. Helen, along with her daughter Georgia Annis and granddaughter Natalie, was in the coach house with a hairdresser. She was looking forward to seeing Linda McMahon and happy that she would have a chance to make peace after the dreadful way she and Stu both perceived the McMahons were treated at the settlement meeting in Kansas City.

Stu Hart

Later that afternoon, Stu expected Bruce and Ellie to take him back to the house so he could change his clothes for the live TV event. But his son and daughter realized that if their father wanted to attend, a trip back to Hart House was not a good idea.

It wasn't long before Helen called Bruce on his cell to confirm what he already feared: Bret had been there and she would not be attending Raw. She also wanted to know where Stu was. Bruce fudged his response. He knew that if his father talked to Helen he'd end up caving — unhappily — and staying home.

At the Saddledome later that evening, Ross, Diana and Smith joined Stu, Bruce, Ellie and Ellie's daughters, Natalie and Kirstin, Georgia's son Ted and Smith's daughter Tanya for the show. Young, upcoming stars of the Stampede Wrestling promotion were also in attendance. Most of them sat together at ringside, listening as announcer Howard Finkel told the capacity crowd that members of the first family of pro-wrestling were present. Stu Hart stood up in front of his ringside seat in amazement when 18,000 fans began screaming his name. Their chant — Stu, Stu, Stu — undulated in sustained adoration for no less than ten minutes. It began altering itself, changing from Stu to Owen to Bret — in an hypnotic frenzy. The WWF organizers could barely believe it — rarely had they seen such a display of support. *For anyone.* Smith Hart says that every one of the Harts present were reduced to tears. The fans' response only reaffirmed Vince's respect for Stu.

Chris Benoit and Chris Jericho, careful to honour the WWF's policy of not mentioning Owen Hart's name on air (something instituted to appease Owen's wife, Martha), spoke to the audience, off camera, about how they felt about losing Owen. They pointed towards heaven to make who they were speaking about perfectly clear. They also paid tribute to Stu, the man to whom they both owed so much, the man who had taken them to the Dungeon to teach them almost every wrestling hold he knew.

Lord of the Ring

Listening, Bruce Hart smiled, glad that his father would know how people felt after his recent hospitalization. Stu had needed something like this. Both Bruce and Ellie were prepared to accommodate whatever Stu wanted or made him happy — they understood that some people thought that he was no longer entirely aware of what was taking place around him. But this was not the case. Despite an advanced age and the inevitable forgetfulness that often accompanies it, he continues to be his own man. It is only his poor hearing and his compromised physical abilities which sometimes leave a different impression.

That night on Raw the last match featured Chris Benoit battling Stone Cold Steve Austin for the WWF title. Many hardcore WWF fans felt a strong sense of déjà vu, watching a version of the Hitman-Shawn Michaels travesty being replayed, almost move-for-move, with Benoit and Austin in the Hart and Michaels roles respectively. The same referee, Earl Hebner, even officiated. In the heat of the moment, the Hart family did not pick up on it — but the rest of the pro-wrestling world did. Once again, McMahon's perceived insult to his old nemesis seemed all too calculated. Austin prevailed in the match, but he lost to Benoit the next night in Edmonton, where the Canadian performed in front of his own home town.

When the two-hour show was over, the Harts and McMahons gathered backstage for more talk. Bruce had the impression that Vince was now looking at things differently, taking a new interest in developing talent through his and Ross Hart's continuing work in the Dungeon. Given that Hart-trained grapplers are still front and centre in the WWF, the idea of continuing to develop talent in the Hart House basement would have its appeal, especially when the promotion is often criticized for employing too many wrestlers who lack serious skills.

Bret was not happy about Stu's TV appearance. He decided not to attend Stu's induction ceremony in Ottawa later that week.

Stu Hart

Dave Meltzer's "Wrestling Observer Newsletter" implied that Stu had been given the award because of Bret's popularity, and because Bret had commissioned a letter to the Advisory Council to the Order of Canada. But that was not the case.

In fact, a substantial submission, including details of Stu Hart's unsung charity work, his long history as a promoter and his kindnesses to many had been the main thrust behind his Order of Canada. All of which he had already achieved *before* his sons even knew how to wrestle. Supporters included Senator Dan Hayes and Premier Ralph Klein — both had been very close to Stu over the years, and were very knowledgeable about Stu Hart's substantial contributions to his community as well as his accomplishments in the wrestling world.

Owen's widow, Martha, was not pleased either. She called Helen to complain about allowing the family to attend Raw. After Helen put down the receiver, she made quick notes about the conversation on her shorthand pad, bewildered as to what control Martha thought she would have over her adult children and husband — who had minds and opinions of their own.

By July life had settled back into its usual routines. Bruce and Ross began a new session of the Hart Brothers' Wrestling Camp, and the ring once again appeared on the side lawn. Everything started to slip into a relative calm. Several of the children continued to steer clear of each other, keeping waves and ripples in the family dynamics to a minimum.

But the lull did not last.

That fall Diana Hart, the youngest living sibling, published *Under the Mat*. Written with Kirsty McLellan, a local entertainment writer, it arrived amid shock waves, unflattering reviews and questions about Diana's motives, many wondering why she would publish such distasteful and controversial material about her own family. McLellan's reasons for wanting to attach her name and rep-

Lord of the Ring

utation to the project were also baffling. She remained largely in the background, and Diana took most of the heat from the family. Most family members and those close to them were at last in agreement — the book was a coarse blemish on the Hart name and an inaccurate, unfair portrayal of the family.

Martha promptly issued a notice that she intended to sue unless an apology was issued and the book was recalled. Nearly every member of the family endured at least a few lacerations in Diana's book, and no private matter was deemed too personal for public airing.

The publication opened a new chapter in the family's internal relationships. It seemed that Stu had approved of the book because its foreword was credited to him. Ellie noted that the foreword had actually been written by Helen — long before the book was written. And, neither she nor Stu had any idea about the book's contents, or were aware that the volume would amount to a character assassination of most of the family. Stu, in an angry exchange with Diana at Hart House on November 4, made it clear that he did not approve of his daughter's book, or its contents.

In the midst of the furor and controversy, a far more important event was about to unfold. It would leave a permanent mark on every member of the family, and upon their many friends around the world.

On September 26, Helen Hart returned from California. She had been there with her sister Betty, but the trip had been coloured with great sorrow after the tragic events of September 11 had ravaged the beloved home of their youth, New York. Helen remained close to all her sisters throughout her life. Her childhood nickname, "Girlie," was what she was still called by them all — a wonderful example of their closeness and affection. Elizabeth (Betty) Budge resides in Piedmont, California; Patricia (Patsy)

Stu Hart

Forrest near Denver, Colorado; Joan (Joanie) Gudmundson makes her home in Lakeland, Florida. The youngest of Harry J. Smith's five daughters, Diana Osler, also lives in Calgary.

A few days after she returned, Stu started to notice changes in Helen's manner and speech patterns. He immediately called in Ellie, who lives in the nearby Strathcona area of west Calgary. They rushed Helen to Foothills Hospital, where she suffered a series of seizures and slipped into a coma. Helen valiantly fought against the effects of her long battle with diabetes, which had been first diagnosed in 1987 when she was 63 years of age. The Hart children and grandchildren gathered around the woman who had meant so much to their lives.

After more than a month, Helen came out of her coma and managed to communicate, briefly, with members of the family. Everyone realized she understood what was happening around her, especially when Ellie said, "Mom, if you can understand us, please turn your head and look at Dad."

She did.

Stu squeezed her hand and said, "Dear, you just made my day."

The family continued to hope she would rally. But it was not to be.

Helen Louise Hart died on November 4, at the age of 77. Stu, Ellie, Georgia, Bruce, Ross and Diana were all at the hospital in those early morning hours. So were Georgia's husband B.J., and daughters, Angela and Annie and Ellie's daughter, Jenny.

Ellie says that for several days before Helen's death, Stu began to brace himself for what might occur. He remembered a poem he had found in the Long Beach library and read to Helen more than 50 years earlier. On many occasions during the early years of their marriage Stu would repeat a few lines of the poem to Helen because he liked the sentiment.

He was able to recall the first four lines of Adelaide Love's

Lord of the Ring

"Walk Slowly" and he spoke the words from memory as several of his children and grandchildren stood by quietly weeping.

Ellie remembers the last thing her father requested of his wife: "If you could smile for me one more time, it would mean everything to me."

Helen managed a slight smile, her eyes resting on her husband. A look of serenity swept over her face as she silently slipped away.

A familiar veil of sadness descended upon Hart House. For the second time in two years the family prepared a formal farewell for a much loved member.

Stu's daughter Alison, a librarian for the Southern Alberta Institute of Technology, was able to find the full text of the poem a few days later on the Internet. Her brother Wayne read it at Helen's memorial.

Walk Slowly

If you should go before me dear, walk slowly
Down the ways of death, well-worn and wide
For I would want to overtake you quickly
And seek the journey's ending by your side

I would be so forlorn not to descry you
Down some shining high road when I came
Walk slowly dear, and often look behind you
And pause to hear if someone calls your name

The service would have met with Helen's approval in every way. Family and friends gathered to share heartfelt memories. The tributes that poured in from around the world were lovely, but paled in comparison to those from her own family and husband. Bruce, Bret, Georgia, Ross and their uncle, Jock Osler, spoke movingly.

Alison, who had toiled for days before the service, presented a pictorial tribute in a slide presentation. Alberta Premier Ralph Klein, City Councillor Craig Burrows and Ed Whalen also gave touching personal tributes and shared memories of their own. Whalen would suffer a heart attack a month later while holidaying in Florida. His death, at the age of 74, would cause more sadness, both for his family, fans and friends in Calgary, and especially for members of the Hart family.

At Helen's memorial, each of those who payed tribute noted that she was the true "heart" of the family — the glue that held them all together. Helen embodied the optimism, spirit and enthusiasm of the Hart clan. As Premier Klein noted, she was "a shining light, unwavering in integrity."

But it was Bruce Hart who captured the true essence of Helen for all present. He evoked a phrase well known to both the family and wrestling fans around the world. It was usually associated with Bret, but also a perfectly fitting description of his mother: "She was the best there is, the best there was and the best there ever will be."

Finally, Bruce reached out to his siblings — appealing for peace among them as a way to honour Helen Hart's memory.

The Rev. Earl Klotz of Woodcliff United Church gave Stu Hart the last word. He rose slowly from his place at the front of the chapel and, leaning on his son Bret's sturdy arm, made his way to the podium.

Stu paused for a moment, looked around the room filled with flowers and familiar faces and gave his thanks to "All you good people for the kindness and support you have given my family this past week."

He then spoke lovingly of his time with a woman who had

Lord of the Ring

been the centre of his universe for more than half a century, recalling that it had taken him a year and a half and more than one marriage proposal to "trap her." Stu said that from the moment he met her, he knew he wanted Helen to be his wife.

"She made a tremendous impression on everyone. She had so many friends. I'm glad I had this much time with her."

Theirs was a lifelong romance, filled with every manner of pain and joy. Yet they always stood together, never wavering. Their marriage was the kind that others dream about, perhaps because they always put each other first.

When Stewart Edward Hart and Helen Louise Smith stood at the altar before Father Gallagher in a New York blizzard on New Year's Eve 1947, neither of them knew what life had in store. Helen — who in the words of her son Bruce, "Did not know the difference between a wrist lock and wrist watch" — would bring gentleness, warmth and love to the life of a country boy whose life began in the most precarious fashion.

Stu Hart had achieved many things with nothing more than a pair of willing hands, common sense, athletic ability and a warm heart. All of which was complemented by his "Tiger Belle," a woman with a gentle spirit, fine mind and natural grace. Together they shared a most unconventional life.

Stu and his "Tiger" would raise twelve children and offer them a future in a land thousands of miles from where they were wed. On that New Year's Eve they forged a bond that would survive many challenges. They were young and confident and willing to accept what greeted them with a spirit that never truly faltered.

Now, the way Stu misses his "Tiger" has become a heartbreaking testimonial to the love they shared. Eileen Simpkins-O'Neill recalls telephoning the house a day or two after Helen's memorial

Stu Hart

service and asking young Matthew Hart if his Grampie had come downstairs yet.

Matthew replied: "No, he's still upstairs. He's lying on Grammie's side of the bed."

Helen's 17-year-old cat, Sissy Snip, added its own voice to the Hart House sadness by beginning to howl outside Stu and Helen's bedroom door. The little cat has taken a new interest in Stu. Both now share Helen's pillow.

And though Stu's life continues, emptier without Helen, he remains fortified by his many cherished memories.

His favourite riddle is also his legacy.

"What do you get when you wrestle a Tiger? Twelve kids, a wrestling business and a wonderful life."